Twayne's English Authors Series

Sylvia E. Bowman, *Editor*

INDIANA UNIVERSITY

George Henry Lewes

George Henry Lewes

By EDGAR W. HIRSHBERG
The University of South Florida
Tampa

Twayne Publishers, Inc. :: New York

Library of Congress Catalog Card Number: 79–99539

MANUFACTURED IN THE UNITED STATES OF AMERICA

To GORDON S. HAIGHT

Professor of English

Yale University

Preface

I first became interested in George Henry Lewes in 1945 when, as an ex-G.I. who suddenly had become a student of English literature at Cambridge University, I prepared for the Tripos Examination in George Eliot under Professors Joan Bennett and F. R. Leavis. At that time Lewes was to me a shadowy little figure, lurking in the periphery of George Eliot's effulgence, in the anomalous position of being her husband, without being her husband, for the last twenty-five years of his life. Later, at Yale, when Professor Gordon S. Haight introduced me more thoroughly to Lewes, I began to understand that he was a person of real consequence, aside from his relationship with George Eliot, a man whose works were well worth studying for their own sake as productions of one of the nineteenth century's most lively, versatile, and original minds.

This book makes no attempt to appraise all that Lewes did and wrote, nor is it in any sense a biography. For reasons that will become apparent to the reader, I have devoted my attention almost exclusively to his accomplishments in literature and criticism, and to my knowledge this is the first full-length study and analysis of them that has as yet been made. I believe that his most enduring importance lies in his work as a critic. Bernard Shaw considered his dramatic criticism the best that was written between William Hazlitt's day and Shaw's own. As a literary critic Lewes was the first among his English contemporaries to adopt and explicate the theory of realism, and the first to make use of this theory in setting up criteria to judge the quality of fiction. René Wellek and other literary historians have cited Lewes's importance as a critic, and I have tried to show by means of additional evidence that Lewes is indeed a figure to be reckoned with in any study of literary events in the nineteenth century.

My ultimate objective has been to bring about a better understanding than now obtains of Lewes's rightful place in literary and cultural history, aside from his association with George Eliot. What were the extent and worth of his own contributions to Victorian life and thought? What is the real value of his work in literature, in criticism, in science, in philosophy? It is to these questions that I shall address myself in the following chapters, not in the hope of answering them definitively, but with the intention of pointing out and elucidating the areas in which he made his mark.

I wish briefly to acknowledge the efforts and myriad favors of many people, which have made it possible for me to complete this study. In particular, I am grateful to Professor Haight for his unflagging interest in me and in my work. I want also to acknowledge with heartfelt thanks the former and present members of the library staff at the University of South Florida who endured my demands with patience, fortitude, and endless ingenuity: Margaret Chapman, Carolyn Heselmeyer, Dennis Robison, Louise Ward, and the Director, Elliott Hardaway, who gave me a place to work. To the library staffs at Duke, Harvard, and Yale Universities I want also to express my appreciation, and especially to Marjorie Wynne, the tireless factotum of the Beinecke Library at Yale. I wish to thank the members of the Faculty of the Graduate School at Duke University, who saw fit to award me a summer Grant-in-Aid to do research, and my colleagues—including the deans—at the University of South Florida, who extended great financial and material aid to me in the form of a grant for half-time release in teaching load, money for travel, and vital secretarial help when it was needed most. And, finally to those whom I cannot name who have helped and encouraged me, my deepest and sincerest thanks.

EDGAR W. HIRSHBERG

The University of South Florida
Tampa, Florida

Contents

Chronology

1817 George Henry Lewes born April 18 in London; son of John Lee and Elizabeth Ashweek Lewes.

1825 Mother, widowed, marries Captain John Willim, formerly of the East India Company Service. George's first memory of the theater when he sees Edmund Kean.

1833 Last year of formal education at Dr. Charles Burney's School in Greenwich.

1834 Sees William C. Macready act in *Sardanapalus* at Drury Lane; tries various occupations without success, until 1838.

1836 Lectures on the philosophy of the Scottish school at Fox's Chapel, Finsbury.

1837 First acquaintance with William Bell Scott, the artist, who became lifelong friend. Writes drama about Tasso. Meets Charles Dickens, J. S. Mill, Lord Bulwer-Lytton, Leigh and Vincent Hunt.

1838– Two trips to Europe, most of the time spent in Germany.
1840 Sees Karl Seydelmann in *Faust;* meets Ludwig Tieck, German critic.

1840 Returns to England. First known published article appears in the *Westminster Review:* "The French Drama: Racine and Victor Hugo."

1841 April 18, marries Agnes Jervis (born May 24, 1822), eldest daughter of Swynfen Jervis, M.P., for Bridport in 1837, of Chatcull, Staffordshire. Acts in Garrick's comedy, *The Guardian;* possibly his first acting experience.

1842 November 24, birth of his first son, Charles Lee. Association with Thornton Hunt begins. Writes *Ranthorpe,* first full-length novel.

1845 Publication of first two volumes of *Biographical History of Philosophy.*

1846 Publication of last two volumes of *Biographical History* and *The Spanish Drama.*

1847 Publication of *Ranthorpe*. Tours London and the provinces as an actor in Dickens' company of "Splendid Strollers."

1848 Publication of *Rose, Blanche and Violet*. Second tour with "Splendid Strollers." Lectures on Shakespeare's dramatic art at Stoke Newington Institute. Publication of *Life of Maximilien Robespierre*.

1849 February, lectures on historical philosophy at Manchester and Liverpool. March, April, and May, plays Shylock in *The Merchant of Venice* and Don Gomez in *The Noble Heart* at Manchester and Liverpool, first performance of which is on April 16 in Manchester, where he lectures again on philosophy in May. November, plays Shylock and lectures on philosophy in Edinburgh.

1850 Becomes literary and drama editor for the newly established *Leader*. Publication of first play, *The Noble Heart;* opens in London February 18. Start of family troubles with birth of son to Agnes by Thornton Hunt.

1851 Introduced to Marian Evans by Herbert Spencer. *Game of Speculation* opens October 2 at the Lyceum Theatre in London. Enters into agreement with Charles Mathews.

1852 April 12, *A Chain of Events* opens; June 3, *Taking by Storm!* opens; both at the Lyceum.

1853 Publication of Auguste Comte's *Philosophy of the Sciences*. March 29, *A Strange History* opens; May 19, *The Lawyers* opens; both at the Lyceum. October, intimacy with Marian Evans begins.

1854 March 23, *Wanted a She-Wolf* opens (?). April 18, *Give a Dog a Bad Name* opens. June 15, *Sunshine Through the Clouds* opens, all at the Lyceum. July, leaves England with Marian Evans; permanent union with her begins.

1855 March, returns to England with Marian. *A Cozy Couple* opens March 15 at the Lyceum. June 29, *Buckstone's Adventures with a Polish Princess* opens at the Haymarket. October 30, *Life of Goethe* published.

1856 February 11, *Stay at Home* opens at the Olympic. To Tenby and Ilfracombe to do research for "Seaside Studies," published serially in *Blackwood's*. Encourages Marian to start writing fiction.

1857 Concluding installments of "Seaside Studies" published in *Blackwood's*, where Marian's first fiction, *Scenes of Clerical*

Life, also appears. She adopts pseudonym, George Eliot.

1858 Publication in book form of *Seaside Studies at Ilfracombe, Tenby, the Scilly Isles and Jersey.* Part of year spent in Europe with Marian. Occupied with anatomy and physiology.

1859 Publication of *Physiology of Common Life;* continues scientific researches.

1860 Second trip to Europe with Marian, most of time spent in Italy. Writing "Studies in Animal Life" for Cornhill Magazine. Starts "Ariadne."

1861 Starts "History of Science," which he never finished.

1862 Publication of *Studies in Animal Life.* Starts association with *Cornhill* as consulting editor, in which *Romola* is serialized.

1863 Continues editorial work with *Cornhill.* Finishes "Aristotle" as part of "History of Science," on which work continues. Moves with Marian to last permanent residence, "The Priory" in London.

1864 Publication of *Aristotle: A Chapter from the History of Science.* Severs connection with *Cornhill. Captain Bland,* originally started in 1855, first performed at Wallack's Theatre in New York, May 30.

1865 Becomes Editor of *Fortnightly Review* for six hundred pounds per year; also writing and working in advisory capacity for *Pall Mall Gazette.* "Principles of Success in Literature" serialized in *Fortnightly,* which he had begun as "Ariadne" in 1860.

1866 Gives up editorship of *Fortnightly* because of failing health.

1867 Publication of *Selections from the Modern British Dramatists,* for which he wrote Introduction and Biographical Notes. Writes Introduction and Explanatory Text for *Female Characters of Goethe,* from original drawings of William Kaulback, probably published same year, 2nd ed. in 1874. Takes trip to Spain with Marian, who is working on "The Spanish Gypsey."

1868 Working on "Problems of Life and Mind." Trips to Germany and Switzerland. August, invited to meeting of British Medical Association in Oxford to read paper on physiology. Meets Charles Darwin. Ends connection with *Pall Mall Gazette.*

1869 A "wasted and painful" year. October 19, death of son, Thornton. First meeting with John Walter Cross.

1870 Death of mother.

1874–1875 Publication of *The Foundations of a Creed,* first two volumes of *Problems of Life and Mind.*

1875 *On Actors and the Art of Acting* published. Death of son, Herbert, June 29, in Natal.

1876 Continues work on *Problems.* Helps form Physiological Society in London.

1877 *The Physical Basis of Mind,* third volume of *Problems,* published.

1878 June, severe symptoms of cancer, but thinks they are caused by gout. Bad illness sets in November 14. Recovers somewhat. Last letter written to Blackwood along with manuscript of George Eliot's *Impressions of Theophrastus Such,* November 21. Dies, November 30.

1879 Publication of last two volumes of *Problems of Life and Mind.*

1885 First appearance in book form of *The Principles of Success in Literature.*

1896 Publication of *Dramatic Essays,* by Lewes and John Forster.

George Henry Lewes

CHAPTER 1

Biographical Sketch

WHEN George Henry Lewes ran away with Marian Evans in 1854 he achieved immortality—as the husband of George Eliot. Whatever he was or might have been has been overshadowed by his relationship with the greatest woman novelist England produced during the nineteenth century. But, aside from this relationship, Lewes had a life of his own, a very interesting and productive life that contains within itself the seeds of its own greatness and that is worth investigating for its own sake. No full-length biography of Lewes has ever been written, but scholars have been busy ferreting out facts about him that might throw light on his all-important influence on George Eliot. Comparatively little has been done to find out anything about his life that does not make this light shine brighter, but enough is now known about him to form a fairly accurate picture of who and what he was—one accurate enough for the purpose of this biography, which is concerned more with what he wrote than with how he lived.

Lewes was born in London on April 18, 1817, youngest of the three sons of John Lee and Elizabeth Ashweek Lewes. His mother came from a respectable but undistinguished Devonshire family, concerning which virtually nothing has been recorded. His paternal ancestry is much more noteworthy, particularly his grandfather, Charles Lee Lewes. Usually referred to as Lee Lewes, he was a professional actor who managed to make a fairly widespread impression in the hurly-burly of the eighteenth-century English theater, and his name appears often in the stage histories of the time. His chief claim to lasting fame seems to have been his portrayal of Young Marlowe in the first production of Oliver Goldsmith's *She Stoops to Conquer* at Covent Garden in 1773. Indeed, the famous playwright was so pleased with the performance that he wrote an epilogue "in his pleasantest vein" when the play was presented for Lewes's benefit.[1]

There is a certain fascination in Lee Lewes's career because it resembles that of his more distinguished grandson in a few rather striking aspects. An inveterate, if not a very good, actor, he toured the United Kingdom in various theatrical companies almost until the day of his death in 1803. He excelled in comedy roles but was never successful in his attempts in tragic ones, and his grandson displayed the same strengths and weaknesses when he tried acting on the professional stage. Lee Lewes also had a penchant for writing, which his grandson certainly inherited; he was the author of a four-volume collection of *Memoirs* that were edited by his son John—G. H. Lewes's father—and published in 1805. Joseph Knight, his biographer in the *Dictionary of National Biography*, attributes to them "an unenviable precedency of worthlessness" in theatrical writing. The *Memoirs* consist chiefly of items of green-room gossip about long-forgotten minor stage figures. One of them, a dancer named Slingsby, might have supplied the inspiration for the rather peculiar first name of the pseudonym that G. H. Lewes used as a drama critic: "Slingsby Lawrence." Lee Lewes also wrote *Comic Sketches*, or *The Comedian His Own Manager*, which was published as a sort of memorial to him a year after his death. It is a series of stage recitations "sufficient for two evenings' entertainment," according to the title page. The anonymous biographical introduction describes Lewes as an extremely conceited but very engaging personality—again, much like his grandson was to be.

Information about Lee Lewes's family life is sparse. Two daughters by his first wife, whose maiden name was Hussey, were still living when the *Sketches* were published. His second wife was a Miss Rigley, the daughter of a respectable Liverpool innkeeper; and one of his sons by her was probably the John Lee Lewes who was George Henry's father. There was a third wife, but no information about her is available.[2] Our chief interest in Lee Lewes, of course, is in the influence his activities and inclinations might have had on his grandson. Certainly, George Henry Lewes's lifelong fascination with the theater was not simply fortuitous, but must have been inherited at least in part from the mercurial originator of Young Marlowe.

Comparatively little is known about John Lee Lewes. He was also an actor and spent much of his life in Liverpool. For a time he managed the Theatre Royal, and his involvements must have fostered George Henry's interest in theatrical matters. Besides editing his father's *Memoirs,* John Lee Lewes wrote two inconsequential collections of verse, *Poems,* published in Liverpool in 1811, and *National Melodies,* which appeared in 1817, the year George was born. But John Lee did not live long enough to have a very profound effect on his son's early life. Although the date of his death is not known, it must have been before 1825, when young George's mother married her second husband, Captain John Willim, a former officer in the East India Company Service. Mention of his stepfather's name is conspicuously absent from Lewes's later diaries, and his activities seem to have made very little impression on him.

The family lived fairly comfortably, from all indications, though there was a good deal of traveling about from place to place during Lewes's boyhood. Most of the memorable experiences in these early years had something to do with the theater. When he was eight, he recalled much later, he first saw Edmund Kean, either in London or in Liverpool. He could remember vividly the great actor's "looks and gestures" and could "hear his thrilling voice as if these were sensations of yesterday." [3] Two years later Lewes was in Nantes with his brother, stealing into the local theater "with pricking consciences," watching the actors, contributing "a stout British *encore!*" and laughing "at what we understood only in passing glimpses." [4] Back in London at sixteen, he went to Drury Lane to see W. C. Macready in Lord Byron's tragic drama, *Sardanapalus;* and twenty years later he wrote that the actors continue to "live with me," their faces and tones still "vividly impressed on my memory." [5]

Schooling for the boys during these years was peripatetic and intermittent. Various sources agree that George went to school in London, Jersey, and Brittany; and his encounters with masters of varying nationalities probably influenced his interest in foreign languages. When he was sixteen, he finished his formal education at Dr. Burney's famous school in Greenwich.[6] The discipline was good for him, but there is no record of how long he stayed. A strict school, it was conducted along conventional pedagogical lines: plenty of Latin and Greek, liberal birchings, cold baths at dawn, and a brutal "fag" system whereby the upperclassmen reigned as absolute—and sometimes despotic—monarchs over the lives and fortunes of the "new boys." The school was founded in the late 1700's by Charles Burney, Junior, who is sometimes referred to as the "Grand Assertor of the Ancient Discipline." He was a famous Classical scholar and the brother of Fanny Burney, one of George Eliot's most illustrious predecessors. At the time young George Lewes attended the school, it was being run by Dr. Burney's son, Charles Parr Burney, who probably carried on his father's tradition. The instruction Lewes received must have laid the foundation for the substantial knowledge of the Classics that he displayed later—despite his frequent claims that he was largely self-taught. How happy his school days were is, of course, debatable. He never mentioned them in any of his writings, and it seems likely that the sensitive, stage-struck adolescent was thoroughly miserable.

After he left Greenwich in 1833, he showed no interest in going up to one of the universities; apparently, he had had his fill of formal education. He tried the law, business, and medicine, but he found himself unfit for any of them. His natural interest in science might have helped him in a medical career, but his experiences while he "walked the hospitals" convinced him that he could not tolerate the human suffering that is so closely associated with life as a doctor. This sensitiveness to pain later restricted the range of Lewes's physiological experiments, according to one biographer; and it is evident in one of his descriptions of a dissection, written in his Journal in 1857. He had to cut up a dead puppy, which he had qualms about—he called it "a pathetic sight," hardly the reaction of an objective scientist.[7]

There is an appealing glimpse of his youthful days in an article Lewes wrote in 1866, in which he describes an informal club that he belonged to when he was about twenty. It met every Saturday night in a tavern in Red Lion Square, near the present location of the Holborn tube station in London. The members were a secondhand bookseller—"rich in free-thinking literature"; a journeyman watchmaker; a bootmaker; a poet; a man of leisure; and a student of "anatomy and many other things, with vast aspirations and no very definite career before him"—Lewes himself. Lewes's version of a typical meeting reads:

> Sitting round the fire, smoking their cigars and pipes, and drinking coffee, grog, or ale, without chairman or president, without fixed form of debate, and with a general tendency to talk all at once when the discussion grew animated, these philosophers did really strike out sparks which illuminated each other's minds; they permitted no displays of rhetoric such as generally make debating societies intolerable; they came for philosophic talk and they talked. It is more than probable that much nonsense was propounded. . . . The meetings were, however, stimulating rather to the intellect than the vanity; and if the topic under discussion sometimes disappeared in many-voiced confusion, a witticism or a remonstrance quickly restored order.

Lewes's reactions to the retreat from the society of a James P. Greaves indicate the philosophical bias espoused by the majority. Most of the members were glad to see Greaves leave because his metaphysics did not sit well with their rational views. In "striking contrast" was Cohn, or Kohn, a German Jew "whom we all admired as a man of astonishing subtlety and logical force, no less than of sweet personal worth." He introduced Spinoza to the group by expounding one proposition each week, and for Lewes there was a special interest in "this theological pariah—partly, no doubt, because he was an outcast." [8]

At this time, Lewes then records, he had a "rebellious sympathy with all outcasts" because he was "suffering the social persecution which embitters all departures from accepted creeds." He does not go into any detail on the kind of persecution he was suffering, but he hints that one reason for it was his approval of Spinoza's doctrine of the subjective nature of evil.[9] This long-ago encounter with the German philosopher, vivified by the disquisitions of the little Jewish watchmaker, started a lifelong interest in Spinoza. He bought a copy of the *Posthumous Works* and started a never completed translation of the *Ethics*. Later he published a notable article about him which was incorporated in the *Biographical History of Philosophy*.

There is mention of another early philosophical project in the Preface to the *Problems of Life and Mind*, on which Lewes spent the last few years of his life. By 1836, he writes, he had planned a treatise subjecting the so-called common sense philosophy of the Scottish school to physiological interpretation. Originated in the eighteenth century, this school is based on a strong reliance on psychology and the inductive method of research and reasoning.

Sometime during the following year—at the age of twenty—Lewes lectured on Scottish philosophy in Fox's Chapel, Finsbury. There is no other record of this occasion besides Lewes's own account of it in the Preface, written in 1870; and so it is based on a memory that must have been very much dimmed with time.

We catch other glimpses of Lewes's life during these formative, mercurial years in the records of his friends and acquaintances. They picture a young man of wide and various interests, boundless but uncontrolled ambition, and limitless energies. In 1837 he became friendly with William Bell Scott, later a distinguished artist, who supplies an engaging account of him in his *Memoirs*. The two met when Lewes wrote him at Leigh Hunt's suggestion that, as neighbors and as "cordial natures," they should get to know each other. Lewes described himself as "a student living a quiet life" with a "gusto for intellectual acquaintance, with which, I am sorry to say, I am not overburdened." Scott, about six years older than Lewes, found him "an exuberant but not very reliable or exact talker, a promising man of parts," though he "ignored and repudiated" the "high and pure ways of life and habits of body" that Scott himself held to.[10]

The artist supplies an engaging description of a visit Lewes paid to him and his wife soon after Scott's marriage. Lewes, who had written a drama on "Tasso and his unhappy love," had "generously" offered to read it to the young couple. When Scott "took courage" and objected to some of the scenes as being too "full of passion" for authors of their age and experience to be able to deal with, Lewes's "startling" answer was, "Well, do you know, young as I am, I have been all through such experiences! I have had ladies at my feet, and I have myself been next to mad with love and its fallacies!"[11] He was then in his early twenties—and how much experience he had actually had with "love and its fallacies" is, of course, a matter of conjecture.

During these years, Lewes's acquaintance with London literary people was constantly widening. In one of his early etchings, Scott portrays himself and Lewes sitting around a fireplace with Leigh Hunt and his son Vincent for an evening of earnest discussion. Lewes also knew John Stuart Mill, with whom he carried on an important correspondence, and Lord Bulwer-Lytton, who remained his lifelong friend, as did another youthful acquaintance, Charles Dickens.

Between 1838 and 1840 Lewes made two trips abroad. He spent most of his time in Germany, and the beginnings of his interest in German literature probably stem from the experiences he had during this period. They culminated some fifteen years later in his splendid biography of Goethe. Two of the impressions that apparently were most memorable to him later were a performance of Goethe's *Faust,* starring the famous German tragedian, Karl Seydelmann, and a conversation with the critic Ludwig Tieck about Macready's acting.[12]

When Lewes returned to England in 1840, he was deeply involved in writing, and he submitted poems, stories, and essays to many of the reputable periodicals of the day. He was starting in earnest his long struggle for literary fame, reflected fictionally in the experiences of young Wynton, one of the characters in his first published novel, *Ranthorpe,* the initial draft of which he finished in 1842. Wynton relates, "I sent articles, tales, and poems to every magazine then published. I lived month after month upon the delicious cozenage of hope that one of the editors would at last have taste and judgment enough to recognize an unknown genius. . . . I clung to my hopes tenaciously; but at length, in despair, I accepted a situation as private tutor in a rich Gloucestershire family."[13] Lewes seems to have lived the same kind of life at this time that Wynton describes so pitiably, and apparently he achieved the same lack of success. He too became a private tutor to bolster his consistently unsteady income, in the home of Swynfen Jervis, M.P., in Staffordshire. Like the not so fictional Wynton, who falls in love with the eighteen-year-old sister of his pupil, Lewes fell in love with Jervis' eldest daughter, Agnes, an extremely attractive, intelligent, and emotional girl, also eighteen. But Lewes had better luck than Wynton, who was spurned by his wealthy Gloucestershire beauty. In April, 1841, Lewes and Agnes Jervis were married in London, where they quickly settled down to a temporarily happy domesticity.

The following decade saw a tremendous increase in Lewes's literary labors. In addition to another novel, *Rose, Blanche, and Violet* (1848), he completed the first of many subsequent editions of his monumental *Biographical History of Philosophy,* a biography of Robespierre, a history of Spanish drama, and a long verse tragedy, *The Noble Heart.* He was also writing numerous articles for such first-rate magazines as *Blackwood's,* the *Edinburgh Re-*

view, the *British and Foreign Review*, and the *Westminster Review*. His subjects varied, but his best work was in criticism; and by midcentury he had gained solid recognition as one of London's leading literary men. Always versatile and incredibly energetic, we wonder how he found the time to write as much as he did, let alone participate in his other activities as actor, lecturer, husband, and father.

Four sons were born to the Leweses during the 1840's, three of whom survived. The growing family lived near the Phalanstery, a large house in Bayswater, where several young couples led a sort of communal life, sharing expenses and housekeeping chores. They included John and Jacinta Gliddon, Samuel and Anastasia Laurence, and Thornton and Kate Hunt. Kate and Anastasia were John Gliddon's sisters, and two more Gliddon girls—unmarried—joined the circle to help with the housework. To this stimulating and highly intelligent group the up-and-coming young writer G. H. Lewes and his handsome wife were more than welcome. Laurence later became a distinguished painter, and his portrait of George Eliot, done in 1860, is one of the best that has survived. Thornton Hunt, the son of Leigh Hunt, was a prolific writer and journalist. Extremely liberal-minded, all espoused the beliefs of the most advanced freethinkers of the age—the consequences of which were to cause momentous domestic upheavals as time passed.

Lewes is variously pictured in this period of his early maturity. One observer was Eliza Lynn, a girl of eighteen fresh from the country, who later married one of Lewes's friends, W. J. Linton, the artist and engraver. In her recollections of the Phalanstery she describes Lewes as "a singularly plain man, deeply pitted with the small pox, with narrow jaws and somewhat drawn-in cheeks . . . bright, vivacious and well-shaped eyes, a quantity of bright brown hair and a flexible mouth of singular moistness." She calls him "the first of the audacious men" of her acquaintance and the most "extreme"; and she depicts him as very much of a hedonist—sensual, self-indulgent, at home in all social groups, a bold and sometimes shocking conversationalist because of the topics he occasionally chose to discuss in mixed company. But, even as she expressed her dislike, she grudgingly admitted that his "brightness and versatility" and "the wonderful expressiveness of his eyes" made her forget "the unlovely rest." [14]

There were others who were struck by Lewes's appearance or personality. Francis Espinasse, a critic and biographer, mentions too "the ravages of the smallpox"; but he is quick to add that Lewes had "a fine eye and an expressive countenance." [15] Margaret Fuller, who met him at a dinner party at Thomas Carlyle's in 1846, describes him in her *Memoirs* as "a witty, French, flippant sort of man, author of a History of Philosophy, and now writing a Life of Goethe, a task for which he must be as unfit as irreligion and sparkling shallowness can make him." But the energetic Boston feminist admired his ability to tell stories and was glad that he "was allowed to interrupt Carlyle a little"—something that was relatively unheard of.[16] An interesting side glance at this encounter is provided in Lewes's review of the *Memoirs* written some six years later, when he comments that study had improved his first impressions of Miss Fuller's work—even though "the impression *we* made upon *her* seems to have been far from flattering." [17]

We are given a different view of him by another woman writer, one more sympathetic and perhaps more perceptive than Miss Fuller. Charlotte Brontë met him for the first time during one of her rare trips to London at a party at the home of Mrs. Gaskell in the spring of 1850. Though Lewes had just written a rather bad review of *Shirley*, which had upset her, she still liked him. In a letter to her friend Ellen Nussey, she wrote that Lewes "is a man with both weakness and sins, but unless I err greatly the foundation of his nature is not bad; and were he almost a fiend in character I could not feel otherwise about him than half-sadly, half-tenderly. . . . Lewes's face almost moves me to tears; it is so wonderfully like [the deceased] Emily, her eyes, her features, the very nose, the somewhat prominent mouth, the forehead, even, at moments, the expression: whatever Lewes does or says, I believe I cannot hate him." [18] The letter is revealing not only because of its insights into Lewes's character, but also because of the remarkable physical resemblance Charlotte saw between him and her beloved sister—in marked contrast to the picture of the shallow, flippant, French-type man Margaret Fuller had observed a short four years before.

Lewes played another role besides that of the successful and prolific writer and critic. Coming from a theatrical background, he never lost his intense interest in the drama in all its forms and manifestations. Going to plays and writing about them did not satisfy him; and, with typical energy and disregard for the consequences, he involved himself in as many other aspects of the theater as possible, plunging into it at various times as actor, producer, and playwright.

The 1840's saw the climax of his career as an actor and its rather abrupt demise. His first recorded acting experience was in Garrick's comedy, *The Guardian,* in which he is supposed to have performed at the Whitehall Theatre in 1841; but no additional information about this presentation is available.[19] We know much more about his next stage venture, his participation in Charles Dickens' company of "splendid strollers," who gave benefit performances in London and in the provinces in 1847 and 1848 to raise money for such worthy cultural causes as a pension for Leigh Hunt and the endowment of a curatorship for Shakespeare's house in Stratford. In neither case was the money needed—civil authorities stepped in and supplied it as a result of the glare of publicity that Dickens' proposed tours ignited. But the perennial stage-struck "Boz" went ahead anyway, and in his company were some of the illustrious figures in the literary and artistic life of the day—Mark Lemon, George Cruikshank, Mary Cowden-Clarke, John Forster, Dudley Costello, and John Leech, in addition to Lewes.

Dickens' glamorous amateurs attracted large and distinguished audiences who were more interested in seeing who the actors were and what they looked like than in how well they acted. Though imperfect, the performances made up in enthusiasm what they lacked in finesse. Queen Victoria herself and her consort attended the London opening of *The Merry Wives of Windsor* on May 15, 1848, at the Haymarket Theatre—Shakespeare's naughtiest play, it was ironically enough Victoria's favorite. Lewes played Sir Hugh Evans; and, according to the *London Times,* he was "one of the best 'hits' of the piece," despite "a trifling tendency towards exaggeration." [20] After their London triumph, Dickens and his troupe traveled to Manchester, Liverpool, Birmingham, Edinburgh, and Glasgow, where they alternated performances of *The Merry Wives* with Ben Jonson's *Every Man in His Humour.* Lewes played Old Knowell in the Jonson comedy on the 1847 tour and Wellbred the year after, switching roles because he probably liked playing a young spark better than a pretentious fuddy-duddy. In the comic "after-pieces" he took various roles, always showing a decided flair for comic acting—in very much the same style as his grandfather.

The warm reactions of the audiences and some of the reviewers, combined with his own inclinations, built up in Lewes's mind the mistaken notion that he should take up acting as a career. In 1849 he made two serious attempts to establish himself in the profession by playing Shylock in *The Merchant of Venice* and Don Gomez in Lewes's own play, *The Noble Heart*. During March, April, and May, 1849, he appeared seven times in Manchester and Liverpool as Don Gomez and four times as Shylock. In November he went to Edinburgh for two more performances as Shylock. The consensus seems to be that he was not so successful in tragedy as he had been in comedy, and everyone who wrote about him had the same general opinion—that he was sensitive and discerning as an interpreter of his roles, but lacked the physical power and presence that high tragedy demanded of the actor. One of the seasoned professionals in the *Merchant of Venice* company, Barry Sullivan, wrote that Lewes boasted at this time that he felt himself capable of taking Macready's vacant place as England's foremost actor; but, despite his ebullience, it does not seem likely that he ever really made such a claim.[21] In any event, his experiences by the end of 1849 had convinced him that he could never make a success of acting as a career; and he had the good sense to abandon it. But the theater never lost its fascination for him. He took an active part in it for several more years; and he continued to write about it, off and on, for the rest of his life. His theatrical experiences, which had familiarized him with the inner workings of theater, contributed to his later dramatic criticisms a genuineness and authority that they could not otherwise have achieved.

In addition to his writing and acting, Lewes also managed to give several public lectures during these eventful years. Late in 1848 he talked on Shakespeare's dramatic art at the Stoke Newington Institute, a Victorian approximation of an adult-education center. A few months later, in February, 1849, he presented a series of lectures on historical philosophy at Manchester and Liverpool, anticipating by a few weeks his appearances in these cities as a tragic actor in *The Merchant of Venice* and *The Noble Heart*. According to one account, he made "a prodigious sensation" as a lecturer in spite of his "moustachios" which "hurt people's sense of propriety." [22] Later in the same year he again combined acting and lecturing, this time in Edinburgh, where he interspersed his November performances as Shylock with lectures on philosophy at the Edinburgh Athenaeum.

Lewes was involved in yet another project, the launching of a new weekly newspaper, the *Leader,* which occupied much of his time and energy between 1850 and 1855. He became the dramatic and literary editor, and many of his most brilliant critical pieces appeared in the *Leader's* columns. In charge of editorial policies, which were on the extremely liberal side, was his friend Thornton Hunt. Radicalism or near-radicalism in their political opinions distinguished most of the other participants in the venture. W. J. Linton reported on foreign affairs for a short time, but he soon resigned from the staff when he decided that Lewes and Hunt were not extreme enough in their ideas on republicanism. G. J. Holyoke, an inveterate agitator for equality among all classes of men, served as office manager. The guiding spirit and originator of the *Leader* was Edward F. S. Pigott, a radical journalist who managed to convince several of his rich, Socialist inclined friends to contribute financial backing. Chief among them was Reverend Edmund Larken, who had married into a wealthy Lincolnshire family and was liberal in his giving as well as in his thinking. W. E. Forster, who became Secretary for Ireland, was another supporter—as was Minter Morgan, a friend of Robert Owen, the pioneer Socialist.[23]

The picture we have of Lewes in the early 1850's, then, is that of the successful and versatile writer, editor, and critic. He has tried his hand at acting and lecturing, but has made up his mind to stick to the literary life, in which he has so far achieved the most success and satisfaction. He maintains his connection with the working theater, which still fascinates him and always will, by writing brilliant and perceptive dramatic criticisms for the *Leader.* He also begins to write plays for actual production in London, so that he involves himself more and more deeply in theatrical concerns.

In the midst of all this stimulating activity there was one source of deep unhappiness: his domestic situation, which was rapidly deteriorating. During the decade of the 1840's he and his wife Agnes enjoyed an apparently ideal marital relationship. But some time after they moved near the Phalanstery his "human Rose"—as he called Agnes—fell in love with Thornton Hunt, who, as we already know, lived with his wife and growing family in that establishment. Several years older than Lewes, he had an engaging personality and, according to all accounts, was very attractive to women despite his rather unprepossessing appearance. In 1850, when Agnes gave birth to her fifth son, everyone concerned acknowledged that Hunt, not Lewes, was the father. The fact that Hunt was his close friend, combined with his forgiving nature and liberal ideas, prompted Lewes to overlook his wife's infidelity, and he had the new baby duly registered as Edmund Alfred Lewes. But less than two years later, her infatuation apparently unabated, Agnes gave birth to a daughter whose father also was Hunt; this time Lewes could not forgive her, and he no longer regarded her as his wife. He remained co-editor of the *Leader*, but to say that his relationship with Hunt was strained would rival the most exaggerated understatement.

During this period of domestic upheaval in October, 1851, Lewes first met Marian Evans, then a spinster of thirty-four. She was assisting John Chapman, an enterprising if somewhat erratic London publisher, as editor of the *Westminster Review*, in which he had a controlling interest. Lewes was introduced to her by a mutual friend, Herbert Spencer, the rationalist philosopher. Though it was not a case of love at first sight, the relationship between Lewes and Marian Evans gradually became more and more intimate. They had many interests in common. As editor of the *Westminster*, Marian bought several of Lewes's articles. In his turn, as literary editor of the *Leader*, Lewes often wrote favorable reviews of the *Westminster*. Their mutual intellectual interests stimulated a growing affection, and Lewes found himself turning to her for companionship and consolation when he had the greatest need for them. And in him Marian Evans discovered the one thing that her life as a successful magazine editor had lacked—the love of a sensitive, congenial, attractive man.

Lewes's work on the *Leader* occupied most of his time between 1850 and 1854. As drama editor, he spent many of his evenings in the theater, where Marian often accompanied him; and this period saw the ripening of their relationship. It was neither a mere liaison nor a platonic friendship. They finally realized that they were deeply and seriously in love; and, by the spring of 1854, they had made up their minds to live together as man and wife. Under

English law Lewes could not obtain a divorce from Agnes because he had condoned her adultery with Hunt the first time he knew about it. As a result, he and Marian could never be married legally. She was fully aware that, if she lived with Lewes, she would be regarded as his mistress, and would subject herself to social ostracism and to the stern reproaches of her family and most of her friends. But she was convinced that her action was justified: she and Lewes loved each other, and his marriage was no longer a reality. They both felt that the only honest course of action was to live together openly and to suffer the consequences.

In July, 1854, they took the fatal step. To her three best friends Marian wrote, "I have only time to say good bye and God bless you. . . . Weimar for the next six weeks, and afterwards Berlin."[24] This brief note signifies the beginning of one of the grand alliances of literary history. For the next twenty-four years Lewes and she were husband and wife in every sense of those words. There is almost no doubt that, if they had not lived together, Marian Evans never would have become George Eliot; and *Adam Bede, The Mill on the Floss, Silas Marner, Middlemarch,* and *Daniel Deronda* would never have been written.

They spent their first few months together in Germany, where Lewes completed his *Life of Goethe,* the most successful and popular book he ever wrote. It came out in 1855, and in March of that year he and Marian moved back to London. Though they were happy, this was a time of heartache, frustration, and embarrassment because of the circumstances under which they had chosen to live. But they were heavily involved in literary labors, which kept them very busy and were much more productive than an active social life would have been. Lewes was supporting his legal wife and their three surviving sons, and he continued to discharge this financial obligation as long as he lived, so that money matters were of considerable concern.

They both contributed critical articles to the various magazines. Lewes kept up his connection with the *Leader* on a reduced basis, and continued with his playwriting and reviewing. But, from about 1856 on, his interests were turning more and more toward science; and he directed his creative and critical capacities into the fields of biology and physiology during the next decade or so. These years saw the publication of his *Seaside Studies,* based on his investigations of marine plant and animal life at Ilfracombe,

Tenby, the Scilly Isles, and Jersey, where he and Marian resided for short periods between 1856 and 1860. *The Physiology of Common Life* and *Studies in Animal Life* also appeared, as well as many articles about scientific subjects in such periodicals as *Blackwood's*, the *Westminster Review* and *Fraser's Magazine*.

During this period Marian also emerged as a writer of fiction. Her first book, *Scenes of Clerical Life,* was a collection of three short novels that originally had appeared in *Blackwood's* as serials in 1857. Lewes, who had encouraged her to write them, had been instrumental in getting *Blackwood's* to publish them. His *Seaside Studies* also were first published in serial form in *Blackwood's;* and in January, 1857, he wrote in his Journal that his resumption of contributions to the magazine had "formed the proximate cause of Marian's introduction to fiction." For a long time they had "discussed the desirability of her trying her powers in that direction; and the temptation of appearing anonymously and successfully in *Blackwood's* induced her to begin a series of tales the first of which appeared this month." [25]

They were both delighted at the enthusiasm with which *Scenes* was received; and Marian, still with Lewes's strong support and encouragement, immediately started *Adam Bede,* her first full-length novel. At about this time—the latter part of 1857—she decided to adopt a pseudonym. She chose "George" because it was Lewes's first name and "Eliot" because, as she explained later, it was "a good, mouth-filling easily pronounced word." [26]

Adam Bede placed George Eliot's name among the shining lights in England's galaxy of great nineteenth-century novelists. A popular success immediately, it has remained a favorite ever since. On the first page of the manuscript these words are inscribed in the author's handwriting: "To my dear husband, George Henry Lewes, I give the M. S. of a work which would never have been written but for the happiness which his love has conferred on my life." The dedication is signed "Marian Lewes" and is dated March 23, 1859.[27] As her reputation grew with the success of her subsequent novels, George Eliot's demands on her husband's time and energies increased. He conducted her dealings with her publishers, saw that she was not disturbed by bad reviews, attended solicitously to her health, and took care of the family finances. Whether or not he would have accomplished more himself along the lines of his own interests and capabilities if he had not been burdened with George Eliot's affairs is, of course, a question that can never be answered.

One advantage of Marian's success was that their financial worries were ended. Lewes was sending his three boys to private school and giving Agnes a fairly substantial allowance. In spite of these obligations, the increasing income from the sale of Marian's books made it possible for him to engage in his scientific pursuits without having to consider financial remuneration as a primary factor. His Journal during the late 1850's and early 1860's is full of accounts of his experiments in marine biology, and we wonder how Marian took to their constant meanderings in the muck off Tenby and the Scilly Isles, searching for exotic flora and fauna for him to look at through his beloved microscope. He first learned to use the instrument during their stay in Tenby in the summer of 1856 while gathering material for his *Seaside Studies*.

His description of the revelations of the microscope is especially interesting as an essentially literary reaction to a scientific activity. How many scientists would write about looking through a microscope in these poetic terms? The entry is dated July 31, 1856: "What marvels are disclosed by the microscope! It is like looking at the Alps from a distance when nothing but purple masses are discernible, and then approaching we find not only the hills and valleys and streams, but villages, and human dramas—so with the naked eye we discern in Glycera nothing but a pale worm . . . , and under Micro these hairs turn out to be complex organism—feet, gills, and bristles!" [28]

Lewes's love for science dominated the last half of his productive life. From his work in marine biology sprang an interest in physiology, neurology, and psychology; and he made some significant contributions to the knowledge of these then young scientific disciplines. At the same time that he was involving himself more deeply in these activities, he never paused in his unremitting attention to the needs of George Eliot; and his life was always divided between his own interests and his concern for hers. One remarkable aspect of it is that he managed to do as much as he did, in spite of this concern.

The years between 1860 and 1876 saw the effulgence of George Eliot's genius. *The Mill on the Floss*, published in 1860, was followed by *Silas Marner*, *Romola*, *Felix Holt*, *Middlemarch*, and

Daniel Deronda—novels that remain permanent landmarks in English fiction. While these books were solidifying her reputation, Lewes was continuing with his experiments in physiology and psychology; and he had embarked on two ambitious projects which he never finished. One of these was his "History of Science," designed as an all-inclusive account of the lives and works of the great scientists. The other was *Problems of Life and Mind,* a general summary of his research in physiology, the first four volumes of which were published between 1874 and 1878. In addition to books and articles on scientific subjects, Lewes continued to contribute essays on literature and the drama to the magazines; but they lacked the verve, color, and spontaneity of his earlier criticism. Generally, they reveal his retreat from literary interests because of his concentration on science. An inept article on Henry Fielding, for example, published in 1860, is one of his few really serious critical blunders. Others included pieces on Victor Hugo, Dickens, and the actor Charles Fechter. He also started "Ariadne," originally conceived as an essay on the philosophy of art, and developed it into a series of articles that appeared in 1865 in the *Fortnightly Review.* Later these were published in book form as *The Principles of Success in Literature,* an interesting and still useful account of his theories on literary esthetics.

A revealing commentary on the relationship between Lewes and George Eliot is that his scientific and literary accomplishments were just as much a source of pride to her as her novels were to him. Far from being a one-way street, their mutual love and admiration was the source of a constant interflow of help and inspiration to each of them. When Charles Ritter, a Swiss scholar, wrote her in 1874 to express his admiration for Lewes's work, she replied that she was "delighted" to hear praise of "my husband's books."[29] In a later—and very interesting—letter to Harriet Beecher Stowe, Marian writes that she is looking forward to working with Lewes on the manuscript and proofs of the third volume of his *Problems of Life and Mind,* when she will "plunge" herself "into the mysteries of our nervous tissue." With regret, she continues, "My studies have lately kept me away from the track of my husband's researches and I feel behindhand in my wifely sympathies." She concludes with one of her rare confidences: "You know the pleasure of such interchange—husband and wife each keeping to their own work, but loving to have cognizance of the other's course."[30]

During the 1860's Lewes served in capacities of editorial leadership on three important literary periodicals, *Cornhill Magazine,* the *Fortnightly Review,* and the *Pall Mall Gazette.* He discharged these obligations with typical Victorian energy and industry—at the same time continuing with his own writing, helping "Polly" with hers, conducting his scientific experiments, and also managing to take several trips abroad for health, relaxation, and research. The Lewes's domestic life likewise was becoming more complicated. George Eliot's increasing income enabled them to buy a comfortable house in London, "The Priory," where they lived from 1863 until Lewes died. Here they entertained many celebrated literary figures, and their Sunday afternoon gatherings were attended by the social as well as the intellectual elite of Victoria's England—although the Queen herself never invited George Eliot to court because of her anomalous relationship with Lewes.

Their concerns with Lewes's sons also occupied much of their attention. All three boys went to the Hofwyl School in Switzerland, and Lewes occasionally used their attendance there as an excuse for an extra jaunt to the Continent. The oldest son, Charles, had a successful career in the post-office service and brought his parents much happiness; but the two younger boys, Thornton and Herbert—or Bertie—were not so fortunate. When they left school, after much pulling of strings by their influential father, they went to Natal to seek their fortunes as farmers. Unhappily, Thornton contracted tuberculosis of the spine and had to return to London, where he died in 1869—a "wasted and painful" year, according to Lewes's Journal, spent taking care of the boy and watching him waste away. But, sad as the time was, he still could write, "Our deepening love sustained us. It is something as the years pass on, and one feels conscious of declining powers, to know that love increases instead of diminishing."

Certainly his "diminishing powers" must have indicated to him that his health was deteriorating. Never robust, he was always losing precious time to bouts with sickness which increased in length and intensity as time went on. At the age of sixty-one he finally succumbed to cancer. Active almost to the last, he was working on the fifth and final volume of *Problems of Life and*

Mind when he died on November 30, 1878. George Eliot spent the next year finishing it from his notes and seeing it through publication. Her subsequent marriage to John Walter Cross belongs to another story. But her creative life had ceased; and, after Lewes died, she never wrote another line of fiction.

CHAPTER 2

The Writer of Fiction

LEWES did his most distinguished and significant work as a man of letters. Although his contributions to philosophy and science were notable, they were not so original or so lasting as those he made to literature, particularly in the field of criticism. For the sake of clarity, his criticism can be divided into two general types: dramatic and literary. More or less arbitrarily, we will consider his dramatic criticism to include his writing on the drama and related subjects, and his literary criticism to include his writing on all other forms of literature. Such a distinction is appropriate because his writing is so varied and prolific that a straightforward chronological consideration of it would make very little sense. During the 1840's and 1850's he wrote—as the spirit, or the request of an editor, moved him—novels, plays, essays, criticism, and biography; but he never concentrated for long on one particular form. What he did rather than when he did it, and how good —or bad—it was, are the objects of our investigation and appraisal.

For both kinds of criticism his preparation, like so many other things about him, was highly irregular. He did not have the background in Classical studies that a conventional education would have provided, yet he somehow managed to obtain a tremendous knowledge not only of the ancient Greeks but of the modern Europeans as well. His reading was omnivorous and unorthodox. Peripatetic and completely unguided, it ranged from Pliny to Rousseau, from Dryden to Victor Hugo, from Dante to George Sand. In his Commonplace Book, dated 1843,[1] there are notes and quotations from various sources, written in German, French, Spanish, Italian, Latin and English. Such subjects are treated as Truth, Reading, Passion, Death, and Love. Quotations and summaries are entered with no apparent plan or order in mind. The list of writers Lewes seems to have been familiar with reads like a catalogue of authors for a Great Books course: George Chapman, Francis Beaumont and John Fletcher, Goethe, Sir Thomas Browne, John Webster, W. S. Landor, Sir William Davenant, Samuel Daniel, Edmund Cartwright, Francis Bacon, Alphonse Lamartine, Petrarch, and many others.

Leafing through the Commonplace Book we come across extracts from *The Satyricon, Wilhelm Meister* and *The Rehearsal;* quotations from Homer, Ovid, Sallust, Torquato Tasso, Martial, and Giacomo Leopardi; epigrams from François de La Rochefoucauld, Nicolas Chamfort, Blaise Pascal and John Donne; passages from Voltaire, *The Illiad,* Petrarch, S. T. Coleridge, Madame de Staël, Tacitus, Pindar, Laurence Sterne, Nicolas Boileau, Molière, Georges Buffon, Juvenal, Spinoza, and Michel de Montaigne—in just about that sequence, with no attempt to synchronize or relate. Lewes, writing in 1852 about the domination of the Classics in British schools, mentions that "the accidents of our own education" might bias him "in favor of that which it has cost us so much labour to acquire." [2] Certainly the evidence in the Commonplace Book indicates that this "labour" was considerable, that he read with an enormous if erratic appetite, but that he had a strong inclination to pick out the best that was then known and thought in the world—the kind of preparation for a critic that his friend Matthew Arnold would have approved of wholeheartedly.

Another facet of Lewes's preparation for the task of literary criticism was his non-critical writing. A good "creative" writer does not necessarily make a good critic, but the attempt to write creatively often sharpens the critical faculties. Because the artist-critic has been involved in trying to create a work of art, he is perhaps better able to judge the quality of such a work than the critic who simply looks at it from the outside without ever having gained the knowledge that involvement brings. Whether or not he produces anything worthwhile, the mere act of trying to create something original out of the resources of his imagination is an exercise in criticism, even if it functions only to demonstrate how supremely difficult the creative process can be.

Lewes's attempts in the field of belles-lettres were largely unsuccessful, but they acquainted him with this very complex process from the inside, as it were, and made him a more perceptive—and perhaps more sympathetic—critic than he otherwise would have been. For a comprehensive understanding of his qualities as a critic, we should inspect briefly his capacities as a creator, not so much to evaluate what he actually produced as to determine what effects his creative efforts had on his critical capabilities.

Lewes began writing plays and stories when he was still in his teens. None of these early pieces has survived, nor has his play about Tasso and his unhappy love, which he read to his friend William Bell Scott with such amusing results. But he did write a novel, *Ranthorpe*, soon after he turned twenty, which we have referred to previously because of its bearing on Lewes's own youthful experiences as an author. It was published in 1847, although he had completed it five years before. As his maiden attempt in the field of fiction, it retains some interest aside from its biographical content. Dedicated to his wife Agnes, who had "lightened the burden of an anxious life," [3] it includes some fine firsthand descriptions of how things were among the London literati in the 1840's.

Ranthorpe, a young writer who first tries his hand at criticism, makes a small *succès d'estime* with a book of poems and then falls by the wayside as the victim of too much adulation by a coterie of admirers who care nothing about him, but want to achieve a vicarious fame by associating with him when he temporarily becomes a "literary lion." Recovering from deep despair after the failure of his second book of poems, he turns his hand to playwriting. He completes a serious verse tragedy, which is finally produced after much travail only to be mercilessly damned on its opening night. On the verge of suicide, he is rescued just as he is about to leap into the Thames by Richard Thornton, a "queer looking," jolly little old man who takes him under his wing for no really good reason. He resembles Leigh Hunt, whose son—Thornton—was one of Lewes's closest friends at the time he was writing the novel.

Unfortunately, Richard Thornton is murdered. Ranthorpe is accused and then exonerated, but he leaves London because of the notoriety brought on by his implication in the crime. After two years in Germany—where Lewes also spent two years when he was about Ranthorpe's age—he returns to London, marries his childhood sweetheart, and settles down to a life of successful literary activity. Lewes describes Ranthorpe at the end of the book in what is a thinly disguised but a highly idealized picture of Lewes himself:

He has won his spurs. His genius has begun to take its magnificent flight far above the reach of other wings. He is in his twenty-fifth year, and his genius is free to operate untrammeled upon the materials afforded him by experience. . . . After many a giddy faintness, and many a sick despondency, he has reached a tableland, from whence he can look down calmly on the path before him. He has walked up through mists, but has reached a certain height. The storms are below him. The poor attorney's clerk has become an honoured author. . . .[4]

Superimposed on the story of Percy Ranthorpe's rise, fall, and rise again are several others: his laborious love affair with Isola; her fate after he rejects her; Florence Wilmington's fate after she rejects him and marries Sir Frederick Hawbucke, Baronet; Harry Cavendish's marriage to Fanny Wilmington after Ranthorpe regains Isola, who has consented to marry Harry, who gallantly lets her go when he discovers that she really loves Ranthorpe after all. This brief summary of some of the ramifications of *Ranthorpe*'s plot seems complex, but it provides the merest hint of how extremely complicated it actually is. Unhappily, Lewes starts enough plots for several full-length novels, but they never arrive anywhere. The reader loses interest in the characters because he never knows them well enough to find out who they are. Events happen so fast that Lewes's account of them becomes a mere outline, a sketchy framework.

Even more disconcerting are his more or less fortuitous interjections of his thoughts on authorship and its concomitant griefs. Midway in an exciting episode, he may insert some lengthy remarks on the nature of genius or several extraneous paragraphs on the differences between aspiration and inspiration. These digressions would be proper in an essay on literature or writing and many of them found their way into his published criticism—but they are inappropriate in the pages of a novel; and they also make *Ranthorpe* even more incoherent than it would have been without them. Most applicable to its basic deficiencies are Lewes's own opinions on the necessity for organic unity in the structure of fiction, which he expressed many years after *Ranthorpe* had gone permanently—and deservedly—out of print, ironically enough, in his *Principles of Success in Literature.* He concluded that, if the author "stretch[es] together a volume of unrelated chapters—a patchwork of descriptions, dialogues, and incidents,—no one will call that a novel." [5] No one will call *Ranthorpe* a novel; but, aside from the insight it provides into Lewes's own youthful experiences, it still retains some interest for the cultural historian because of its quick, vivid glimpses into the life of a typical apprentice in the industry of manufacturing salable but worthwhile literature, an industry with which Lewes had an intimate and longstanding acquaintance.

His only other novel to be published in completed form was *Rose, Blanche and Violet,* which appeared in three neat and rather elegant volumes in 1848. At this time one of his critical favorites was George Sand, whose first successful novel was *Rose et Blanche.* Whether her work had anything to do with Lewes's choice of a title is, of course, conjectural; but we hope that it did. *Rose, Blanche and Violet* shows some improvement over *Ranthorpe* and is not so dependent on Lewes's own personal experiences, but it still has many biographical elements and contains many of the same faults. There is the same overcrowded plot in which too many things happen in too short a time for characterization and motive to develop sufficiently. Again there is a lack of transition between events, so that the reader is left with the impression that the novel consists of a series of more or less disconnected incidents. And there is also too much authorial comment, even in an age when a certain amount of such comment was acceptable, indicating that Lewes often was more interested in driving home a point about art, marriage, genius, or whatever interested him than he was in telling a tightly knit story about an integrated group of characters. And, like *Ranthorpe,* the book is marred by a general preciosity that is emphasized by the author's obvious effort to impress his readers with the depth and breadth of his intellect.

It is dedicated to "M. Benjamin Morel (de Dunkerque), comme un affectueux souvenir de l'auteur," with no hint as to who M. Morel might be or why he was singled out for such an honor. In addition to references in German and French, there is a plethora of allusions from Latin and Greek writers, particularly in the conversations involving the three girls' elderly father, Meredith Vyner. He is a classical scholar who has for several years been engaged in writing a new and definitive edition of the Odes of Horace, which he never gets around to finishing. His character might have lent inspiration to George Eliot, years later, when she created Dr. Casaubon in *Middlemarch,* who also was a scholar of the trivial and also—like Vyner—was married to a woman much younger than himself.

Despite its imperfections, the novel has aspects that deserve consideration for the light they throw on Lewes's own character and capabilities. Some of the characters are well drawn and would grace many a better novel by their presence. For example, his description of the "Walton Sappho," Hester Mason, and her coterie of worn-out poetry lovers is a masterpiece in satiric destruction—as is his picture of Sir Chetsom Chetsom, the "wigged and whiskered baronet" who becomes her unfortunate paramour. There are also some good individual scenes in the book which illustrate Lewes's skill in dramatic construction, so useful to him when he wrote his plays. The gambling den, in its detailed analysis of the poor wretches who have "caught the bug," is a fine description and a subtle piece of foreshadowing. Whether George Eliot read it—and might have had it in mind—when she wrote the first scene of *Daniel Deronda,* also a gambling den, is an interesting question. The later gambling scenes in *Rose, Blanche and Violet* are equally effective, if a little overdrawn. Several of the book's depictions of passion are vivid and authentic, such as the encounters between Marmaduke Ashley and Mrs. Vyner. The scene in her bedroom, when Lewes examines the motivations and cross-purposes of the two antagonists with an almost Proustian intensity, achieves a high point in genuine dramatic feeling. There is also a certain cleverness in some of his narrative devices, such as his employment of the works of Petrarch and Leopardi—about whom he was then writing critical articles—to convey messages between lovers.

Many of Lewes's digressions are in themselves interesting; but, as in *Ranthorpe,* they sometimes interrupt the action and mar the construction of the novel. In the first volume there is an entire chapter devoted to "The Disadvantages of Ugliness," in which Lewes describes Julius St. John, one of the three suitors, who is handicapped by a lack of physical attraction that is more than compensated by his possession of other sterling qualities such as intelligence, sensitiveness, virtue, and grace. Aside from the obvious base in Lewes's consciousness of his own physical disadvantages, the unusual nature of this digression gives it a certain appeal; moreover, it becomes a contribution to the reader's understanding of Julius' character and later actions. But, when Hester Mason discusses the "unholy institution" of marriage, or when the author puts by his story to embark on a short dissertation on the proposition that "life is short and art is long," the reader may be struck with admiration at the cogency and truth of the observations, but he also realizes that the digressions are badly misplaced in the context of this particular novel.

Some of the descriptions of places present isolated if—again—unintegrated examples of Lewes's literary capabilities. Mrs. Tring's boarding house has all the depressing aspects of something out of Balzac. In fact, we wonder if, when Lewes wrote it, he had in mind a recent recollection of *Père Goriot,* which appeared as part of the "Comédie Humaine" in 1843. The year following saw publication of a substantial article by Lewes about Balzac and George Sand, and so his memories of the French novels were fresh.[6] But, whatever his debt to Balzac, the description is a vivid depiction of a sordid side of nineteenth-century lower middle-class London life not often presented in contemporary English fiction.

One of the few light touches in the book is the delineation of Miss Blundell, a harpist in one of Hester Mason's musical *soirees.* It shows that Lewes might have done better in his novel writing, if he had concentrated more on the comic instead of the serious aspects of life; for his flair for comedy also characterized his dramatic writing as well as his acting:

> Miss Blundell was not handsome. Of an age so uncertain that it is denominated "a certain age," she wore her black hair in a girlish crop. On a low, square, rugged forehead sparkled a *Sévigné.* Wondering eyebrows overarched two sunken eyes; a graceless nose and insignificant mouth did *not* tempt an artist. . . . In accordance with the juvenility of her style, she was robed in white muslin, displaying a scraggy tawny neck, fierce and protuberant shoulder blades, and disreputable arms. . . . She began by a rattling sweep over the strings, and an audacious display of elbows. . . . A few seconds of silent invocation brought down the muse, and she flogged the harp into the Gustavus galop.[7]

The most interesting contemporary reaction to *Rose, Blanche and Violet* that I have come across is in a long letter written by Charlotte Brontë in April, 1848. Since Lewes had been one of the few critics to recognize the extraordinary abilities of the author of *Jane Eyre,* Charlotte was perhaps a little prejudiced in his favor.[8] Yet her comments have the ring of sincerity and obviously were not meant for publication. She regarded his second novel as a possible improvement over *Ranthorpe,* which she also had liked very much because it "had a pith, truth, significance in it which gave the book sterling value." [9] In *Rose, Blanche and Violet* Charlotte considered Lewes himself the most original character. His didactic passages are "far the best," she felt, even though the reader sometimes resents the manner in which his "doctrines"—sagacious as they might be—are presented. "You acknowledge that he offers you gems of truth," but "why do you keep perpetually scrutinizing them for flaws?" It is in Lewes's style, not in what he says, that Charlotte finds weaknesses. She sees in him "a touch too much of dogmatism: a dash extra of confidence," yet when the reader puts the book down and thinks about it, he is glad to have made a "fuller acquaintance" with "a fine mind and a true heart, with high abilities and manly principles." Lewes's emotional scenes are sometimes handled in a "too unfairly vehement" way and could have been "more subdued"; for he occasionally "takes a French pen into his hand"—which, however, does not "mislead" him far, since he "wields it with British muscles"—not a very happy figure. But, as she concludes with the hope that Lewes will write another book soon, she expresses the opinion that this novel deserves a reception "far beyond anything due to a Bulwer or D'Israeli production." [10]

A few days after she had written this letter she wrote another to Smith Williams, dated May 1, 1848, answering his criticisms of *Rose, Blanche and Violet.* In it she deplores Lewes's constant use of quotations from Classical and foreign writers to embroider the texture of his English, agrees with Williams that Lewes lacks delicacy and imagination, and concedes that he is too anxious to impress his readers with his "acquirements," desiring to excite the pleasant feelings which incline the taught to the teacher "more for reasons of reverence than of friendship." If she could address Lewes directly, she would say, "You have a sound, clear judgment as far as it goes, but I conceive it to be limited; your standard of talent is high, but I cannot acknowledge it to be the highest; you are deserving of all attention when you lay down the law on principles, but you are to be resisted when you dogmatize on feelings." Charlotte concludes that Lewes can go to a certain point intellectually, but no further. Not all his learning, reading, sagacity, or perseverance can help him over a boundary that is "as impassable as it is invisible" into a sphere within which a man must be born; "untaught peasants have there drawn their first breath, while learned philosophers have striven hard till old age to reach it, and have never succeeded." [11]

Here Charlotte is ruling Lewes out of the charmed circle of inspired writers of imaginative prose—in which she herself belonged—and her reasons for doing so are perfectly valid. Lewes—in love with the facts of life, a determined rationalist in his philosophy—was never one to soar on the viewless wings of poesy. Rather, he stood almost too foursquare on the solid ground of actuality. To use one of his own expressions, he was high on aspiration but low in inspiration in his fiction writing; and, though he had a truly remarkable facility in the use of words, he was never able to wield and shape them into the original imaginative conceptions with which the true novelist must weave his narrative web.

Charlotte's criticism of the main characters in *Rose, Blanche and Violet* also illuminated Lewes's faults. Hester Mason, the ill-fated "rustic poetess," she considers a "dreary picture" doubtless drawn from life, but hardly a worthwhile figure for fictional treatment. Julius St. John and Captain Heath, who to her are unconvincing, receive short shrift. She is also skeptical about Mrs. Vyner, who, though "a portrait from life," is characterized as so thoroughly wicked that she is scarcely credible as a human being. Unlike "Mr. Thackeray's Rebecca," who is very much a person in spite of her vanity, heartlessness, and falsehood—and so "infinitely more impressive" in the lesson she teaches—Mrs. Vyner is simply a demon, from whose "strange fantasies" we can learn little, since "we are not of their kind." [12]

In all these opinions Charlotte was in agreement with her correspondent, Smith Williams; but she differed strongly with him about one of the characters, Cecil Chamberlayne, Blanche's brilliant but unstable husband, who ends his life as a disgraced suicide. In Charlotte's passionate defense of Lewes's depiction of Cecil there is the sincerity bred of intimate, firsthand knowledge. Surely she was thinking of her brother Branwell when she wrote these lines:

You say that . . . men of genius and talent may have egregious faults, but they cannot descend to brutality or meanness. Would that the case were so! Would that intellect could preserve from low vice! But alas! it cannot. No, the whole character of Cecil is painted with but too faithful a hand; it is very masterly, because it is very true. Lewes is nobly right when he says that intellect is *not* the highest faculty of man, though it may be the most brilliant; when he declares that the *moral* nature of his kind is more sacred than the *intellectual* nature. . . . You probably never knew a Cecil Chamberlayne. If you had known such a one you would feel that Lewes has rather subdued the picture than overcharged it; you would know that mental gifts without moral firmness, without a clear sense of right and wrong, without the honourable principle which makes a man rather proud than ashamed of honest labour, are no guarantee from even deepest baseness.[13]

Charlotte Brontë's spirited defense of the characterization of Cecil Chamberlayne throws some interesting light on her attitude toward errant genius, deeply affected as it must have been by her unhappy experience with Branwell's many frailties. Lewes's realistic account of the effects of moral weakness on intellectual strength apparently struck a deep and intimate chord in her nature. In any event, notwithstanding the novel's many defects, she felt that it was well worth reading—and discussing at more than usual length.

Another famous novelist who felt that *Rose, Blanche and Violet* had some positive merits was Charles Dickens, some of whose talents as a storyteller Lewes could have put to very good use. Dickens might have read it as a gesture of friendship toward one of his "splendid strollers," or perhaps he was simply curious. He was sufficiently impressed with it to write to Lewes in May, 1848, after finishing Volume III, that "it affected me extremely, and manifests I think very great power." Like Charlotte Brontë, he too admired the history of Cecil Chamberlayne and his wife, which "swallowed up" all the other things he had noticed and left him "in a damned black brooding state." [14] But another friend was far differently affected: irrepressible Jane Welsh Carlyle wrote to her husband that she thought the book was "silly" and a waste of time; and she regretted that she had not put it aside "in the first half volume"—which she would have done if she had not "felt a pitying interest in the man" that made her read on "in hope of coming to something a little better." [15]

Soon after *Rose, Blanche and Violet* was published in 1848, both it and *Ranthorpe* were reviewed in the *British Quarterly Review*.[16] The anonymous critic's tone is one of respectful if uninspired praise. He sees the intellectual power of the author of the recently published *Biographical History of Philosophy* reappearing in his fiction in the form of philosophical generalizations and didactic observations and analyses of character and motivation rather than "in the invention of stirring incidents." *Ranthorpe* is throughout "instructive, and delineated with a firm and masterly hand." *Rose, Blanche and Violet*, aimed more at the circulation library audience, is written in a style that is "always lively, often witty, never dull." Obviously more interested in the "moral nature" of both books than anything else about them, the reviewer fills up a tremendous amount of his space with excerpts to illustrate the point that Lewes had made in his rather perfunctory Introduction: the moral aspect of man's nature is more important than the intellectual. Value judgments based on any esthetic considerations are conspicuously absent. Like much contemporary literary criticism, the review is inept and ineffective as a comment on either the faults or the virtues of Lewes's artistry and is written in a dull and wooden style. Happily, Lewes's own criticism suffers remarkably little from these egregious faults.

Ranthorpe and *Rose, Blanche and Violet* are the only full-length novels Lewes ever completed; most of his other ventures into fiction were stories of varying length and quality. One was a translation—evidently hackwork—of a short novel by George Sand, done in 1844 when Lewes, still in a precarious financial situation with a growing family, was willing to turn an honest shilling at any odd literary job that came along. This rather gaudy story of a borderline love affair, laced with romantic mystery, was called in George Sand's original version *Le Sécrétaire Intime;* but it was retitled for British consumption *The State Murder: A Tale.* It ran in two installments in *Fraser's Magazine;* but the novel was adapted and abridged along the lines of a revealing footnote, which appears on the first page of the opening episode: the version in the *Magazine* "is not defaced by any of those faults usually so offensive to English tastes. It has been, however, deemed necessary to soften the colouring of one or two scenes, and to omit others as superfluous. By this means the female reader is enabled to enjoy a novel of the celebrated George Sand, without danger and without distrust." [17]

Here is a typical example, of course, of Victorian censorship. Lewes, perfectly willing to cooperate, apparently felt that by omitting "offensive" faults and softening the "colouring" of certain scenes he was not impinging on anyone's freedom to read but was helping in the noble task of educating young British womanhood while protecting it from the baneful influence of French sensuality. In any event *The State Murder,* abridged and emasculated as it is, has always remained in the well-merited obscurity of *Fraser's* yellowing pages.

Another of Lewes's early—and slight—efforts at fiction was a short story called "A Night in a German Swamp," which appeared in *Douglas Jerrold's Shilling Magazine* in 1847.[18] Probably based on an experience recollected from his youth—he had spent most of 1839 and 1840 in Germany—it is a pleasant little account of a mishap that occurred on a walking trip: the descriptions are sprightly, the style easy and readable, the narrative sustained and interesting. In a later number of *Jerrold's Magazine* during the same year, yet another of Lewes's stories appeared, "The Gallant Glazier; or the Mystery of Ridley Hall." [19] Influenced perhaps by Lewes's recent acquaintanceship with *Jane Eyre,* it concerns an isolated country seat—much like Thornfield—where also resides an imprisoned woman whose name—coincidentally—is Jane. She is the beautiful sister of cruel and greedy Squire Templeworth, who has confined her as a lunatic because he does not want to share the estate with her—the circumstance that is "the mystery of Ridley Hall." It is solved by Harry Meadows, the gallant glazier, who rescues Jane in a daring sortie over insurmountable obstructions. She insists on marrying him, sweeping aside the worthy workman's humble protest that she is "not meant for such as me" because of the wide difference in their "stations." This kind of development is in line with Lewes's ideas on social equality, which, for a Victorian, were on the radical side. They appear again in his description of Squire Templeworth's luxurious but lonely life—at his solitary dinner, waited on by a corps of servants, his wealth "wears not its air of insolent prosperity—it only makes the scene hideous." Aside from these attempts to convey some sort of social message, the piece is not very effective. It suffers from the same defects that plague Lewes's longer fiction: the characters are not sufficiently realized, the events are mechanically contrived, the narrative is reduced to the dimensions of an outline, and reader interest and involvement are lacking.

Social rather than esthetic concerns likewise dominate his next venture into fiction, *The Apprenticeship of Life*, which ran as a serialized novel in the *Leader* from March to June, 1850. In its original conception it was to have had three divisions: "The Initiation of Faith," "The Initiation of Love," and "The Initiation of Work." The chapters on Faith and Love appeared, but there is no trace of those on Work in the succeeding issues of the *Leader* after the conclusion of the sequence on Love.

In *The Apprenticeship of Life* Lewes deals with the formative years of its hero, Armand, who bears a striking resemblance to Ranthorpe. But the writing is better than that in the earlier novel, and Armand's character is more fully developed. "The Initiation of Faith" tells the story of Armand's unique switch, under the influence of his friend Stavros Frangipolo, from complete skepticism, to a strong faith in unorthodox Christianity. In real life, Frangipolo was Stavros Dilberoglue, whom Lewes had met during one of his lecture tours in Manchester in 1849. A Greek refugee of great charm, he had taken up temporary residence in England because of his revolutionary activities against the Turks. Lewes admired him enough to delineate him in considerable detail in his creation of Frangipolo, whose portrayal has the breath of life lacking in many of the other characterizations.

Armand's "Initiation of Love" takes place in Paris, perhaps a more suitable location than London for the events that transpire. Banished by his rich uncle because he has too much religious faith —the irony of this situation either escaped Lewes or he chose to ignore it—Armand is befriended by Hortense, a handsome St. Simonian several years his senior. She believes in the doctrine of love as the sole bond of marriage, and probably was a projection in Lewes's mind of George Sand, a conscientious practitioner of this doctrine, who in the late 1840's was his favorite French author. Events gallop apace, as they always do in his stories: Hortense and Armand become lovers, but he eventually rejects her for a younger girl; he feels—like Shelley—that "progressive natures, patriots as well as poets, are inconstant almost inevitably." Armand gets mixed up in French politics with his friend Frangipolo, and there are again radical overtones in his yearning for free democratic institutions for the people as well as free love for himself.

The ideas Armand espouses in *The Apprenticeship of Life* were, of course, Lewes's. Liberal in his thinking about both politics and marriage, Lewes used the form of fiction as a means of self-expression. The fact that he never finished the novel—though it can hardly be called one—probably indicates that he lost interest in it as a method of propaganda. Once Armand has delivered himself of his opinions on love and politics, he has little more to say. The unwritten third section, "The Initiation of Work," presumably would have been about his experiences as an apprentice in the literary or artistic world—and this subject already had been exhausted, as far as Lewes was concerned, in *Ranthorpe* and in *Rose, Blanche and Violet*. We can regard Armand, then, as an approximate projection of what Lewes would like to have been in the late 1840's and early 1850's: free of conventional marriage ties, active in liberal politics, intimate with important people. Already his life was pointed in these directions, and this projection became more and more of a reality as time passed—in a way that Lewes certainly could not have anticipated when he wrote *The Apprenticeship of Life*.

Though he turned most of his energies during these years toward criticism, much of it dramatic, he was also writing plays, or, as we have seen, adapting them from French originals. Most of them were produced, and we shall consider them later in the context of his activities in the theater. But two of them never appeared on the stage, for one reason or another; and with typical persistence and ingenuity he converted them into stories which eventually were published as serials in *Blackwood's Magazine*. Based on the works of other authors, they do not reveal so much about him as his previous fiction, which was largely autobiographical. But they are interesting as examples of Lewes's strengths—and weaknesses—as a writer of fiction. Perhaps more important, he made some comments while working on them about his own limitations that shed light on his unique capabilities as a literary critic—capabilities that enabled him to recognize and help bring to fruition George Eliot's talent, just then beginning to assert itself. Her first work of fiction, *Scenes of Clerical Life,* also ran as a serial in *Blackwood's* only a few months after the appearance of the first of Lewes's two pieces, "Metamorphoses: A Tale," which was published in the May, June, and July, 1856, issues.[20]

Adapted from a French play that is no longer extant, as far as I have been able to determine, the tale concerns the adventures of a nondescript group of Frenchmen—and women—caught in the toils of intrigue and conspiracy during the eventful days of the First Republic. The hero-villain is Victor Marras, whom Lewes originally had wanted to "do something novel with" by making him a "semi-humbug." [21] A poor boy of humble origins, Victor is in love with Adrienne, the beautiful daughter of rich, aristocratic, but reputedly liberal Count de Chateauneuf, who has "none of the prejudices of his race or caste," can read Rousseau, and discuss the rights of man "with great temperance." [22] He has himself educated Victor in his own liberal tradition, and, when he and his family summarily rebuff Victor in his quest for Adrienne's hand because he is not of noble blood, the irony and shame are compounded. Bitter and rejected, Victor runs off to Paris where he is involved in various shady dealings connected with the Revolution.

Years later, as one of Robespierre's trusted commissars, Victor returns to his native village in search of the Chateauneufs, who, captured after many escapes and adventures, finally fall into his hands. He not only lets them escape, thereby betraying the Republic, but refuses Adrienne's passionately proffered favors despite the fact that he still is hopelessly in love with her. Beneath his apparent depravity, Victor is the noble but lowborn hero of sterling worth and integrity. She sees these qualities, but too late. She leaves the country, eventually returns, but never marries; Victor simply disappears in the mists of his ambivalent revolutionary fervor. The melodrama's seriousness is lightened by Goulard, the barber, and Nicotte, the milkmaid, who provide the comic relief. But, like the rest of the characters, they are so obviously borrowed from the stage that they never ring true as people of the book.

Lewes himself, aware of the weakness of the story, wrote Blackwood that its defect was that of "the original play from which I altered it, in that neither hero nor heroine have sufficiently marked *character.*" In a subsequent letter he wrote that the story "is too curt and hurried; indeed I was afraid of getting lengthy and have fallen into the opposite extreme." [23] The observation is true, and the fact that Lewes himself recognized his own failings is an indication of his critical acumen. The delineations of Victor, Adrienne, and the other characters are unconvincing; and, though Nicotte and Goulard are occasionally lifelike and amusing, they are not important enough to improve the piece as a whole. Events move too fast, motivations are inconsistent and insufficient, and the story simply lacks interest because Lewes was unable to breathe life into his people.

The only other unproduced play by Lewes that appeared as a magazine story started out as a comedy called *The Fox Who Got the Grapes.* Originally completed in 1854, it was an adaptation from a comédie-vaudeville, *Alexandre chez Apelles,* which had been produced in Paris some two years before.[24] When Lewes was unable to find a market for it, he put it aside; then in January and February, 1859, he rewrote it but still could not get it produced. Finally he converted it into a short story, changed the name to "Mrs. Beauchamp's Vengeance," and sold it for twenty-three pounds to *Blackwood's,* where it finally appeared in May, 1861.[25]

During its seven-year evolution *Alexandre chez Apelles* underwent substantial alterations. The play concerns the efforts of a French painter, Sénasar, to seduce Clotilde, who he thinks is safely married to his best friend. At the height of his protestations she informs him that she is not really his friend's wife but his mistress. But he has been unfaithful, and so, she cries in triumph, "Je suis accepter la main que vous m'offrez. . . . sans crime!" [26] ("I accept the hand which you offer me . . . without offense!"). Sénasar's dismay is, of course, considerable; and he spends the rest of the comedy trying to forestall marriage to Clotilde. Lewes's version is very much watered down. In *The Fox Who Got the Grapes* Mrs. Beauchamp is not Easy Rackit's friend's mistress but his fiancée, and there is no hint of an illegal liaison between them. Apparently such a liaison, in Lewes's judgment, might have been a fit subject for the sophisticated tastes of Parisian theatergoers, but it was certainly not for staid Victorian Londoners. The change in relationships takes most of the starch out of the comedy; and, although it is one of Lewes's most original adaptations because he had to make so many changes, it is not very funny or dramatic—which probably is why it was never performed.

The other alterations in "Mrs. Beauchamp's Vengeance," as it finally appeared in *Blackwood's,* were even more damaging. To make it completely respectable, Lewes cut the best comedy scene in *The Fox Who Got the Grapes,* in which Mrs. Beauchamp offers to compromise herself by moving into Rackit's apartment to prove her sincerity. When her personal belongings arrive, they include just "a few trifles"—several trunks, a large Tambour Frame for worsted work, a parrot, a harp, a cat, and some bandboxes, which she calls merely "the things that are indispensable." [27] Eliminating humorous situations like this one inevitably reduced "Mrs. Beauchamp's Vengeance" to a rather dull story. But Lewes felt that even vague references to extramarital relationships would be improper matters for *Blackwood's* subscribers to read about, and so he dispensed with most of the lively incidents and flattened out the characters into conventional Victorians.

Ironically enough, Lewes knew very well—even while he was converting *The Fox Who Got the Grapes* into "Mrs. Beauchamp's Vengeance"—that, as a fiction writer, he was dealing in an entirely different medium of communication from that of the dramatist. He also knew the precise nature of the differences between the two media. In one of his *Leader* reviews that appeared in 1853 he observed that the details in a drama "should be few and striking, rather than abundant and trivial," while in a novel the author must construct "a large work out of minute details." Effects in a play "should be distributed in masses" because of "the very fact of representation in an hour or two [of] the events and feelings of a large episode in life." The novelist, on the other hand, can take his time to build up to "the complete exhibition of the idea" by means of the "exhaustive details" necessary to the whole but individually "too minute and familiar to be of great interest." [28]

The trouble with Lewes's own fiction was that he usually failed to build up details for "the complete exhibition of the idea" because he had neither the imagination nor the inclination to do this kind of writing. His stories are largely made up of the "few and striking" pictures that drama demand. They lack, therefore, the "abundant and trivial" details that he claimed a good novel needs in order to provide complete conceptions of character and action. As we have seen, *Ranthorpe* and *Rose, Blanche and Violet* suffer from this deficiency. Events are generalized, and characters are insufficiently analyzed. The shorter fiction suffers from the same malady.

The significant difference between Lewes and any other unsuccessful fiction writer is that he was acutely conscious of his own ineptitude. He knew why his novels and stories were generally ineffective, but he lacked the imagination—or, more accurately, the talent—to do with them what he fully realized needed to be done. No criticism that he ever wrote is more applicable to himself than this observation about novel writing, which appeared many years after he had given up the idea of ever becoming a novelist: "The novel may be more popular and more lucrative, when successful, than the history or the essay; but to make it popular and lucrative the writer needs a special talent, and this . . . seems frequently forgotten by those who take to novel writing."[29] Lewes lacked this "special talent." Yet his unsuccessful attempts at fiction contributed materially to his understanding of the novel as a form of literature, and made him a better critic of it—just as his experiences as a playwright made him a better dramatic critic than he otherwise would have been.

CHAPTER 3

The Literary Critic

I *Principles and Practice*

THE important thing to remember about Lewes's literary and dramatic criticism is that it is firmly based on philosophical principles. He rarely passed judgment on any artistic work—a novel, a play, a painting, or a symphony—simply on the basis of personal preference. In this one respect he was different from most Victorian critics, and from all minor critics of any era. The basis of specific esthetic principles elevates his criticism above the ordinary and the temporal, and it accounts to a great extent for the enduring validity of his judgments.

Dominating his esthetic philosophy were his conceptions of truth, reality, and sincerity. Related as these three conceptions are, they result from what might be regarded as the scientific bias of Lewes's mind. The chief aspect of his uniqueness among purely literary men was his knowledge of and interest in science, and his approach to the esthetics of literature was essentially scientific. It insisted on logic, reason, and facts as bases for its assumptions, observations, and conclusions. His insistence on using the scientist's mode of thought clarified all of his criticism, but it also imposed certain limitations; it may account to some extent for the patent superiority of his judgments about fiction and drama over those concerning poetry. But the fact that Lewes was both a scientist and a literary man had, on the whole, a salutory effect on his criticism because it increased its effectiveness and its honesty.

The principle of sincerity, perhaps the dominant element in his esthetic system, permeates all of his criticism—as, indeed, everything he did and wrote. The idea of sincerity occupies a primary place in the first critical essay he ever had published, an article on Shelley written in 1841, when he was only twenty-four years old; and it was one of the main points in what can be termed his final critical testament, the *Principles of Success in Literature*, which first appeared in the *Fortnightly Review* as a series of articles a quarter of a century later.

Lewes's early definition of sincerity in the Shelley piece has a significant bearing not only on his subsequent criticism but on the conduct of his own life as well. He admired Shelley as "eminently virtuous because he was eminently sincere." [1] Shelley—in obeying his own rules of conduct, regardless of the social acceptability of these rules—was living virtuously because he had the integrity to do what he sincerely thought was right. Here, Lewes felt, was the kernel of the whole idea—the real virtue is in the doing, not merely the thinking; and in this sense Shelley was completely sincere. Despite the general vilification of the poet as an immoralist because of his extramarital relationships, Lewes admired him for this "one quality" that "distinguishes him pre-eminently": "an unyielding worship of truth" as Shelley saw it.[2]

Sincerity becomes a principle of effective artistic endeavor, as well as a way of life, in Lewes's later declaration in the *Principles of Success in Literature*. The man who does his best work is the one who is most sincere about it. Whatever his attributes in the way of talent, imagination, or insight, they must be sincerely guided to the creation of the absolute truth. The artist's genius—such as it is, and no matter how humble—is related to the moral qualities of patience, honesty, courage, and simplicity. If the artist does not possess these qualities in his participation in artistic activity, he will not be able to direct his abilities sincerely; consequently, he will fail in his attempts to achieve the very best of which he is capable. The specific application of this principle to the writer's art, Lewes's concludes, is in "placing before the reader intelligible symbols of the thoughts and feelings in the writer's mind" as they really exist and in as true, simple, accurate, and sincere a style as possible. He despises "fine writing" for mere ornamentation not only because it is esthetically inadmissible but also—and much more important—because it is a violation of the writer's sincerity.[3]

The principle also applies in matters of taste. Lewes refers to Emerson in bolstering his contention that the artist should depend on his own instincts and nobody else's, and should stick to his own opinions even if they disagree with those of the majority. The fact that the artist honestly believes in his opinions is the key to his sincerity, regardless of the opposing tastes of others. When he violates his own taste to cater to what he thinks will enhance his popularity, when his eyes are fixed on the public reaction to his work instead of the work itself, he is insincere and can produce nothing but "claptrap." Whether his insincerity is prompted by conventional "idealism" or simply by the "insidious flattery of public prejudice," it is still inexcusable. The sincere artist loves his art as "the splendour of truth." He is insincere when he prefers effects to reality, when he tries to create "arresting phantasms" instead of "visions of his own soul." [4]

Closely allied to his principle of sincerity and heavily dependent on it is Lewes's second esthetic mainstay: the function of truth. Associated with this idea in turn is his conception of reality, which to him is a necessary part of the artists's integrity. As we read Lewes's criticism of both drama and fiction, we discover that these two conceptions—truth and reality—are the starting points, as well as the foundation, of most of his judgments. There also is a consistent relationship between them and his conception of moral virtue. What is true and therefore beautiful, says Lewes, is also good; what is untrue and consequently ugly is evil. These Keatsian conclusions are of course oversimplifications; but, by examining some of their implications, we can trace the development of Lewes's esthetic ideas and at the same time determine what contributions he made to the history and techniques of criticism.

As early as 1841, in his first ventures into the field of critical writing, Lewes was equating the power of good with the existence of truth. In the article on Shelley, he was still reasonable and consistent enough, despite the adulatory tone, to attribute his feelings to definite causes. In comparing Shelley to Byron, he considers that Shelley was essentially good because he believed in the ultimate power that good has over evil. With a "true poet's spirit" he devoted himself to helping mankind. Though he was a dialectical skeptic, he was still an ethical believer. Though he had no faith in man's religions, he had complete faith in man—unlike Byron, who had no faith in anything. Shelley was the only poet to devote himself completely to the truth of man's power for good—to the "dominant idea" of the age, characterized by "progression, humanity, perfectibility, civilization, democracy." [5] Shelley's stature as a poet is equated by Lewes with dedication to truth and the progress of mankind—an essentially Romantic idea, with overtones from Carlyle.

But Lewes's adulation of Shelley's moral superiority did not blind him to the poet's weaknesses. Ironically foreshadowing some of Shelley's detractors who thrived a century later, Lewes saw that the poetry suffers from a want of "*objectivity*"—Shelley cannot describe objects because his mind is "sensitive and reflective, rather than plastic and creative." His descriptions are dreamy, but they are not realistic. In using such words as "objectivity" and "realistic" Lewes was indicating the way his critical path was to lead—away from Romantic philosophizing toward a rationale based on esthetic is well as exclusively moral truths.

The same tendency is evinced more distinctly in Lewes's criticism of George Sand and Balzac, written a few years after the Shelley article. Though he felt that the critic should examine a novel for its truth and morality, as well as for its capacities to amuse, he no longer equated morality with the author's attitudes about life but rather with the novel's approximation to truth. In turn, truth depends not merely on the credibility of the events in the story but on "the probability and consistency of the motives, passions, and characters." For truthful rendering of human passions supplies more lasting delight than the artifices of narrative and the excitement of exceptional happenings. Balzac's great distinction is in his discovery that "the true source of human interest" lies in human nature.[6]

But it is in his appraisal of Charlotte Brontë's *Jane Eyre* that Lewes articulates most clearly and most forcefully the meaning of his conceptions of truth and reality. Written in 1847, the Brontë criticism is part of the article "Recent Novels: French and English" in *Fraser's Magazine*. Originally he had wanted to write it only about *Jane Eyre*, which had just been published, because he recognized the book's transcendent and unusual superiority; and, when the editors of *Fraser's* would not allow him to devote a major article to a first novel by an unknown author, Lewes dismissed the other "recent novels" with a few comments, then embarked on a remarkably perceptive and prophetic account of the excellencies and imperfections of *Jane Eyre*.

His estimate is based on the premise that the correct representation of real life is the most important criterion in judging a novel —that, above all, it must be "true to nature." On the basis of this criterion *Jane Eyre* is an excellent book: "Reality—deep, significant reality" is its "great characteristic." The action of the story, though based on the author's own experience, invests this experience with an added charm and interest, so that the novel becomes an utterance "from the depths of struggling, suffering, much enduring spirit." Lewes, generalizing to prove his point, speculates that, if the unknown author has not had much experience, her future works must be carefully planned because, "unless a novel be built out of real experience, it can have no real success." Ordinary novels, he continues, attract readers temporarily if they have an interesting plot; but they do not last and are never reread. But if, to mere curiosity about the events in a story, are added "scenes which, being transcripts from the book of life," affect the reader as all truth of human nature must affect him, "then the novel rises, as *Jane Eyre* does, from the poor level of street conjuring into the exalted region of art." [7]

Lewes particularly admired the characterization of Jane herself, who is a woman, not a pattern, with "very fleshly infirmities and very mortal excellencies." Rochester and St. John Rivers are not so well depicted, for both are obviously portraits of men drawn by a woman. Helen Burns he calls "eminently ideal and accurately real," an antithesis that is interesting if a little hard to accept. He spends little time on the descriptions of landscape but accords them the accolade of truth—they are realistic, clear, and picturesque. The author's delineation of life in the country among the higher social classes is distinguished by "ease and accuracy," though Lewes hastens to add that this delineation is accurate only in the sense of "being represented from the governess point of view." [8]

He also admires the unknown writer's power of "subjective representation," and in doing so he is one of the first critics to acknowledge and recognize the importance of the psychological aspects of the novel. He elaborates on her ability to connect "external appearances with internal effects" on a character by "representing the psychological interpretation of material phenomena." [9] This capacity to unite the physical and psychological implications of an episode or event Lewes illustrates by citing the scene in which Jane is punished as a child by being shut up in the old red room at Gateshead Hall, and the consequent effects on her imagination—certainly a pertinent example of the psychological results of a physical circumstance.

Lewes praises the book's style along much the same lines as he does its other qualities. Despite minor objections, the style, though not "fine," has "the capital point of all great styles in being *personal,*—the written speech of an individual"—not the "artificial language" of books. His final injunction to the author is to persevere in this rejection of artificiality. He advises her to "keep reality distinctly before you, and paint it as accurately as you can: invention will never equal the effect of truth."

Throughout his entire appraisal of *Jane Eyre* we note Lewes's persistent adherence to the principle he has enunciated for himself at the very beginning, his "brief confession" that is to "give our criticisms their just significance": "What we most heartily enjoy and applaud is truth in the delineation of life and character; incidents however wonderful, adventures however perilous, are almost as naught when compared with the deep and lasting interest excited by any thing like a correct representation of life. That, indeed, seems to us to be Art, and the only Art we care to applaud." [10] Though Lewes had used the terms "real" and "realistic" before, this statement was his first elaborate explanation of what he meant by their implications in his criticism of the novel as "Art." His opinions about plot, characterization, and style were all influenced by his conception of the meaning of realism, which remained constant as a basic criterion in his evaluations of fiction.

Three years after the publication of Lewes's perceptive review of *Jane Eyre*—and he was almost the only contemporary English critic to recognize its author's exceptional talents—he wrote an adverse criticism of her next novel, *Shirley*. He did not reverse his previous high opinion of Charlotte Brontë's genius, but he did show a consistent application of his own critical standards. He had praised *Jane Eyre* because it was real and truthful; he depreciated *Shirley* because it was not. The basis of his opinion he first laid down as a principle, in accordance with his usual procedure, that relates to the difference between truth and art. Truth is not necessarily acceptable simply because it is the truth; consequently, the mind must be prepared to accept it. The imagination helps in this process of preparation not because of a departure from truth but "only because it presents the recognized attributes of our nature in new and striking combinations." Art, then, should not deal with the idiosyncrasies of human nature but with the generally acceptable characteristics. As "recognized attributes" in "new and striking combinations," the peculiarities of a character in fiction should still be acceptable as natural. Simply saying that a character is copied from nature—as the author of *Shirley* does—is not enough if he strikes the reader as "unnatural." The artist, then, must base his conception of truth on nature; and his imagination must not depart from it even while creating "new and striking" manifestations of it.[11]

Basing his evaluation on this distinction between art and nature, Lewes concludes that *Shirley* lacks the quality of truth that distinguishes *Jane Eyre*. The second novel fails to "hurry" the reader through its "improbabilities" with "so keen a sympathy in its reality" because the author's imagination is not consistent enough to make the essentially unbelievable events at least acceptable.[12] Relying on the principle that what is artistic is natural, Lewes details his reasons why Miss Brontë's imaginative inconsistency prevents *Shirley* from being a true work of art.

First, the point of view is too indefinite, so that the artist paints a panorama and the readers become mere spectators, not participants in the action. Second, the scenes are disparate and there is no coherent movement or sense of life, so that the novel lacks unity, and interest in it as a complete work of art diminishes. Third, though the characters themselves are realistic and true to life in some ways, they are not related directly enough to the story. The curates, for example, are "boors," not curates—their attributes as social misfits emerge much more clearly than their attributes as clerics; therefore, they are simply "not true" as believable people. Fourth, Lewes concludes that *Shirley* is not a work of art because the artist was not sure of what she wanted to do in writing it; as a result, she created a "portfolio of random sketches for one or more pictures" rather than a single, coherent whole.[13] We see artistic unity in this instance as yet another aspect of Lewes's conception of truth as a standard of excellence—what is not whole is not true, and, consequently, is not admissible as art.

Lewes applied this principle of artistic unity as a criterion of excellence in a later article on Fielding's *Tom Jones*,[14] in which he sought to prove that it too, like *Shirley*, is not a work of art because of its faults in construction. Unfortunately, this evaluation was one of Lewes's rare—and worst—lapses in critical judgment. Published in 1860, it was a radical turnabout from the opinions of Fielding that he had expressed long before when he wrote in 1847 that "Fielding and Miss Austen are the greatest novelists in our language" and that he "would rather have written *Pride and Prejudice* and *Tom Jones* than any of the Waverley novels." [15]

Just why Lewes's attitude changed so much about Fielding—though it did not about Jane Austen—is difficult to determine. By 1860 he was spending much of his time on his experiments in psychology and physiology. What thoughts he gave to literature were devoted more to his esthetic theories about it than to concrete judgments. In his depreciation of *Tom Jones* he cites two principles to substantiate his opinion that the book's structure violates its unity as a work of art. These are the "Principle of Economy" and that of "Selection," and he goes into considerable detail in describing them. Eventually, they were incorporated into *The Principles of Success in Literature*. Though the principles of economy and selection are perfectly valid as precepts for writers to follow, their application to *Tom Jones* is only partially relevant. Lewes uses the novel as one of several examples to elucidate them; and, as long as he sticks to this purpose, he remains straightforward in his reasoning. He explains the "Principle of Economy" as the requirement that the writer free his work of all superfluities, with the qualification that it restricts the dramatist more than the novelist because of the time limitation inherent in the form of a play. The "Principle of Selection" obligates the author, first, to pick events that are not obvious coincidences manufactured to help him out of his plot difficulties, and, second, to avoid converting his characters into mouthpieces to voice his opinions by making sure that what they say results from their own thoughts, not his.[16]

Tom Jones is guilty on both counts, according to Lewes; and his strictures are along much the same lines as his previous comments about *Shirley*. He considers that *Tom Jones* is largely episodical, a collection of separate tales strung together in a series of more or less unrelated events. Tom passes from place to place and always arrives at the right time to meet the appropriate set of characters who will best help the plot along. There is no unity in Fielding's variety, and the book is full of coincidences and superfluous scenes that "violate the most elementary rules of construction." The characters also lack emotional depth and are unrealistic, and the reader only sees and hears them by means of Fielding's "dramatic ventriloquism," without ever knowing them or believing in them.[17] Because of its inept construction and unconvincing characterization, *Tom Jones* violates both the principles of economy and of selection.

Lewes's criticism is not completely fallacious. Certainly, the novel is episodic and loosely constructed; and his remarks would have been innocuous if he had been content to leave it at that. But he goes too far in his summarizing verdict and displays a singular lack of appreciation for the qualities of humor and satire in *Tom Jones.* Terming Fielding a "painter of manners and amusing story-teller," Lewes attributes to him an "intensely unpoetical mind," which is unable to portray humanity because of a "deadness to Nature" that is a typical eighteenth-century deficiency. He misses the point of Fielding's exaggerated handling of some emotional situations and asserts that Fielding simply is incapable of "serious" writing when he describes scenes in which "poetry" or "sentiment" is called for. As for his morality, Lewes will "not dwell" on it—enough to say that Fielding is completely insensible to the "disgracefulness" of Tom's liaison with Lady Bellaston.[18]

In conclusion, *Tom Jones* has "not one surpassing excellence" among its many merits. The construction is bad, the characters have no real depth, and Fielding shows no profound knowledge of human nature. The humor, though abundant, is coarse. Irony and animal spirits keep the reader amused, but the book's only "real merit" is as a picture of eighteenth-century manners. Before readers pass final judgment, Lewes suggests that they peruse the book themselves and that they try to read it as impartially as they would the novels of Balzac. In what might have been an attempt to temper his disapproval, he admits that he expects many will disagree with him on some counts, but at least he has proved his point about the construction of *Tom Jones,* which nobody can deny is palpably faulty.[19]

Certainly Lewes makes a strong case, but at too great a cost to the realities of Fielding's stature. Modern criticism recognizes *Tom Jones* for what it is—an imposing if somewhat disunified edifice. For all its faults in this regard, it still remains one of the greatest English novels ever written, because of its wonderful, lusty characters and its earthy picture of contemporary life. In view of Lewes's usually perceptive judgments about so many other books, we can only wonder at his derogation of *Tom Jones* on the basis of the additional reasons he cites besides construction. Perhaps one explanation is that, as he grew older, he became more conservative in his criticism as well as his morality, as his liaison with George Eliot became more respectable, and he was unable to tolerate Fielding's relatively loose standards. In any event, his judgment is a pertinent demonstration of one of his own critical precepts, that the moral and esthetic standards of one age should not be used to evaluate the works produced in another.

Though he was mistaken about *Tom Jones,* he went astray on few other occasions because he managed to stay consistent in his adherence to truth and reality as the foundation of his esthetics in practically all of his literary criticism. He defines literature as "the expressions of the forms and order of human life," and he specifies that its quality is measured by these expressions in proportion as they are "the forms of universal truths, of facts common to all nations or appreciable to all intellects." His conclusion is that the best literature is that "which has reality for its basis." [20] As long as his conception of "reality" remained steady—as it did most of the time—his criticism retained its validity. Most contemporary novels, Lewes felt, suffer because they tell stories about people and events that have no relation to reality. But, he claims, "Art is a Representation of Reality"; and the novelist is therefore obligated to make his characters true to life—not mere puppets used to bring out the points of a particular story. The writer must paint what he actually sees, completely. If one of his characters is a dressmaker, she must make dresses, and not just be a beautiful consumptive. If his characterizations are to be interesting or believable, then the "*actualities* of life" must impinge on them.[21]

This principle applies not only to the appearance and actions of the characters but also to their inner lives. In 1858, when Lewes comments again on the place and importance of the psychological aspects of the novel, he elaborates upon his observations in his earlier criticism of *Jane Eyre*. True psychology in a novel "consists in the presentation of actual emotions, motives, and thoughts at work in the action of the drama." By "drama" Lewes means the inner as well as the outer conflicts that take place in and among the characters. He sees the ultimate excellence in the novelist who can portray both types of conflict accurately: "In Art, as in Life, there is high and low, great and little; and everything that is truly represented is interesting in proportion to its truth of representation and its objective value." To illustrate the degrees of excellence, he concludes that "a well-painted table-cover is better than an ill-painted face but a well-painted face . . . is the highest reach of art, as the human soul is the highest thing we know." [22]

Lewes uses the same kind of striking imagery in his *Principles of Success in Literature* when he illustrates the differences between false and true realism by discussing the importance of high objectives to the artist. Again, the deciding factor is how lofty the artist's vision is, how deeply he can peer into the human soul—and the nobler the soul, the better—but no matter how lofty, the vision must above all be true:

Titian's portrait of "The Young Man with a Glove" is a great work of art, though not of great art. It is infinitely higher than a portrait of Cromwell, by a painter unable to see the great soul of Cromwell, and to make us see it; but, it is infinitely lower than Titian's "Tribute Money," "Peter the Martyr," or the "Assumption." Tennyson's "Northern Farmer" is incomparably greater as a poem than Mr. Barly's ambitious "Festus"; but the "Northern Farmer" is far below "Ulysses" or "Guinevere," because moving on a lower level, and recording the facts of a lower life.

Titian and Tennyson were great artists because they could see the truth and depict it as they saw it—but, the loftier their subjects and the higher their sights, the greater their art.[23]

Lewes's insistence on esthetic truth and his awareness of the psychological aspects of characterization are very much in evidence in his negative criticism of Victor Hugo, one of his examples of the artist whose talents, extraordinary as they might be, never are devoted to the "service of truth." Hugo is a scene-painter, not a dramatist; and his greatest weakness is his inability to depict true characters. The bishop in *Notre Dame de Paris* is a typical illustration: he is "meant to be good, and is only 'goody.'" Really good men, with all their faults and idiosyncrasies, are proper subjects only for the real artist—one who will not shrink from the truth and "replace it by an impossible ideal of passionless morality." The virtue of Hugo's bishop "springs from moral *maxims* instead of from feelings; from abstractions, instead of from complex individualities," so that the reader is unable to sympathize with him because, like all "goody" people, he simply does not exist—he is not a true human being.[24]

Hugo's handling of situations and events also does not seem real to Lewes, who drives home his point with one of those complacent Victorian generalities which occasionally mar his usual objectivity. French writers, he claims, simply cannot trust the truth. Hugo, being "eminently French," cannot trust it either; and he exaggerates and intensifies his situations so much that the reader's credibility is strained to the breaking point. Lewes uses the case of Fantini in *Notre Dame* to substantiate his opinion. The characterization makes too many demands on the reader and relies too heavily on Hugo's deplorable law of antithesis: "It is one thing to rejoice over the repentant sinner, and to recognize that much goodness may accompany both profligacy and crime; another thing to consider the profligacy a necessary basis for goodness." [25]

As for Hugo's style, "elaborate, colored, polished . . . often brilliant" as it is, it is "not the strong, healthy, inspiring eloquence of a serious and beautiful mind, but rather the turbulent and factitious power of a strong talent loosened from all control: a debauch of diction, not a draught from Helicon," because it is "essentially untrue." Hugo shoots off fireworks of rhetoric at the expense of reality, by which "fancy may be dazzled, but reason is irritated." To Lewes, Hugo is the prime example of what the true artist should *not* be: his characters are not real people; the situations they get into and their actions once in them, are incredible and contrived; and his writing is falsely rhetorical.[26]

In contrast, Lewes cites Jane Austen as a truly great literary genius because her art is the essence of reality. Where Hugo's characters and plots have no basis in truth, Jane Austen—within the limits of her "two-inch bit of ivory"—is "the greatest artist that has ever written, using the term to signify the most perfect mastery over the means to her end." Life, as she has seen and experienced it as an English gentlewoman, "is mirrored in her works with a purity and fidelity that must endow them with an interest for all time." Lewes agrees with Macaulay's appraisal of her as a "prose Shakespeare" because her delineations of character have so much "truth and felicity." To Lewes, reading one of her books "is like an actual experience of life; you know the people as if you had lived with them. . . . The incidents, the characters, the dialogue—all are of every day life, and so truthfully presented, that to appreciate the art we must try to imitate it." Lewes's final accolade is that, of all imaginative writers, Jane Austen "is the most *real.* Never does she transcend her own actual experience, never does her pen trace a line that does not touch the experience of others. Herein we recognize the first quality of literature." [27]

Though Lewes later qualified these encomiums of 1852, he continued in his admiration of Jane Austen as a realistic artist. In 1859, he still felt that her genius lies in her power to produce sympathy and interest by means of her ability to represent life, but that she does not have the "culture, reach of mind and depth of emotional sensibility" of—for example—"Mr. George Eliot." He proceeds to prove his point by quoting a rather long passage from the recently published *Scenes of Clerical Life.*[28] In consideration of the fact that Lewes and "Mr. George Eliot" had at this time been living together as man and wife for five years, his praise in the context of a piece on Jane Austen seems at least pardonable —if a little misplaced. But he was sincere, and his opinions about Jane Austen's weaknesses as well as her strengths are well founded and have borne the test of time.

Lewes's conclusions in his 1859 article about Jane Austen are largely concerned with the level of her genius, not its quality. Though her characters have "truth and felicity," they are not noble, and though she is a great dramatist, the dramas themselves are of a "homely common quality." Her genius is not on the highest level because her aim is not high, and here Lewes uses the same kind of reasoning as he did in his comments about Titian and Tennyson. Jane Austen's dramatic instinct is superb in her handling of characters and motive, but the situations she invents are not in themselves dramatic. Consequently, the reader's "pulse never throbs, his curiosity is never intense; but his interest never wanes for a moment." Though her art of telling a story is "incomparable," she often has only "an indifferent story to tell." Her charm is in her "exquisite" art of representing life and character; but her powers of description and the "general vigour" of her mind, as exhibited by her extraneous comments and "illumination," are lacking. Lewes concludes that her place is still among the great artists because her books possess what he consistently considers the "first quality" of literature—reality. But her place is not high; she "sits in the House of Peers . . . as a simple Baron." [29]

In these appraisals of Hugo and Jane Austen, as well as in most of his other critical judgments, reality is his first criterion of excellence. To term Lewes "the first English exponent of the theory of realism in the novel," as René Wellek has done, is but to give him his due.[30] He used the terminology of realism earlier than any other writer who applied it to the criticism of literature. Franklin Gary has observed that Lewes's articles represent "the transition from one set of critical principles to another" long before this transition becomes evident in general critical practice, and George Ford has stated that in 1855 Lewes was the "first English critic to use the word *realism.*" Ford is correct, but, as we have seen, the term crops up in Lewes's writings several years earlier than 1855. Gary also claims that Lewes's espousal of realism influenced the whole course of English drama and fiction during the nineteenth century, and in this claim we must agree with him.[31]

Certainly, Lewes influenced George Eliot, one of the first articulate realists among the English novelists, and deeply committed to truth in her fictional depictions of human nature. Concerning the relationship between art and truth, she wrote in 1856 that "Art is the nearest thing to life; it is a mode of amplifying experience and extending our contact with our fellow-men beyond the bounds of our personal lot." [32] This statement is an elaboration on the same idea that Lewes had expressed in several of the critical articles that had appeared during the previous decade or so. That he also had a direct influence on the thinking of others among his contemporaries there can be little doubt, for his criticism was well known and highly respected during the 1850's and 1860's. The tide of realism in fiction might well have run slower in the later years of the century if Lewes's forthright comments had not contributed to its flood.

II *Style*

Lewes's comments on style, another important aspect of the writer's art, also are keen and perceptive. Acutely conscious of it in his own work, he referred to it often in his criticism of the work of others. One of his first and most striking statements about it is in an essay on Girardin, the French critic, that was written while he was still in his twenties. He describes style not as "the mere dress of thought, the outward and insignificant material" that clothes it. Style is rather the inner form, "the shape assumed by the thought . . . the vase which contains the thought, and if made of earthenware, the light of the thought will fail to penetrate it; if made of alabaster it will shine softly; if made of crystal it will shine resplendently." The greatest writers have the clearest style, Lewes concludes. In this discussion, in which he chides German scholar-critics for their clumsy use of language, he observes that most of them use the "commonest earthenware" to contain their thoughts—with the exceptions of Goethe and Lessing, whose ideas shine through lucidly from their "crystal" containers.[33] Though this analogy might sound like an advertisement for glassware, Lewes's point is clear enough: no matter how brilliant the light of an idea might be, it illuminates nothing if it is hidden behind the opaque wall of a turgid, murky style.

Lewes's later observations remain consistent with this idea. In *Principles of Success in Literature* he maintains that the writer's primary obligation is to express himself in such a style that his words and meaning will suffer the "least possible retardation from the inevitable friction of the reader's mind." [34] He prescribes five "Laws" for beauty of style: the law of *economy,* the rejection of whatever is superfluous; of *simplicity,* the consistent use of the simplest rhetorical means to secure the fullest effects; of *sequence,* the arrangement of sentences and paragraphs in logical progression. They should lead, according to the law of *climax,* to a suitable rhetorical climax at the proper juncture, and should be written, according to the final law, with an appropriate *variety* of structure. These "laws," as Wellek remarks,[35] are oversimplifications; and Lewes's earlier and more specific pronouncements about style are more valuable.

Long before he ever thought of any definitive system or prescription for "success in literature," he set forth in one of his Journals some common-sense guidelines for clarity; for example, "*Short sentences* should always be employed to convey the important points; long sentences for illustration or limitation." He calls "Precision" the writer's "highest quality"—not "the pedantic precision of Pope," or "the overweening importance of trifles; not precision in small but in great things. . . . It is a pruning knife. It abhors sterile abundance." [36] An interesting elaboration on the emphasis he placed on clarity and precision in his own writing is in a letter he wrote in 1842 to John M. Kemble, then editor of the *British and Foreign Review,* concerning an article on Goethe that Lewes had submitted for publication.

When Kemble objects to some of his "points of manner" as being characterized by "carelessness of composition," Lewes replies that these "points" were "deliberately planned"; and he continues with a detailed description of how he always wrote his critical pieces: ". . . as Sir Positive Atall would say 'if there is *one thing* in which I am *superlatively* endowed' it is carefulness! I always consider an essay a work of Art. I draw out a program of my intentions, dispose the parts, then work off a careful cartoon and then finally get to work at the picture. Error there may be, and shortcoming but not carelessness. Whenever particularly dull as Swift says there is some design in it—whenever flippant there is some serious intention. . . ."[37]

The Goethe article eventually appeared in the January, 1843, issue of the *British and Foreign Review;* and it received high praise, despite Kemble's strictures, though Lewes probably reworded his original manuscript as the editor had suggested.[38] At least two distinguished contemporaries, Arthur Helps and John Stuart Mill, wrote Lewes laudatory letters about it—and Mill singled out the style particularly, as being "infinitely nearer to excellence" than any of Lewes's previous writings.[39]

The Kemble letter indicates how deliberately Lewes planned his articles, and almost all of them demonstrate that he was indeed "superlatively endowed" with carefulness. The form is usually worked out on the basis of a consistent framework. He starts with generalities, sometimes of a startling kind, to gain attention. Then he backs up the generalities with specific points, leading to whatever critical conclusions he wants to make. He uses examples from the work or works he is criticizing to demonstrate the validity of his judgments. The number and length of the illustrations depend on the space he has available. Never is his planning haphazard—despite the considerable pressure under which he often had to work—and lapses in logic or sequence are rare.

One of Lewes's most detailed declarations about the importance of style is in his review of Macaulay's *History of England,* first published in 1849, which has survived as a landmark in nineteenth-century historiography. Lewes's appraisal of its worth as history is perceptive, but his observations on writing are interesting in themselves.[40] He considers that style, as art, demands of the writer both genius and labor: "genius, to further the matter; labor, to give the form." Some men have one capacity or the other, but the great writer must have both. Genius and labor unite to make a truly superior style, and these are both qualities of the man who possesses them. Lewes not only agrees with Buffon's saying that "le style, c'est l'homme," but he goes further when he says that the writer's style will be a reflection of his mind: "a great mind cannot altogether dwarf itself, a small mind cannot greatly exalt itself." The best style—which is also the most original style—must show the mark of a strong personality: "that peculiar impress which is given to the style by every mind which thinks for itself, and writes as *it* thinks, not as others have thought." The artist—the man himself—as well as his intellect shows through his style. No matter how lucid, how precise, style must also have originality to be truly great; and inevitably the style will be an indication of the greatness or smallness of its creator's mind.

On the basis of these generalities Lewes makes an interesting comparison between Macaulay and Carlyle. Macaulay's lack of "speculative or meditative power" and intellectual depth prevents him from exerting any real influence on his era. Though his style has "unsurpassed clearness" and "unrivalled powers of illustration," coupled with "picturesqueness of selection" and "a sense of grace and harmony," he has "materially bettered no one," has "deepened no man's convictions . . . given fresh strength to no human soul." In contrast, Carlyle—despite his roughness, abruptness, and disdain for the "ordinary rules of composition" and the "elegancies, graces, and *shams* of life and literature"—has "produced a visible influence on the minds of his contemporaries."[41] And Lewes prophesies truly, for the rugged Carlyle has survived the rigors of succeeding critical storms much better than the smooth, urbane Macaulay. Despite the difficulties of simply reading Carlyle, he still is read; and he has retained the respect of students of nineteenth-century literature and thought. Macaulay's reputation, on the other hand, rests on the fact that his style is a fine example of contemporary rhetoric and not—as Lewes foresaw—on any basis having to do with his contributions to the intellectual or philosophical life of his times.

In a later criticism Lewes weighs the qualities of another distinguished stylist, Thomas De Quincey, whom he terms unequivocally "the greatest of English prose writers." Though his reputation and influence have been inconsiderable, Lewes attributes to De Quincey "magnificent" intellectual powers. But he lacks resolution: his writings are purposeless, and he needs an inner central control to carve his reveries and dreams into something concrete and consistent. He writes song, but no symphony. Lewes suggests that his pieces in *Selections, Grave and Gay* be subtitled "dreams of an opium-eater of genius." But where De Quincey's "matter" is vagrant and erratic, though deep, his style, considered exclusively as "Form," makes him a master of the English language, and it is in this sense that Lewes calls him the greatest prose writer. Without reference to "Composition," his style has splendor, variety, ease, idiomatic richness and grace. Not only does it vary with the message it conveys, as all great styles should do; it also is a "passionately eloquent" prose, affecting the mind like poetry with its "organlike grandeur and variety of its cadence." De Quincey has every quality that a great writer should possess, Lewes concludes, but he lacks the will power to use his capacities to create great works.[42]

This opinion is not quite consistent with some of Lewes's other ideas about style. De Quincey, with all his grandeur, splendor and variety, still is not clear and precise at all times. As Lewes points out, the absence of proper direction prevents him from scaling the heights of true excellence. Perhaps we should apply Lewes's criterion of precision, though he did not do this himself. Certainly De Quincey would be found wanting if we did. Lewes's admiration of his style strictly as "Form" seems incompatible with his previously expressed opinion that a great style demands both "genius, to further the matter" and "labor, to give the form." Apparently, De Quincey had the labor but not the genius, and so did not live up to Lewes's requirements. We can conclude that, when Lewes termed De Quincey "the greatest of English prose writers," he meant "greatest" in a very limited sense; or perhaps that he temporarily was dazzled by the haunting magic of De Quincey's effusions.

But both Carlyle and De Quincey, each in his own peculiar way, were exceptions; and Lewes was much less tolerant of turgidity and aimlessness in the writings of others. For example, he often took the Germans to task for their lack of clarity and concision, and found them almost illiterate in comparison to the French. The German who "can write with clearness and elegance" is rare; and he seems, Lewes claims, to be more intent on punishing his readers than on pleasing them because he is terrified lest clarity be mistaken for shallowness. The Frenchman, on the other hand, wants to be both exact and profound; but, knowing that he won't be read unless he has an agreeable style, he aims also at eloquence and finesse.[43] Even professors, Lewes insists, who write highly technical or scholarly books, should not be immune from the obligation to communicate as clearly as possible—and the importance of a subject is no excuse for confusion or needless obfuscation. The professor "should write intelligibly and carefully, as society requires that he should wash his face and button his waistcoat."[44] If Lewes could read some of the writing in today's scholarly journals—on both sides of the Atlantic—he certainly would not change his mind on this point.

Ironically enough, Lewes's own writing is so clear and easy to read that critics sometimes have mistaken ease of understanding for superficiality of idea. What is easy cannot be profound, many scholars feel; therefore, lucid explanations of any concept, complex or simple, are immediately suspect. That Lewes's reputation has actually suffered in some quarters because of the simple clarity of his style and the apparent ease with which he wrote is an ironic commentary on scholarly presuppositions concerning the necessity of a heavy, complex, involuted manner for the expression of any idea, be it big or little, important or trivial, profound or superficial. In any event, Lewes's comments on good style still hold true as valid criteria for writers as well as critics of writing; and his own style, for the most part, is a convincing demonstration that he could practice what he preached.

III *Contemporary Fiction*

Lewes's ideas about the function of the critic of contemporary fiction changed considerably as he grew older. During the *Leader* days he viewed himself as a "guide, philosopher, and friend" who helped his readers select the right books to buy, interchanged "friendly ideas" with them, and often told them what they could just as well have told themselves but sometimes what they are "glad to know."[45] But he later adopted a more serious attitude about book reviewing. In 1865, while he was editor of the *Fortnightly Review,* he wrote a strong protest against the laxity of the critics, declaring that the chief reason for the deterioration of the novel was their failure to maintain high standards of excellence in judging fiction. They were using the same terms of commendation to appraise the latest incidental piece of fictional "fluff" as they were to evaluate a book of acknowledged superiority, such as *Vanity Fair* or *Pride and Prejudice,* thereby debasing their standards of judgment and making criticism completely meaningless:

> Even in the best journals poor novels are often praised in terms strictly applicable to works of genius alone. If a thoughtful reader opens one of these novels, he sees such violations of common sense and common knowledge, such style and such twaddle, as would never gain admission into the critical journals themselves. . . . The reason generally is that critics have ceased to regard novels as Literature, and do not think of applying to the style and sentiments of a fiction those ordinary canons which would be applied to a history, an article, or a pamphlet.[46]

Regarding himself as a sort of elder statesman among the critics, Lewes advises his younger colleagues to employ only those standards of taste and judgment that are appropriate to the works they presume to evaluate. The critic should not demand from the writer "qualities incompatible with, or obviously disregarded by his method." For example, in a story that depends on "wild and startling incidents," it is patently absurd "to demand a minute attention to probabilities," as long as the imagination is not taxed to ridiculous lengths. On the other hand, if the story "lies among scenes and characters of familiar experience," if the writer tries "to engage our sympathy by pictures of concrete realities, and not by *abstractions* of passion and incident," then the critic must demand "a closer adherence to truth and experience." The second kind of writer works in a higher form of artistic expression, but both are legitimate forms and should be judged according to appropriate standards.[47]

By applying both sets of standards to them and finding them wanting on all counts, Lewes demolishes two contemporary novels, *Maxwell Drewitt,* by F. G. Trafford, and the anonymous *Sir Jasper's Tenant.* He concludes with another exhortation to the critics—one just as applicable in the 1970's as when he wrote it a century ago. If the critics would be more "stringent" about minor points in matters of insight and truth, authors would be more careful and their conceptions would improve:

If critics were vigilant and rigorous, they would somewhat check the presumptuous facility and *facundia* of indolent novelists, by impressing on them a sense of danger in allowing the pen to wander at random. It would warn them that rhetoric without ideas would lead them into ridicule. It would teach them that what they wrote would not only be read, but reflected on; and if their glittering diction proved on inspection to be tinsel, they would suffer from the exposure. . . . Let criticism only exact from novels the same respect for truth and common sense which it exacts from other literary works. . . .[48]

Almost always Lewes wrote his own evaluations with these ideas of truth and common sense uppermost in his mind. Seldom was he the friendly philosopher—despite the easy-going self-portrait cited above—leading readers from bookstall to bookstall, innocuously sampling whatever came along. On the contrary, he applied the most rigorous standards to everything he appraised. As a consequence, he reserved his favorable criticism only for work of the highest quality, and the overwhelming majority of his qualitative judgments have stood the test of time. During his nearly five years as literary editor of the *Leader,* and the much longer period when he was writing miscellaneous pieces for the magazines, he evaluated literally hundreds of books. Titles abound like *Time the Avenger, The Daughter of Night, The First Angel,* and *George Geith,* to list a random few among the many that have long since been forgotten. Lewes evaluated them for what they were worth with almost unerring accuracy, with an instinct for what was worst—and best—that seldom failed him.

Comparison of his criticism of an anonymous novel entitled *The Bachelor of the Albany* with that of *Jane Eyre* provides a typical demonstration of his discriminatory powers. Both were published in 1847, and he reviewed them in the same article in *Fraser's Magazine.* To *Jane Eyre,* as we have seen, he gives the wholehearted but perceptive approval that it deserved; and his judgment has been vindicated if we consider the novel's subsequent reputation. But *The Bachelor of the Albany* he regards as the inconsequential product of an accomplished teller of tales who caters to the public taste by dazzling the eyes and exciting the blood but who contributes nothing to the reader's "pleasant store-house of fiction." It is a book "to read, to laugh over, and forget. You cannot help forgetting it." It titillates the reader only temporarily because it lacks consistency and reality, and it sins against the laws of art and common sense in its conception and in its execution. Despite some good descriptive writing and several amuseing incidents, it is a farce, not a novel.[49]

In arriving at this conclusion Lewes is consistent and obeys his own critical precepts by applying the same high standards to this novel as he did to *Jane Eyre*—and as he would to any other. Again he was right in so doing; the bachelor of the Albany—forever nameless—has long since found his permanent place where forgotten heroes lurk unmissed. Jane Eyre, as Lewes foresaw she would, continues to fascinate her followers after well over a century. As we have noted, he based his judgment of Miss Brontë's next book, *Shirley,* on the same criteria, and found it not up to the standard of excellence she had established for herself in *Jane Eyre.*[50] Again he was correct in his judgment, and his criticism still stands as one of the fairest and most perceptive ever written about *Shirley.* Even today we find scholars saying substantially the same things about it that Lewes did back in 1849—that, despite its obvious qualities as a realistic depiction of life in rural England, it has too many artistic defects in plot and characterization to stand comparison with *Jane Eyre* as a complete novel.[51]

In *Villette,* when it came out three years later, Lewes saw some recovery of Charlotte Brontë's powers. In his *Leader* criticism, he wrote that the novel shows great strength and originality, though it lacks the unity of *Jane Eyre* and contains some stylistic infelicities. But Currer Bell is speaking—not the echoes of the circulation library: she "has looked at life with a saddened, yet not vanquished soul," and has written "what *she* has thought, and felt, not what she thinks others will expect her to have thought and felt." Though her characters are sometimes personally unpleasant and do not always behave in good taste, they are real people, free from sham, representing the triumph of "sterling over tinsel," of the "essential" over the "collateral." In his observations about the characterization of children in *Villette,* Lewes anticipates similar reactions from later critics. Almost for the first time, he writes, they are portrayed as people, not dolls, with faults as well as virtues. Miss Brontë's children are complete depictions and not merely catalogues of cute tricks and precocious remarks—a great improvement over the usual sweet but unreal portraits; for "no true pudding is made only of plums." [52]

In a later, more detailed criticism published in the *Westminster Review* in 1853, Lewes compares *Villette* with Mrs. Gaskell's new novel, *Ruth;* and he embarks on an interesting discussion of the place of morality in fiction. His general conclusion is that fiction, like any art, should not necessarily always demonstrate a moral, though it can make some appeal to the moral sense. When we read a good novel or hear a beautiful sermon, we do not expect the events of the story or the illustrations of the discourse to prove anything. Yet, though "Art *proves* nothing," the details of a narrative "may be so grouped as to satisfy the mind like a sermon." In one way or another the novelist can exert a moral influence simply by illustration, either directly through the events of the story or indirectly by means of the way the characters express themselves.[53]

In *Ruth,* the moral is "carried in the story." It concerns a seduction, which Lewes investigates in considerable detail. He praises Mrs. Gaskell's frank treatment of a delicate subject, but he wonders about the logic of portraying Ruth as so innocent, as so completely the victim of circumstances, that she can scarcely be regarded as blameworthy. The author's position would have been stronger, he feels, if Ruth had been older and able to see more clearly the consequences of her transgression. Her guilt has so many extenuating circumstances that, "although she has much to regret," she "cannot in her conscience have much to repent"—peculiar sentiments for a proper Victorian to express. He also expostulates about Ruth's unusual charms, indicating that Mrs. Gaskell might have shown "a more simple trust in the principle involved" if she had made a less obvious attempt "to interest and propitiate the reader by all manner of graceful accessories." He also objects to Ruth's young son's behavior when he discovers that his mother is unmarried. The intensity of his grief is "unnatural" and altogether too "conventional"; and his language is "sheerly impossible." Lewes chides Mrs. Gaskell for not realizing that "in our day" the brand of irrevocable disgrace no longer marks the illegitimate child—a most reasonable viewpoint for Lewes to adopt, when we consider the storms then rocking the structure of his own domestic establishment.[54]

He sees two "morals" in *Ruth:* that men can be rehabilitated only by "noble and pure" women, who can show them that "no action is final" in this world; and that the only path that will lead into the light is "the straight path of truth," however "dark and difficult" it seems. These two straightforward Victorian sentiments were ones with which no reader of Mrs. Gaskell's books could disagree, and in his criticism Lewes shows the respect for them that they deserved. Interestingly enough, though he does not see nearly so distinct a moral message in *Villette,* he obviously likes it better than *Ruth.* He claims "many morals" for *Villette,* but discusses none of them. Instead, he sees it as "a work of astonishing power and passion," springing "from the independent originality of a strong mind nurtured in solitude," and showing a contempt for conventions "in all things, in style, in thought, even in the art of story-telling." Though there are some "defects" in plot and characterization—and here he elaborates on those he remarked on in his previous criticism in the *Leader*—the book as a whole he admires, both for the "prose poetry" in some of its great passages and for the depth of the author's "capacity for all passionate emotions." When we compare *Villette* and *Ruth,* Lewes concludes, we compare "sunlight with moonlight, passion with affection." Except for George Sand, there is no author "of our day" who has "the glory and the power which light up the writings of Currer Bell." [55]

Lewes ends his observations on *Villette* with the injunction to the author to "bestow more pains on her story." Coupled with her great "power of transmitting experience into the forms of enduring fiction," an interesting plot is all she needs to surpass the popularity of *Jane Eyre.*[56] Perhaps, if Charlotte Brontë had lived for a few years longer, she would have taken this advice and tried to write a better story in her next novel. He recognized the strengths and weaknesses of her talent as few others did among her contemporaries; and, by and large, his judgments about her have retained their validity in the face of later and more sophisticated criticism. *Jane Eyre* still ranks as her best book; *Shirley,* as her least successful. Critical opinion of *Villette* also has remained in general agreement with Lewes's original appraisal of it—that it is a powerful if imperfect manifestation of her growing genius.

Lewes showed an unusual interest in many of the other "lady novelists" besides the Brontës; indeed, he was one of the few respected critics who took them seriously as writers of fiction. His relationship with George Eliot is consistent with this interest, and the faith he showed in her capabilities, along with her ultimate vindication of this faith, is in a sense a demonstration of the truth of much that he had often said about the potentialities of women as authors. His *Westminster Review* article on "The Lady Novelists" appeared in 1852, while George Eliot was editor; and the introductory paragraphs must have had a particular appeal for her. Lewes hails the "appearance of Woman in the field of literature" as "a significant fact," and his defense of this "fact" provides come revealing information about nineteenth-century feminism from a fairly liberal masculine point of view.[57]

Lewes liked women—there is no doubt about that. But he also had respect for them as intellectuals, if they deserved this kind of respect, regardless of their sex. In this attitude he was unusual. Most men were—and of course many still are—unwilling to acknowledge women as their intellectual equals. A demonstration of such an attitude is typified by Lewes's hypothesis of the "intellectual Jones," who plaintively asks, "Where is our supremacy to find a throne if we admit women to share our imperious dominion—Intelligence?" Lewes does not attempt to answer this delicate question, but he poses another of greater pertinence to his immediate concern when he asks, "What does the literature of women really mean?"[58]

In his reply to it, he first subscribes to a principle to base his judgments on—his usual critical procedure. The principle, one we have referred to previously, concerns the definition of literature itself as "the expression of the forms and order of human life." It is "permanently good and true" in proportion as it expresses these forms, and it is "effective" only if it has "reality for its basis." Women can contribute to an understanding of this reality by bringing a "new element" to literature: "woman's view of life, woman's experience," essentially different from—and not necessarily inferior to—man's. The difference lies mainly in her mental and emotional makeup. In general, a woman is better fitted "to give expression to the emotional facts of life" because her emotions usually are dominant over her intellect, while the opposite is true of most men. As a consequence of women's superior emotional sensibility, they are best suited by nature to the creation of fiction; and Lewes calls on them to provide a "genuine female experience." Heretofore their weakness has been in their almost universal attempt to imitate the literature of men by writing like them. Their great strength, on the contrary, lies not in literature of imitation but in the creation of their own, from their own unique point of view: "to write as women, is the real office they have to perform." [59]

Encouraging women to do what they can do best, Lewes is specific in delineating what these things are. Because of the "predominance of sentiment" in the feminine mind, women are most capable of handling that "staple of fiction," romantic love, as well as the "joys and sorrows of affection, the incidents of domestic life, the aspirations and fluctuations of emotional life," all of which "assume typical forms in the novel." Women also do better with "*finesse* of detail" and in the expression of "pathos and sentiment," while men are more successful in plot construction and character delineation. To illustrate his points, Lewes cites several pertinent examples: "Such a novel as *Tom Jones* or *Vanity Fair* we shall not get from a woman; nor such an effort of imaginative history as *Ivanhoe* or *Old Mortality;* but Fielding, Thackeray, and Scott are equally excluded from such perfection in its kind as *Pride and Prejudice, Indiana* or *Jane Eyre;* as an artist, Miss Austen surpasses all the male novelists that ever lived; and for eloquence and depth of feeling no man approaches George Sand." [60]

Lewes concludes his general remarks about women's special capabilities as novelists by citing one more of their unique characteristics: "the influence of Sorrow" on their writings. When they are not imitating, women usually turn to literature as a solace for some sorrow that "in silence wastes their lives." They escape by withdrawing from it intellectually, or by transmuting their "secret anxieties into types"—certainly in 1852 a rather advanced view of the psychological reasons why women write. Perhaps Lewes had the Brontë sisters in mind when he contended that women also turn to literature at times when "domestic disquiet and unfulfilled expectations" influence them to take up "intellectual activity." [61] In any event, his observations about the special capabilities of women in portraying "depths of feeling" and "pathos" seem more pointed than those about the "influence of Sorrow" which perhaps applied more generally in the nineteenth century than they do today. But his remarks show a forward-looking view of the ultimate place that women have taken in the writing of fiction—if they are not in the forefront, they are very near to it.

In Lewes's detailed criticism of individual women, he ranks Jane Austen "first and foremost" on the basis of her adherence to reality. As we have seen, his judgments of her were modified with the passage of time, but his placing her even as "a simple Baron" in the literary "House of Peers" indicates pretty accurately the subsequent progress of Jane Austen's reputation, which has remained high, within the limited scope of her "bit of ivory." But he also admired her "womanliness" in "tone and point of view," considering it another reason why her novels are so "durable" as examples of the best that "female literature" has produced.[62]

He designates feminity as the saving grace of another genius of "incomparably deeper experience" than Jane Austen, who represents woman's literature "more illustriously and more obviously," in spite of her continued attempts to mask herself as a man. Here Lewes refers to George Sand, whom he never ceased to admire. In her writing he sees the "abiding consciousness of the womanly point of view" and the essentially feminine "influence of Sorrow" as dominant impulses. Because so many of the actual facts of her life enter her stories, they have the "charm of reality," along with a richness in variety that her wide range of experience has brought to them. Lewes also has high praise for her style, using one of his favorite images: "like a light shining through an alabaster vase, the ideas shine through her diction." Above all, her works "fulfil the primary condition of all literature" by being "original . . . transcripts" of truth, deeply influenced by the "forlorn splendour of a life of passionate experience," which has made her books the products of an exclusively feminine genius, for the simple reason that no man could have had her unique experiences.[63]

Lewes's consistent admiration for George Sand, in spite of the generally low opinion of her morals that most Victorians held, is a commentary on the independence of his judgments as well as the liberal cast of his thinking. Defending her in an earlier article against critics who condemned her for trying "lawless love" after her unhappy marriage had broken up, he points out that she always preached against extramarital attachments in her writings by making her heroines resist the temptation to involve themselves in them and by attacking St. Simonianism as a "dangerous sophistication." [64] She never condoned the social abuses she described, such as those inherent in the institutions of marriage and the church, but simply pointed them out without offering solutions. The only sense in which her works could be called "immoral," Lewes claims, is that they tend to unsettle men's minds by making them dissatisfied with current conditions.[65] On the other hand, Lewes deplores George Sand's over-frank treatment of her liaison with Chopin, easily recognizable in some of her later fiction. He considers that her inclusion of this kind of experience in a novel is a device to obtain sympathy for herself; he terms it an "illegitimate employment of experience." [66] In attacking George Sand's writings for this reason, he was not judging her moral right to live with Chopin as his mistress; he was condemning her breach of confidence and lack of taste in revealing the details of their relationship in a novel.

Lewes makes some interesting observations about several other "lady novelists" in his *Westminster Review* article.[67] Maria Edgeworth he sees as a fine observer of human nature, but unfortunately deficient in "*Sentiment.*" Fanny Burney has a quick eye for details, a "certain broad vulgar gauge of human nature"; and in her lifetime she managed "to write one or two novels that admirably reflected the passing manners of her age." But, when she resorted to "Sentiment," her "failure," as exemplified by *The Wanderer,* was "hopeless"—a rather cavalier tribute to the one lady novelist whom many critics have regarded as almost the only predecessor of Jane Austen worthy of notice. The element of "serious Sentiment"—by which Lewes means "deep feeling"—also is missing in the "fashionable novels" of Mrs. Gore, who has "Observation" and "gaiety of style," but no pathos, poetry, or psychology.

Continuing with his use of "Observation" and "Sentiment" as criteria by which to judge quality, Lewes considers the work of two minor ladies in whom he had a personal interest. He was polite but not very prophetic. The first was Geraldine Jewsbury, whom he came to know during his visits to Manchester in the 1840's. Though she has both observation and sentiment in equal proportions, she "does not work them harmoniously together"; and her novels therefore lack unity. She "excells in subtle and sometimes deep observation of morals as of manners," and Lewes hopes she will produce "still finer works than any she has yet written." In this hope, he was disappointed; the erratic Miss Jewsbury's chief claim to fame is as a friend of the Carlyles, and her novels have been forgotten. The other personal friend among the ladies whom Lewes politely criticizes was Eliza Lynn, later the Mrs. Lynn Linton who wrote so scathingly about the relationship between him and George Eliot.[68] He praises her for her scholarship and for a "daring voluptuousness" of diction, but he admits that her novels lack "Observation" and so fail to achieve reality. They too—as Lewes probably foresaw without comment—achieved quick and deserved obscurity.

Lewes concludes his "rapid flight over the large field of female literature" by expressing the hope that he has "proved the right of Woman to citizenship in the Republic of Letters." [69] Certainly his high opinion did no harm to the "lady novelists" whose claims to this "citizenship" were justified, such as Jane Austen, the Brontës, and George Sand. Perhaps more important was his insistence, at this comparatively early date, that women should not be discriminated against as novelists simply because they are women. Also exceptional was his candid admission that women by nature are better equipped to write about matters of love and sentiment than men are, and that they have a unique contribution to make to the art of fiction because they provide an altogether "new element"—the woman's point of view of life and of human experience.

Lewes's criticism of the novels of his masculine contemporaries was limited by his low opinion of most of their works. He was more severe with them than he was with the ladies, perhaps for reasons of chivalry; but he devoted comparatively few of his major periodical pieces to the criticism of fiction. He was also writing about poetry, drama, philosophy, and science, among other things; and he seemed to feel that he should devote the bulk of his time to these subjects rather than to fiction, for the simple reason that so few high-quality novels were being produced.

One of the few exceptions among the generally inferior run of novelists in Lewes's estimation was Thackeray, to whom he gave considerable attention. His review of *The Book of Snobs* in the *Morning Chronicle*, written in 1848, was one of the first really perceptive examinations of Thackeray's theory of fiction; and it prompted a quick and rather detailed rejoinder from the author himself. As always, Lewes bases his criticism on a principle—that the serious purpose of the social satirist is a proper subject for the critic's inspection, even though the satirist may operate under the innocuous disguise of a clown. Thackeray's style and wit are so felicitous and his art is so "unfettered" by political or philosophical loyalties that his works throw the reader off his guard—a mere jester cannot be taken seriously. But the "semblance of truth has more effect in a jest, because we do not look for it there, than a demonstration in a serious essay." It behooves the critic, then, "to watch very narrowly the doctrines which the jester desires to disseminate." [70]

On this logical basis—the fact that the jester who laughs at serious things needs to be taken seriously if he is a writer of Thackeray's stature—Lewes considers two "reprehensible" aspects of Thackeray's work. The first is his intense concentration on the evil side of human nature, to the exclusion of the good. Tearing away the mask from life, he "shows us *everywhere* corruption under it." Though he recognizes "the finer portion of our nature," he fails to honor it enough; and, though his heart sometimes responds to what is noble, he "almost seems ashamed of it." In his greatest work, *Vanity Fair*, "how little is to love!" Its people are all "scamps, scoundrels, or humbugs." The only ones who show any vestiges of paternal affection are Rawdon Crawley and old Osborne—and "by what bitter irony are this foolish blackleg and this coarse brutal old wretch selected as the sole exhibitors of such an affection!" Dobbin, who possesses the only noble heart in the book, "is made ridiculous."

To Thackeray there is nothing in Vanity Fair except the sad, perpetual laughter that has "something terrible" in its impartiality. But to Lewes this perpetual laughter is "blasphemy against the divine beauty which is life." If, as Thackeray says, his final object is simply to "*be perfectly miserable in private,*" then the moral of his books is that everyone—himself included—"is no more than a funny, miserable pretender; that most of our virtues are pretences and when not pretences are only kept up because removed from temptation." This to Lewes—typical Victorian optimist as he is—is no moral at all, but a violation of both art and nature. All the people in the world simpy are not that bad, and the artist has no conceivable right to presume that they are.

The second count against Thackeray is his conviction that nobody is naturally honest because the only people who are honest are those who do not need to be otherwise. Lewes particularly deprecates Thackeray's speculations in *Vanity Fair* about Becky, which he quotes in the *Chronicle* review. She tells herself that it is "only her poverty that makes her vicious." Thackeray comments that she was probably right, and he draws a comparison between her and a respectable alderman who will not step out of his carriage on his way home from a feast to steal a leg of mutton—"but *put him to starve, and see if he will not purloin a loaf.*" Lewes, italicizing this immoral injunction, exclaims in horror: "Was it carelessness, or deep misanthropy, distorting that otherwise clear judgment, which allowed such a remark to fall? What, in the face of starving thousands, men who literally die for want of bread, yet who prefer death to stealing, shall it be said that honesty is only the virtue of abundance!" How many of the poor are "heroically honest" in the face of temptation, while the comparatively wealthy "face conviction for their crime!" Of all false ideas, "that about honesty being a question of money is the most glaring and the most insidious," cries Lewes. "Blot it out, Thackeray; let it no longer deface your pages!"

But Thackeray did not blot it out, though he did try to explain it. On the morning that the *Chronicle* criticism appeared, he wrote a reply to the anonymous reviewer, through Andrew Doyle, then the newspaper's editor. Concerning the disputed passage about Becky and the alderman, Thackeray writes that he meant only to emphasize that the wealthy man in a gig should be "chary of despising poor Lazarus on foot, and look very humbly and leniently upon the faults of his less fortunate brethren. . . ." But he still feels that Becky would have been respectable if she had had five thousand pounds a year and had never been in the embarrassing position of having to resist temptation—for "What satire is so awful as Lead us not into temptation?" [71]

Turning to Lewes's first objection—that the evil in Vanity Fair is too unrelieved and the good insufficiently recognized—Thackeray replies, "God forbid that the world should be like it altogether," but he is still afraid that the world and Vanity Fair are very much alike, after all. He must carry his story forward "in this dreary minor key" because his object is to "make every body engaged, engaged in the pursuit of vanity," and he can only hint of better things.[72] Of course, Thackeray does not budge from his original position—he would have had to rewrite *Vanity Fair* if he had; and he remains the satiric realist. Lewes is the earnest idealist here—a paradoxical role for him to play, perhaps, in view of his constant insistence on realism as a criterion of excellence in writing.

When he applies this criterion to Thackeray, once he has finished scolding him for his attitudes about corruption and temptation, Lewes finds, with approval, that the "strong sense of reality" that pervades his writings distinguishes him from "almost all his contemporaries." He also has praise for Thackeray's characterizations, his humor, and for the impartiality of his satire, particularly in the *Book of Snobs*. The conclusion of the review is an encomium on Thackeray's "power of pathos," one comparable to Sterne's "exquisite" touches. Lewes cites the passage from *Vanity Fair* in which Amelia takes leave of her boy—"though it is difficult to read it, our eyes are not dry enough." This praise is a wide departure from Lewes's strictures on Thackeray's unrelieved irony in the first part of the review, and it perhaps indicates that, the longer he thought about Thackeray, the less Lewes really objected to most of what he wrote.

Lewes retains this ambivalent attitude in his review of *Pendennis*, which appeared in 1850.[73] He admires Thackeray's truth and style, but he chides him for the carelessness of his construction and for the timeliness of the topics he deals with, which will make the appeal of his novels temporary rather than lasting. To a great extent Lewes was correct in what he prophesied—the least durable parts of Thackeray's works are, with few exceptions, those concerning contemporary events. But Lewes still feels that *Pendennis* is a masterly work, containing "beautiful thoughts, caustic, subtle, pathetic, varied with unrivalled pictures of human life and character." The style is "incomparable" and has strength, ease, delicacy and clarity—it is a "flowing garment which robes his thoughts," taking appropriate shapes to convey different impressions. This compliment, a high one for Lewes to pay, indicates his appreciation of one of Thackeray's most universally acknowledged qualities.

Lewes feels that the general appeal of *Pendennis* is to people of experience, who can laugh at their early follies and who can understand Thackeray's characterizations, which are "marvellously true to nature," exposing as they do all sides of their subjects. His hero, for example, has the gout; and the villain is not completely bad. Miss Fotheringay Lewes selects as a special instance of a completely true-to-life characterization—a splendid actress and a beautiful woman, but ignorant as a horse. He hastens to add in a disgression, one that may relate to his own experience, that intelligence is not necessarily essential to good acting. In summary, he finds that Thackeray shows more of a loving than a mocking spirit in *Pendennis;* and, though he scorns pretense, he admires true worth. His view of humanity is more generous than in *Vanity Fair,* and the characters are more high-minded. The depiction of society is unflattering but true in the novel, and so is not immoral. But it does not tell such a good story—"Pendennis is not so strong a thread to hang pearls on as Becky." The book's chief defect is in its carelessness of construction—a defect modern critics still recognize.

When Lewes reviewed *Henry Esmond* late in 1852, he considered it an advance in Thackeray's art over that of *Vanity Fair* and *Pendennis.*[74] The construction is much tighter; and the spirit of mockery, even less evident, marks a new phase in Thackeray's growth as a novelist and artist. *Esmond,* which displays a "kinder and juster appreciation of life," is altogether a more serious work than his previous ones. Lewes is "touched and delighted" by it, as all should be who have lived and loved. Perhaps significantly, the lengthy passages he chooses to quote as examples of typically good writing concern the disillusionment and bitterness accompanying the breakup of Lord and Lady Castlewood's marriage, and we wonder if they did not appeal to Lewes with particular poignancy as descriptions of the state of his own marital relationship during the early 1850's. But he also particularly admires Thackeray's ability to depict the men and events of the past as they really were, giving verisimilitude to the book as history. However, most of the characters, including Esmond himself, lack complete development. He considers that the exceptions are Lady Castlewood and Beatrix, who are well-drawn, full-length portraits. In these opinions about Thackeray's characterizations many later critics also have agreed with Lewes.

Another contemporary whose works were the subject of Lewes's perceptive evaluation was Benjamin Disraeli. Despite the high position he occupied in the government, Lewes was uncompromising in his general denigration of his abilities as a novelist. The fact that Lewes disagreed violently with Disraeli's politics may have influenced his critical judgments. In any event, his outspoken disapproval is an example of his courage and intellectual integrity. He thoroughly condemned both Disraeli and his books in a lengthy review of the 1849 edition of *Coningsby,* calling him an "adventurer in politics" and an "acrobat in literature." [75] Recalling Disraeli's past failures in his attempts to write poetry and drama as well as fiction, Lewes attributes to him only the "*will* to greatness," without the ability to achieve it. His life and works are a "prospectus" of genius, never realized but always anticipating some worthwhile accomplishment that never evolves. The same is true in politics—Disraeli has good ideas but can never carry them to fruition. Despite his weaknesses, Lewes foresees—correctly—that he will become Prime Minister. Though Lewes's low opinion of Disraeli's political abilities is ill-founded, his perception of his worth as a literary artist is a fairly accurate prophecy of his present reputation. Disraeli's novels retain some interest as literary curiosities, but they do not rank among the great works of nineteenth-century fiction.

In his criticism of another contemporary, Wilkie Collins, Lewes also was unusually discerning. He recognized Collins' major strengths and weaknesses long before the appearance in the 1860's of *The Woman in White* and *The Moonstone,* the two novels which contributed most to his ultimate reputation. In a review of *Basil,* published in 1852, Lewes sees Collins as a serious "man of Letters, who regards his Profession with respect, and his Art with love." Even at this early point in his career, Lewes considers Collins more than merely a writer of intensely fascinating stories, of which *Basil* is a remarkable example. He quotes at length from Collins' account of how he happened to write the novel and what he hoped to accomplish, directing his characters and story "toward the light of Reality" whenever possible and basing them on the facts of life as he has seen them.

The trouble develops, in Lewes's view, not in Collins' intention but in his execution. His failure is in the "human and aesthetic aspects" of his story. The characters fall short of reality; and, "however true as a matter of fact the main incident may be," an "air of unreality" pervades the book, so that even commonplace incidents become "improbable." And the obligation of the novelist is to make these events at least reasonably believable, whether they are based on truth or not. Also in characterization the question is not, as Lewes points out, "Did you have a living model?" Rather, it always must be "Have you created a living figure?"—an intriguing distinction. Collins does fail in his attempts to create living figures—the reader cannot accept the various characters in *Basil* because they are not presented in such a way as to be able to exist in the reader's mind as real people. Likewise the events in the story are incredible as Collins presents them, even though the reader cannot leave the story unread because of "its marvellous narrative power." Lewes cites several examples of Collins' failure to supply his incidents with enough reality because of their faulty presentation, and he then concludes that Collins has thrown too much of his energy into the "one great requisite—narrative" but has neglected other "equally important requisites." The review ends with the expression of Lewes's hope that Collins in his future works "will turn his eloquence, his observation, his reflection, and his imagination, to better account by transmuting realities into real-looking fictions." [76]

Whether Collins actually read Lewes's criticism or not—and it is quite possible that he did—it is certain that the success of his two most famous novels depends heavily on the fact that he acted —consciously or unconsciously—on Lewes's suggestions. Collins makes the wildly improbable events in *The Woman in White* and in *The Moonstone* credible by presenting them in as realistic a manner as possible through minute descriptions of actual physical details. He also makes his characters believable because he takes unusual pains to endow them with certain unmistakably human traits. People like Miss Clack, Betteridge, Godfrey Ablewhite, Count Fosco, Fairlie, and Marian Halcombe may not be real; but they definitely are "real-looking fictions." Thereby they satisfy Lewes's requirements—and become the characters of two very fascinating books.

Lewes's flair for prophecy was not evident in his criticism of Collins's best friend, Charles Dickens. Probably because Dickens and Lewes knew each other personally from the early days of their careers, Lewes never wrote any considerable detailed criticisms of Dickens' books during the novelist's rise to fame. The two had first met in 1838, when Dickens invited Lewes to his home for a visit because, as Lewes explained much later, "Something I had written" about Pickwick "pleased him." [77] Just what Lewes had written about *Pickwick Papers* that was so pleasing to Dickens, and where it appeared, I have been unable to discover; but, from this time on, their friendship, though never intimate, remained constant. As we already have seen, Lewes participated as a "splendid stroller" in Dickens' amateur theatrical ventures in 1847 and 1848 to raise money for various worthy literary causes. In late 1852 and early 1853 they had an interesting and animated correspondence about Dickens' use of spontaneous combustion as a way of killing off Krook, one of the villains in *Bleak House*. Lewes objected to the method on scientific grounds, which he elucidated in open letters in the *Leader;* and he thereby prompted Dickens to add a note in the Preface to the 1853 edition of *Bleak House* about "my good friend Mr. Lewes" and his arguments "that Spontaneous Combustion could not possibly be." [78] Several years later, when Dickens negotiated with Lewes about the possibility of publishing one of George Eliot's novels as a serial in his magazine *All the Year Round,* nothing came of the idea; but he and Lewes continued in their pleasant relationship.[79]

Lewes's only sustained evaluation of Dickens as a novelist appeared in an article in the *Fortnightly Review* in 1872, two years after Dickens' death. It was written at the request of Chapman and Hall, then publishers of the *Review,* as a criticism of John Forster's monumental *Life of Dickens,* the first two volumes of which had just been issued. In Lewes's comments he has little to say about the *Life,* but several important things about criticism in general and Dickens' reputation in particular. He begins with a discourse on the nature of critical perception and on the difficulties most critics have in expressing themselves. He reproaches them because of their lamentable tendency to pass off their own personal opinions as absolute judgments, and he emphasizes the necessity for evidence to substantiate general critical verdicts, calling attention particularly to the "great difficulty, sometimes a sheer impossibility, in passing from the individual to the universal" in either praising or condemning any work of Art, because of personal feelings. These remarks on criticism lead into the one paragraph that Lewes devotes exclusively to Forster, whom he considers by implication a prime example of a critic whose judgments are deeply influenced by personal feelings, although he praises Forster's long-standing regard for Dickens, pointing out that his esteem "was expressed long before all the world had acknowledged Dickens's genius, and was continued through the long years when the majority of writers had ceased to express much fervor or admiration. . . ."[80]

This disapproval of Dickens by the critics Lewes uses as in-troduction to his own comments. He wonders why Dickens' genius, in view of his vast popularity, "was so little *appreciated* by the critics." Even his detractors admitted, "because it was indisputable, that Dickens delighted thousands, that his admirers were found in all classes," and that "he stirred the sympathy of masses not easily reached through Literature, and always stirred healthy, generous emotions." Even more, by impressing a whole "new direction" on popular writing, he "modified the literature of his age, in its spirit no less than in its form." Yet "private readers" as well as "public critics," eagerly as they perused each new installment when its "well-known green cover" appeared, were reluctant to praise Dickens and lavish in their scorn of what he wrote.[81]

Why then, in the face of his acknowledged weaknesses which so many readers were so quick to recognize, was Dickens so enormously popular? Lewes considers two primary causes for his success: his "overflowing fun," which makes even his most uncompromising opponents break out in uncontrollable laughter, and his "imagination of marvellous vividness" which is immeasurably strengthened by "an emotional sympathetic nature capable of furnishing that imagination with elements of universal power." Lewes, after a long digression on the psychology of the imagination, concludes that Dickens' imagination was aided by such extreme vividness of sensation that his mental visions approached the intensity of hallucinations—although, Lewes hastens to add, there is no trace of insanity in the evidence of his hallucinatory powers. Rather, they sharpened his perceptions to an extraordinary degree:

> What seems preposterous, impossible to us, seemed to him simple fact of observation. When he imagined a street, a house, a room, a figure, he saw it not in the vague schematic way of ordinary imagination, but in the sharp definition of actual perception, all the salient details obtruding themselves on his attention. He, seeing it thus vividly, made us also see it; and believing in its reality however fantastic, he communicated something of his belief to us. He presented it in such relief that we ceased to think of it as a picture. So definite and insistent was the image, that even while knowing it was false we could not help, for a moment, being affected, as it were, by his hallucination.[82]

This "glorious energy of imagination" was something that Dickens had in common "with all great writers," and enabled him to create characters that "established themselves in the public mind like personal experiences." Their falsity was "unnoticed in the blaze of their illumination," so that "every humbug seemed a Pecksniff, every nurse a Gamp, every jovial improvident a Micawber, every stinted serving-wench a Marchioness." With a power against which criticism "was almost idle," Dickens originated a group of types that fired the popular fancy—the vividness of their presentation "triumphed over reflection" because he "managed to communicate to the public his own unhesitating belief in them." Lewes put his finger on the secret of Dickens' success in characterization when he pointed out that his uncanny ability to embody some one "real characteristic . . . some well-marked physical trait, some peculiarity of aspect, speech, or manner" had the effect of excluding all doubts; as a result, Dickens' unreal characters impressed his readers "with the force of reality." The fact that many of them are wooden makes no difference. Dickens brings them "within the range of the reader's interests," and from these interests they receive a "sudden illumination," like the puppets of a drama "every incident of which appeals to the sympathies." [83]

In addition, Lewes continues, Dickens had a "fine felicity of instinct" that prompted him to use situations "having an irresistible hold over the domestic affections and ordinary sympathies." He wrote "in the mother-tongue of the heart," painting "the life every one knew." Though the scenes and manners might be unfamiliar, "the feelings and motives, and the joys and griefs, the mistakes and efforts of the actors were universal," so that even "critical spectators" could not "wholly resist their effective suggestiveness." By touching on "the domestic affections," he "set in motion the secret springs of sympathy." Though there was nothing ideal or heroic in his pictures, and the world of thought and passion "lay beyond his horizon," he had in his grasp "all the resources of the bourgeois epic"—the "joys and pains of childhood, the petty tyrannies of ignoble natures, the genial pleasantries of happier natures, the life of the poor, the struggles of the street and back parlour. . . ." [84]

After this detailed analysis of what Lewes regarded as the sources of Dickens' power, he examines the other side of the coin

—the reasons why critics, even though they have recognized Dickens' qualities, have so often denigrated his work. Lewes offers "the bias of opposition" and "the bias of technical estimate" to account for this critical eclipse. The former results from opposition to the artist's evident failures, which causes critics to overvalue these failures at the expense of his successes. The latter evolves because the critic is inclined to overvalue technical skill at the expense of the artistic accomplishment as a whole. These two "biases," acting together, caused critics to "overlook in Dickens the great artistic powers which are proved by his immense success; and to dwell only on those great artistic deficiencies which exclude him from the class of exquisite writers." [85]

Lewes answers this objection by again calling attention to Dickens' excellencies in the context of what he tried to do rather than what critics claimed he ought to have done, judging him by standards that were not applicable to him. He "worked in delf, not in procelain"; and from this cruder medium his "prodigal imagination" created images that "stir the universal heart"—the murder of Nancy is "unforgettable"; the deaths of Little Nell and little Paul "were national griefs"; the seduction scene in Peggoty's boathouse "burns itself into the memory"; and Captain Cuttle, Dick Swiveller, Tilly Slowboy, and Tiny Tim "may be imperfect presentations of human character, but they are types which no one can forget." For Dickens appealed to all classes of readers. The refined and the uncultivated alike were affected by his pictures, his "fertile invention, his striking selection of incident, his intense vision of physical details." [86]

Balancing these encomiums on Dickens' strong points, which receive clear and generous acknowledgment, is Lewes's appraisal of his defects, which stem almost wholly from Dickens' lack of intellect. Though Dickens has a mind of "singular force," sensations in it "never pass into ideas" because he sees and feels, but does not think. In his books there is a "pervading commonness" and "a marked absence of the reflective tendency," indicating that he was never concerned with the past history of mankind. He observes objects but never "connects his observations into a general expression" or takes interest in "general relations of things." Finally, he had "merely an *animal* intelligence, *i.e.*, restricted to perceptions," so that his early education—or lack of it—was "more fruitful and less injurious" than it would have been to a "more reflective and intellectual" nature; and his life provided him with "rare and valuable experience," developing in him "sympathies with the lowly and struggling" without starving him intellectually, since he "never was and never would have been a student." [87]

These strictures, though damaging, certainly do not obliterate the appreciation and understanding of Dickens that Lewes displayed in the preceding and much longer section of the article. Lewes's admiration of Dickens' virtues admittedly was tempered by his recognition of his faults; but, as an over-all estimate, this criticism ranks among the fairest and most perceptive that were written during the nineteenth century. What Lewes did was to see Dickens and see him whole, discovering certain strengths and certain weaknesses that he tried unprejudicially to elucidate. Consequently, his comments are balanced and thoughtful, giving praise where it was due, censure where it was deserved.

But when John Forster read them in 1872 in the *Fortnightly Review* he was furious; and he added a five-page attack on Lewes in his chapter on "Dickens as a Novelist" in the biography that he was then completing. In it he de-emphasized Lewes's wholehearted praise of Dickens' good points and concentrated almost exclusively on Lewes's estimate of what he considered Dickens' weaknesses. By means of his own extraneous remarks and insertions in Lewes's text, Forster managed to distort almost beyond recognition what Lewes actually wrote; he accused him of "scattering . . . rubbish" over "an established fame" and called him a "delicate monster with two voices." [88] Succeeding critics have followed his lead, among them Swinburne, who lumped Lewes with all the other "malignant boobies" so presumptuous as to question Dickens' supremacy on all counts.[89] George H. Ford reflects current opinion by terming Lewes's article "the most effective attack on Dickens ever written," [90] although he acknowledges that it is "an extremely sophisticated piece of irony" [91] and cheerfully concedes that most twentieth-century critics have been engaged in the "reiteration or refutation" of the same points that Lewes listed originally as Dickens' primary defects, with the exception of an added reference to sex.[92] Ford also admits in his conclusion that, at least in a sense, "some of Lewes's objections to Dickens have been not so much answered . . . but by-passed." [93]

But, to a great extent, Lewes's criticism of Dickens, both laudatory and adverse, is still valid in the context of modern appraisals of him. One of Lewes's main points is that the reason for Dickens' popularity is that he has something for everyone, despite his intellectual shortcomings; and this statement is as true today as it was when Lewes made it. To class his criticism as the jealous complaint of an unsuccessful author, as Forster did, is to misread almost everything in the article. To term it a classic example of the many attempts that have been made to damage Dickens' reputation, as several succeeding critics did, is a complete misinterpretation of Lewes's objectives in writing the piece. The one thing that he did not intend was that it should be construed as an attack on his old friend. Trollope, with whom he discussed the whole matter of Forster's violent reaction, later wrote that Lewes was deeply disturbed by Forster's remarks because they "seemed to indicate unfairness toward a fellow-author who was dead." [94] Instead, the article is what it purports to be: an attempt at a judicious and thoughtful evaluation of the true nature of Dickens' genius, with some additional comments on his personality and extreme sensitivity that were based on Lewes's study of psychology.

Surely a critic cannot be accused of defaming an author when he says about him, as Lewes does about Dickens, that he was bent on using the power of his genius to help mankind, that he gave unstintingly of his best in whatever he did and wrote, that, along with his limitations, he had "great qualities" and "supreme powers." [95] This language is not that of the carping fault-finder, jealous of his rival's fame; it is that of the critic who tries to remain unbiased in spite of his deep respect and admiration for the great writer who is the subject of his criticism.

Lewes's evaluations of authors such as Dickens and Thackeray are more interesting than those of the many lesser writers of fiction who plied their trade during the middle 1800's. Our survey has concerned itself chiefly with his opinions about those authors whose reputations have survived. The remarkable thing about these opinions is that by and large they too have survived as valid judgments. About books that deserved lasting reputations Lewes was seldom wrong, and he often anticipated that an author would achieve fame and success long before he actually did so, as in his appraisals of the Brontës. He also anticipated changes in critical taste that, as Ford has observed, "were to welcome Tolstoy, Flaubert, Meredith, and James." [96] And, of course, Lewes was right about George Eliot, whose talent never would have developed in the direction that it did if his critical acumen—as well as his love—had not been everpresent in her conceptions.

His general precepts about fiction were both perceptive and prophetic, although he made some serious mistakes. But on such subjects as the art of the novel itself, the place and promise of women as writers of fiction, and the functions of critics and criticism, he was indeed—in the truthful if lugubrious terminology of Professor Ford—"one of the most important figures in the history of novel-criticism in England." [97] By his creation and employment of a consistent and valid esthetic that was concerned, as we have seen, with style, construction, verisimilitude, and the uses of the imagination, Lewes was able to arrive at the kind of judgments that should have earned him a much more substantial reputation as a literary critic than he now enjoys.

IV *Poetry*

i. CRITICAL THEORIES. Underlying Lewes's criticism of poetry is the same concept that underlies his criticism of prose—that the criterion of excellence is reality. An esthetic with such a basis is perhaps better suited to the judgment of prose, but Lewes was at least consistent. At "the root of all aesthetics," he wrote in 1851, lies the difference between feigning and creating, or between imaging scenes which others have experienced and "taking from the world of *our* experience things which Art raises into its own world of plastic beauty." [98] More specifically, commenting on an edition of Elizabeth Barrett Browning's poems, "Experience alone forms the substance of real poetry," and even "lyric" poetry demands that the writer should have "seen, felt and thought much" if he produces first-rate work.[99] The fact that Mrs. Browning's poems are pure fantasy and have no relevance to the world of reality is to Lewes her chief weakness.[100]

He judges the quality of a poem on the basis of its relevance to some aspect of "reality"; and in his concept of reality, there are such factors as observation, feeling, experience, and thought, as opposed to fantasy, which in Lewes's mind has no relationship to the kind of reality that constitutes the stuff of good poetry. Furthermore, the true poet must be able to see clearly and be able to project what he sees—his vision—through the power of his imagination, which is his "distinguishing superiority." But his imagination will produce no good poetry "if conjoined with inferior faculties, or if deprived of the requisite materials which are to become plastic in his hands." [101]

In addition to these extraordinary powers of vision and imagination, the poet must have the ability to express what he sees in truly great and inspired language. He is "a Seer and a Singer," and his rank will be determined "by the clearness of his vision and the melody of his song." Lewes's emphasis is on the indispensability of both qualities. The ultimate criterion whereby the poet is to be judged is not the "grandeur and depth" of his conceptions, nor "the beauty and melody of his song," but "the degree in which the two are *united.*" [102] Except for Lewes's insistence on "reality" as the proper source of the materials that the poet makes use of as his subjects, Lewes's ideas on judging the quality of poetry are essentially the same as those of many of the Romantic poets who were his immediate predecessors, a mixture culled—consciously or unconsciously—largely from Shelley, Wordsworth, Coleridge, and Goethe.

Lewes also insisted—as the Romantics did—on verse form as essential for poetry, asserting that the poet expresses emotions in verse in the same way that the painter does with color, the musician with melody, and the sculptor with clay. Though verse may often not be poetry, poetry "as Art" always must be in verse.[103] He remained consistent in his later elaborations on the nature of poetry in the *Principles of Success in Literature,* defining it as "the metrical utterance of emotion, having beauty for its result, and pervaded by a religious Idea which it thereby symbolizes." [104]

But these elaborations develop other aspects of his early ideas about poetry that are not altogether consistent with them. Concerning the language of poetry, he claims that it must be different from that of prose because prose is the language of thought, which in poetry is subservient to emotion. If it is to have beauty, the language of poetry cannot be the "ordinary language of mankind," because it must be suited to ideal minds and fit for the expression of ideal thoughts. As a consequence, ordinary words with ordinary associations must be avoided. Lewes not only rejects Wordsworth's theory; he modifies his own conception of "reality," which, if it includes thought at all, must place thought on an "ideal" level. He again insists on the necessity for meter; and, borrowing from Hegel for emphasis, he considers verse to be the "form and incarnation" of poetry. Lewes asserts that rhythm is not accidental, but the expression of man's soul in poetry and its only possible form—one evolved from man and not invented by him.[105] In this later definition of poetry, Lewes remains consistent concerning its language, but not about his conception of reality.

The inclusion of a new element—a "religious Idea"—as an attribute of poetry relates to his increasing interest in the moral influence that all literature should exert. Poetry should have to do with the "great concerns" of the times in which it is written. In the nineteenth century these are liberty, equality, and humanity, aspects of a "poetic Idea" that is a partial expression in abstract of the spirit of the age. By religion, Lewes does not mean Christianity or any one creed, but generally speculation of any kind, as long as it pertains to these great concerns.[106] Though this conception did not appear in its final form until 1865, Lewes had been thinking along much the same lines for many years. In one of the first critical articles he ever had published, he praised Shelley because of his devotion to what Lewes termed the truth of man's power for good, the "dominant Idea" of the age, embracing "progression, humanity, perfectability, civilization, democracy"—bywords in the code of Victorian optimism which supplied the intellectual and spiritual nurture of so many of Lewes's contemporaries.[107]

Consistent and characteristically Victorian in his attention to religion in its abstract, moral implications, Lewes concluded that the chief function of poetry is to teach. Because of its nature, it does not teach directly; it "*indirectly* establishes the end of all morality," not by means of "*moral instruction,*" but by "*moral emulation,*" or, he elucidates, not by prescribing doctrine but by providing inspiration. Each poem performs a different function as the "beautiful phasis of a religious Idea." The ideas expressed in poetry, concerned as they are with faith, science, or virtue, "become realized in religion, philosophy, and art." The poem does not exist exclusively as the expression of an esthetic or emotional experience, then, but to enunciate some aspect of the "Dominant Idea" of the epoch in which it appears. For this reason, the times exert a profound influence on poetry: different epochs require different expressions, and great events have inspired great and stirring poetry because of their historical significance. Lewes cites the ages of Homer, Elizabeth, and the French Revolution as examples of moments in history when the juxtaposition in time of inspired writers and epic events precipitated the creation of great poetry.[108]

But he did not believe that a work is necessarily great simply because it concerns epic events, or is composed while such events are occurring. Many inept and ill-conceived poems have been written about epochal happenings in history, and the greatness of a subject has been no assurance that its treatment in artistic form —music, painting, or poetry—will reflect the same greatness. Lewes expressed this opinion in several contexts; and it relates to his attitude toward the Classics, concerning which he made some of his most original and interesting pronouncements. They anticipate in some respects those of a much more famous critic, Matthew Arnold.

ii. ARNOLD AND THE POETRY OF THE PAST. In 1853 Lewes wrote a review of a new edition of Arnold's *Poems*, in which he took Arnold to task for emphasizing in his Preface the dominance of action, or subject, over other factors—such as form and rhythm—as a criterion of excellence in judging poetry. Arnold's conclusion is that the works of the ancients are better than those of the moderns because the actions they describe are nobler. To Lewes, actions are a means, not an end, to Art; and good poetry fluctuates with varying moods of thought and language. The poet should not consciously imitate any model, ancient or modern, nor should he revere the Past just because it is the Past and for no other reason.[109] Rather, he should study both the Classics and the moderns, taking care to avoid "the rudeness and baldness of one" as well as "the rhetoric and glitter of the other!" To respect only the Classics as models, as Arnold advocates, is to be one-sided and undiscriminating. The works of Homer, Virgil, and Aeschylus often are rude, obscure, and feeble, possessing artistic qualities that are bad in any age and certainly not worthy of imitation.[110]

Nearly thirty years later Arnold expressed substantially the same sentiments in "The Study of Poetry," first published in 1880, when he cautioned readers against using the "historic estimate" to judge the poetry of the ancients, thereby overrating it as art simply because it is important as an aspect of a nation's historical or cultural development, regardless of its qualities as good or bad poetry.[111] This attitude is, of course, very different from the one which Arnold had adopted in his Preface to the 1853 edition of the *Poems*. Whether or not Lewes had anything to do with this change is an interesting question, but he certainly played his part in the "reaction" to the Preface which, according to one recent literary historian, "helped to direct Arnold the critic toward becoming the most adequate of the Victorians." [112]

Lewes's appraisal of the 1853 edition of the *Poems* is colored by his opinions about the Classics and their influence. He regards Arnold as a scholar rather than a singer; as a creator of the kind of poetry that appeals only to the cultured few who can appreciate its classic qualities. "Sohrab and Rustum" is the best of the collection because it has an intrinsically interesting story relatively unspoiled by the "Graecisms," which Lewes considers "ornaments of questionable taste." Whatever excellencies the poem might have are not derived from Greece, though the defects are, such as the long, Homeric similes that "retard and encumber" the action. They are examples of "rude art," illustrating the error of imitation, the natural tendency to fasten on "the fleeting modes, and not the eternal spirit" of the Classics. If Homer had lived now, Lewes concludes, "he would not write like Homer's imitators." [113]

Though Lewes's criticism of the 1853 edition of Arnold's *Poems* is in general agreement with contemporary and subsequent opinion, the principles he laid down for judging the relevance of the ancient writers to nineteenth-century culture were shared by few of his fellow critics—and certainly not by Arnold. Yet the attitudes he expressed in the 1840's and 1850's anticipated some of those that Arnold had made Victorian verities by the 1860's and 1870's. When Lewes observed in 1845 that Sophocles' art is second only to Shakespeare's, that finding out why this is so takes painstaking study and analysis, and that such art should not be considered good just because it is Greek,[114] he was again anticipating Arnold's warnings in "The Study of Poetry" about overrating the Classics without properly evaluating them as literature. When Lewes remarked in 1853 that poets should read both the ancient and modern writers with the objective of emulating what they find is best in both,[115] he was illustrating the point that Arnold made in 1864 in "The Function of Criticism at the Present Time": critics should try to facilitate the flow of "fresh and true ideas" by learning and propagating "the best that is known and thought in the world." [116] And, when Lewes saw in 1947 that Victoria's was an age of application, not invention, characterized by a distinct lack of heroes and of heroic actions to write about, and therefore not an environment conducive to the creation of great and original poetry, he[117] was recognizing substantially the same conditions that Arnold did in 1864 when he wrote that the present age was not one in which "the exercise of the creative power in the production of great works" was possible.[118]

Interesting aside from their resemblance to—and anticipation of—Arnold's are Lewes's ideas about the effects of the atmosphere of an era on the works its artists produce. They are the basis of a general principle that dominated most of his critical judgments: all truth—and consequently all valid criticism—is relative. In one of his first published articles, written in 1842, commenting on the poetry of ancient Rome, Lewes makes the point that modern criticism has shown that truth in the abstract is "subject to temporary influences." Likewise poetry, if it is "the collective voice of an epoch," necessarily must "partake of the pecularities of that epoch"; and, if it is in the language of the epoch, it also speaks "with its ideas." [119] Poets, then, are not mirrors of eternal truth, but of what the truth is to them in their own era. Contemporary opinions are of value in judging how people felt about them when they lived, but critics of later times have difficulty in judging the poetry of the ancients because they are unacquainted with the circumstances of ancient life. To Victorians, the works of Seneca, Phaedrus, Persius, Juvenal, and Martial—though interesting because of the information they supply about the epoch in which they were written—often seem exaggerated, turgid, and obscene. But they were what the Romans wanted as a reflection of their own lives. Evolutions in taste, Lewes concludes, illustrate the idea that "the fastidiousness of one age becomes the pruriency of the next." [120] Though it might be difficult to conceive of the ancient Romans as "fastidious," the point is clear: tastes change; and critical evaluations, to have any validity, must reflect the changes.

Lewes's ideas on critical relativism are more fully developed in a review written in 1946 of Leigh Hunt's *Stories from the Italian Poets.* Though he has comparatively little to say about Hunt, he says a good deal about what he regards as a new class of critics "who, when judging a work of art, endeavor to throw themselves back into the era in which it was produced"—to look at it as the people did for whom it was produced. These new critics try to "penetrate into the spirit of that age, to understand its language, —its beliefs—and its prejudices; in order that the imagination of the poet who utters the language may have its influence over their minds unimpeded by any want of sympathy, which ignorance would create." This relativistic view differs from that of eighteenth-century criticism, which was "absolute, without reference to the era" in which the works being judged were produced. Lewes, opposing this absolute view, contends that men and their works should be judged by the standards of their own age, not those of any other. For example, men like Walter Raleigh and Philip Sidney, eminently acceptable as gallant courtiers in Queen Elizabeth's court, would seem ignorant barbarians if they could be resuscitated to appear in modern society. And Shakespeare, if he were writing his plays for today's theater, would write them in entirely different form in order to accommodate today's tastes. In judging the works of the past, Lewes concludes, critics should make allowances "for the characteristics of the past" and their implications.[121]

Lewes was more capable of applying his relativistic principles to the criticism of drama than of poetry, as we shall see in our consideration of his dramatic criticism. He was particularly inept in his attempts to apply them in his judgments of the works produced in the eighteenth century, a period which he neither understood nor appreciated. He refrained from writing very much about it, and when he did—as in the case of *Tom Jones*—his opinions as often as not were prejudiced and unperceptive. He not only disagreed with the "absolute" views of its critics, but he considered the period itself immoral, indelicate, and "*ungentlemanly,*" as represented by most of its authors, who had no conception of literature except as an arena in which to display their wit and dexterity. In this respect eighteenth-century writing differed radically from the "passionate" and "poetic" productions of the seventeenth century—which Lewes understood much better than he did the eighteenth—and from the "*consciously* moral" literature of the nineteenth.[122] Consequently, Lewes's observations on the works of such figures as Swift, Dryden, and Pope contain little of substance or value; and they illustrate very well Lewes's own precept: a critic must understand the age in which a work of art is produced in order to evaluate it properly.

iii. THE NINETEENTH CENTURY. Lewes's criticism of the poetry of his contemporaries and immediate predecessors indicates that he was a man of his own age. By his definition, as we have seen, the nineteenth century was an unfavorable environment for poets; and his opinions reflect this view. Vastly more at home himself in the medium of prose, as his few attempts at writing poetry amply demonstrated,[123] he lacked both the capacity and the inclination to deal intimately and understandingly with some poetic conceptions. A pragmatist and a realist, he looked for meaning and specificity in poems, as well as for a certain kind of beauty. When they did not meet the requirements of his own critical precepts, he was unhappy with them.

His first extended criticism of a contemporary was a major article on Browning, prompted by the publication of *Pippa Passes* in 1847. Within the severe limitations of Browning's times and his talents—something of a qualification—Lewes considers him an "original" artist but certainly "not a great poet." Though he has significant powers of observation, he is "neither a deep thinker nor a musical writer"; and he is not to be compared with Tennyson. Commenting on Browning's major works up to that time, Lewes feels that *Paracelsus,* though still considered his best poem, is marred by its unfortunate choice of a subject and by the harshness and inelegance of its versification. He sees no improvement in *Sordello,* despite the high hopes inspired by *Paracelsus.* The meaning is obscure, the music grating: "Walking on a new-ploughed field of damp clayed soil, would be skating compared to it." As for the poems in *Bells and Pomegranates*, they are "always readable, if not often musical, and are not often insults to our ears"—surely measured praise; but the versification is spotty and irregular both in rhyme and rhythm, and the subject matter often inappropriate. *Pippa Passes* Lewes finds marred by an obscurity that is not suggestive but simply tiresome, and the long monologues are flatly "unintelligible." In *Flight of the Duchess* there are some admirable isolated passages; but, in general, the poem seems to consist mainly of "the musical embodiment of some strong emotion or deep thought" that defies rational expression.[124]

The conclusion Lewes arrives at in his 1847 article is that Browning, though possessed of a clear, open mind, is "rather a thinker than a singer." His thoughts are noble and original, but he would do better to express them in prose than in poetry because mere thoughts cannot take the place of the beauty that his poetry lacks. The larger works are "weak and wavering" in conception, their originality borders on eccentricity, and the style is spasmodic and "obscure from mere indulgence." Though Lewes concludes the piece with a long quotation from that "much-admired romance," "How They Brought the Good News from Ghent to Aix," he sees little to praise or even extenuate in most of Browning's poetry.[125]

Lewes remains consistent in this attitude in a review of "Christmas Eve and Easter Day" written in 1850, repeating more or less the same sentiments he had expressed three years before. Browning has everything, including originality, except for the "magic and mystery of Beauty," which "constitutes the grand peculiarity and enduring delight of Poetry." Though "Christmas Eve" concerns a great theme powerfully conceived and "picturesquely, sometimes grotesquely handled," and though it is written in a sincere and earnest spirit, the poem is not a work of art. Admirable as Browning's rugged verse is, facile as he sometimes is as a rhymer, and eminently suitable as his style of poetry is to expound his thought, he still is "not a Singer." Lewes's concluding observation is meant to summarize his over-all feeling about Browning's poems: "Realism in Art has Truth as an aim, Ugliness as a pitfall." [126] As far as Lewes is concerned, Browning is trapped in the "pitfall" much more often than he manages to achieve his aim.

One circumstance explains to a considerable extent Lewes's uncompromising lack of appreciation for Browning's work. Lewes never had an opportunity to comment on many of the best poems because they did not appear until long after his interests had turned away from literary criticism. *Pauline, Paracelsus,* and *Sordello,* amazing as they are as manifestations of Browning's exceptional talents, were the products of his youth; by themselves, they were not enough to provide more than a foretaste of his future fame. And, although *Bells and Pomegranates* contains such famous poems as "My Last Duchess," "Soliloquy in a Spanish Cloister," and "The Bishop Orders His Tomb at St. Praxed's," there was so much else of less merit in the collection that Lewes can scarcely be blamed for regarding Browning, at this stage in his career, as something less than a poetic genius. The religious and philosophical content of "Christmas Eve and Easter Day" was not enough to inspire any substantial change in Lewes's opinion, one that was shared by many others during the 1850's. Only after the publication of *Dramatis Personae* in 1864 and *The Ring and the Book* a few years later did Browning's reputation begin to establish itself. Lewes's estimate of his early works probably seemed fair enough to most of his contemporaries—unused as he and they were to the unique ruggedness, unevenness and obscurity of Browning's poetry. These characteristics were enough to blind Lewes to its many great qualities. Subsequent critics needed years of familiarity with Browning to come to a full appreciation of the nature of these qualities. Lewes's reactions, which can be said to be typical of his time, do not show either unusual sensitivity or exceptional perceptiveness.

Lewes makes some further observations about Browning in another context. In 1852, in a review of Browning's Introductory Essay to an edition of some newly discovered Shelley letters, most of which were almost immediately revealed as forgeries, Lewes comments extensively on the relationship between a poet's works and the biographical facts of his life. He agrees with Browning's observation that Shelley's letters reveal "no discordance between the author and the man" and that we see in them "the germs of which the poems were but the full and necessary blossom." This relationship is "a beautiful manifestation of the sincerity and unity of his nature." Lewes regards Shelley as "the nearest approach in life and works to the ideal of a poet," though his reputation has suffered because of the charges that have been leveled against his personal life. His fame "has lived down calumny," but every tribute from those "who speak with the authority of commanding intellects and unsullied lives" is useful in dissipating the "lingering prejudices" that still reflect on him. It is therefore regrettable that the "loving but wise appreciation of such a man as Browning" should be vitiated by the discovery that the letters are forgeries.[127]

In this review Lewes shows a growing respect for Browning, both as a man and as a thinker; he also restates his long-standing opinion of Shelley, whom he had praised extravagantly as a "pure" and "sincere" poet many years before in one of his first critical articles, to which we already have referred. He elaborates further on his principle that "the Poet is at once Seer and Singer," in the sense that both the conception and the execution of a poem are important; no matter how exceptional the one, lack of either makes for a less perfect art: "As a fine landscape painter is superior to a poor historical painter, although historical painting is in itself a higher reach of art, so a fine lyrical poet is infinitely superior to a mediocre dramatist or epic poet." The conception without the ability to realize it is not enough, and "the highest poet is not he who *aims* at the highest subjects, but he who fitly *represents* the highest subjects." [128] This idea is closely related to Lewes's criterion of excellence in the criticism of fiction as well as of poetry, as we have seen.

Lewes's observations on the greatest of his other contemporaries, Tennyson, are neither so extensive nor so opinionated as those on Browning. He wrote a cordial review of *In Memoriam* when it first appeared in 1850, placing it above Milton's *Lycidas* as an elegy in the degree of feeling it expressed; but he did not imply thereby that Tennyson rivaled Milton as a poetic genius.[129] He terms *In Memoriam* the "musical utterance of a noble loving heart," and praises its form as "exquisitely adapted" to its "burden." The poetry is free from conceit but rich in imagery, but some of the rhymes are false and labored. Lewis sees the poem as a "solace and delight of every house where poetry is loved"; and, with a typically Victorian fondness for moral implications, he admires its "true and hopeful spirit" because it elevates sorrow to the lofty position of a moral teacher, thereby enlarging the reader's capacity to feel and sympathize. On the philosophical implications of Tennyson's references to evolution and religion Lewes did not see fit to comment, though he certainly must have seen and understood them. Apparently, he felt that the real importance of *In Memoriam* was as an elegy—not as an allegory. His recognition of its lyric qualities indicates that he appreciated those aspects of the poem that still survive as most noteworthy in the minds of its readers.

But Lewes did not hesitate to condemn the *Ode on the Death of the Duke of Wellington* as an "intrinsically poor performance" when it appeared in 1852.[130] He backs up his opinion with lengthy quotations from the poem, terming it inappropriate because it consists of commonplace reflections in a form that lacks "redeeming splendor" of imagery, indicating hasty and thoughtless composition. Lewes concludes that Tennyson obviously wrote the ode simply because he was poet-laureate, and not on any basis of poetic fervor or inspiration—an observation that was evidently true, though neither Tennyson nor the poem deserves such truculent opprobrium.

A young poet whom Tennyson admired and who was to gain future fame as a novelist also came to Lewes's attention at this time. The first edition of George Meredith's *Poems* was published in 1851, and Lewes gave the work a brief notice in the *Leader*, adding some lengthy quotations.[131] In his evaluation Lewes recognizes nothing exceptional: the poems are elegant trifles. Though the workmanship is fanciful, the verse is quaint rather than artistic; and the execution is careless and commonplace. Some of the poems are bright and musical, Lewes concedes, and have considerable emotion, delicacy of expression, and charm; but he sees little depth of insight or feeling. His conclusion is that the chief distinctions displayed by Meredith's early work are elegance and felicity of expression—a verdict with which later critics have had no substantial disagreement.

Yet another young poet, Alexander Smith, received the benefits of Lewes's criticism; in praising him, Lewes showed even less prophetic bent than he did in depreciating Browning. But his defense of Smith gave rise to an interesting insight into Lewes's ideas on the freedom of the artist to operate in society as he sees fit. In 1853, at the age of twenty-three, Smith published his first book of poems. Several had appeared previously in the *Leader*, and charges of gross immorality had been leveled against one of them because it included the following lines:

> On a bosom white
> Which came and went beneath me like a sea,
> An Emperor I lay, in empire bright,
> Lord of the beating heart. . . .[132]

Admittedly on the lurid side for Victorian tastes, Lewes defended these lines energetically against the storm of scandalized protest they precipitated. Terming them "truthful" examples of "luxurious imagery," he claimed that the real question is not whether they are immoral, but whether poetry should "give utterance to real emotions, to real passions, or must it shrink from the truth lest the truth be thought immoral?" In answer, he makes an impassioned plea in behalf of the artist for freedom from the trammels of conventional morality.

If passion is the expression of real love, it is not mere "animalism," Lewes maintains; and the artist has the right to portray it vividly because he has a more elevated nature than the mere thrill-seeker: "Art purifies everything, not by keeping what is essential in the background, not by ignoring, but by elevating it into the region of Beauty. It chastens and refines by *training* the passions, not by suppressing them. It cannot, like fashion and ethics, ignore humanity: from human passion it draws its life, its strength, its usefulness. All is permitted to it, because its aims are noble." Consequently, the work of a true artist is consecrated by the fact that it is art; and true poetry, as art, elevates love above the sphere of ordinary human passions and must deal with love frankly and honestly, or "betray its function." This view was an extremely liberal one for Lewes to adopt concerning such a delicate matter—at least to the Victorians—as describing a lover's experience in such terms. The *Leader*'s columns were overflowing with protesting letters for weeks after he expressed it, but he conceded nothing and maintained his position.

Right in principle as we may feel that Lewes was—and certainly we must agree with him about the purifying and beautifying function of Art—his choice of Alexander Smith as an exemplar was unfortunate. Lewes followed his defense of Smith's morality with an adulatory review of the 1853 edition of the *Poems,* in which he calls Smith "a born singer"—his highest accolade—and a "man of genius," worthy of a place "among the foremost of English poets" if he vindicates the promise he has so far shown. Lewes praises the young poet's imagery, despite its "over-luxuriance," and his sensuousness, despite its youthful "voluptuousness," which he does not find objectionable. Elaborating on the theme he had treated in the *Leader* article, he again defends Smith's "passionate" muse because it is "sincere and reverent." The poet is bound to use "the language of passion" when he performs the legitimate function of "beautifying and ennobling such feelings," which Smith, as a "pure" and "earnest" poet, conscientiously tries to do. After more encomiums in a similar vein, Lewes advises Smith to "deepen and extend the nature of his passion" in his future works, but not to "tame the impassioned fervour of his language"—which he claims is reminiscent of the best of both Shakespeare and Keats.[133]

The long excerpts Lewes quotes from Smith's *Life-Drama* have a "rare felicity of expression" and an "intensely musical feeling" that "everyone will recognize," according to Lewes; but he could scarcely have been more ill-advised in his expression of this opinion. And it is hard to conceive of a less perceptive prophecy than his concluding observation that in Alexander Smith is the "faculty devine" that, "when moved by the momentum of richer experience, will create great poems." [134] Along with a few others of his ilk, Smith was permanently relegated to what W. E. Aytoun, a contemporary satirist, called "the Spasmodic School" of poetry, known chiefly through its excesses of verbiage and the expression of exaggerated emotion.[135] Smith never brought to fruition whatever promise he might have shown, and Aytoun's judgment has stood the test of time much better than Lewes's extravagant, misplaced praise.

Ironically enough, though Lewes could see qualities of greatness in Smith's bombastic effusions, he was unable to discern them in the poet Smith imitated most slavishly, John Keats. To Lewes—the Victorian critic with scientific leanings and the realistic disciple of Auguste Comte—Keats's sensual love for the physically beautiful and his dependence on feeling and emotion were completely inimical. In his review of R. Monckton Milnes's *Life, Letters and Literary Remains of John Keats*, first published in 1848, Lewes revealed his attitude fully; and, in so doing, he made another esthetic miscue of major proportions.

Lewes's main contention is that, although the book adds to our knowledge and understanding of the pitiful story of Keats's life, it does not provide any evidence that he would have been a much greater poet than he was if he had lived longer. To substantiate this contention, Lewes goes to considerable lengths to show why Keats "will always remain in our literature as a marvellous specimen of what mere sensuous imagery can create in poetry." But he will never scale the heights of true greatness, because he lacked the "creative and o'ermastering power of thought," which is even more indispensable to the poet than the "plastic power" that he had in so much abundance:

> Affluent in imagery, he was meagre in thought. He passed through life the creature of sensations; throwing off poems which were the transcripts of those sensations; but he seems not to have had his eye open to the universe before him, except as that of a mere spectator, lux-

uriously contemplating its ever-changing hues, and myriad graceful forms. The mystery of life was no burden on his soul. Earth spread out before him, and was fair to see. To him it only presented flowers; and those flowers only presented their beauty. He questioned nothing; he strove to penetrate no problems. He was content to feel, and to sing.[136]

Intimately related to this incapacity for thought is Keats's inability to cope with reality, and here again he falls short of the requirements of Lewes's criteria. His love poetry, dealing with real feelings and emotions, is inferior to that which concerns fanciful subjects, according to Milnes; and Lewes agrees. Consequently, Keats fails his most significant test. The "highest effort of art," writes Lewes, is "to mould into shapes of beauty all that we have felt, thought and suffered"; but "to mould the caprices of our fancy," as Keats did, is "comparatively easy." Not "strong enough" to deal successfully with "the highest difficulties of his art," Keats instinctively preferred "subjects of fancy rather than reality," as in the case of Endymion, Lamia, and Hyperion, who were borrowed from the "remote antique world rather than from the living breathing world around him." In saying this, Lewes does not want to shut Keats out from the antique world but "simply . . . from the merely fanciful employment of antiquity," for the poet

is not limited to time and space; but he ought to be limited to those materials of human experience which alone have any poetic value. Poetry is *vision,* not *caprice;* the poet is a Seer, not an intellectual Acrobat. He addresses the human soul, and does not merely titillate the fancy. . . . True it is, that Keats infused into ancient mythology a more poetic spirit than had most of his predecessors; because he did not regard mythologic persons as mere abstractions, but as living beings. The objection to his creations is, that they are neither Greek nor human.[137]

Keats, then, is the victim of his own fancy; and he is unwilling to work in terms of real attitudes, real emotions, real experiences —the unpardonable sin in Lewes's scale of esthetic values, enough to lead him to the surprisingly inept conclusion that Keats's poetry, despite its sensuality and exquisite imagery, "is by far too unsubstantial ever to nourish one single soul." [138] Just how far off the mark Lewes was is obvious in the light of Keats's subsequent reputation. As one knowledgeable modern literary historian, Albert

C. Baugh, has stated, "After 1848, the year when R. M. Milnes's biography . . . appeared, the poetry of Keats became the greatest single influence upon the poetry and painting of the Victorian generation. Emphasis upon the value of Keats's thought is a phenomenon of the criticism of our own day." [139]

Besides the strictures on Keats's poetic and intellectual capacities, Lewes's article contains little that is noteworthy. There is brief mention of the tragic love affair with "a lady who is still alive, and of whom therefore the biographer gives us the vaguest possible glimpses." The lady was, of course, Fanny Brawne; and Lewes apparently wanted more information about her than Milnes chose to reveal. Lewes also chides Keats for his "intolerable coxcombry" in adopting a patronizing attitude about selling an article to the *Edinburgh Review*, something which Lewes himself was glad to do whenever he could.[140] He concludes the review by praising Severn's friendship with Keats, quoting long excerpts from Severn's letters and finding a moral—in typical Victorian fashion—in their "pictures of disinterestedness" and "examples of self-sacrificing love" that will teach men to "resist the encroachments of egotism, and of the too common indifference to the mysteries of our destiny." [141] Severn emerges as the hero, not poor Keats; but the observation is of a piece with Lewes's appreciation and understanding of the entire book. He sees nothing of the extraordinary elements of Keats's genius that are revealed both in the letters and in the poems that Milnes quotes, and little of the pathos and bravery that characterized his life. One of Lewes's most respected friends, Leigh Hunt, called Keats "a poet of the most poetical kind";[142] and it was this highly poetical quality that might well have prevented Lewes from getting close enough to him in mind and spirit to arrive at a valid vision of what he really was.

Lewes's attitude about Keats did not change in later years. In his comments on Browning's edition of the Shelley letters, written in 1852 and already referred to, Lewes alludes to Milnes's book by way of comparison; and he again remarks on Keats's completely "sensuous nature." To "sum up" Keats, he suggests one sentence out of the letters—"*I look upon fine phrases as a lover!*" The implication is not that Lewes thinks more highly of Keats because he is a lover of "fine phrases" but that he feels that the creation of such phrases is the best Keats can do. Lewes finally concedes that "many a felicitous phrase, and many a suggestive thought" in the *Literary Remains* imply "far greater range and variety in Keats's mind than one had given him credit for." [143] It is just possible that Lewes had second thoughts when he reread Milnes's book, in connection with writing the later article on Shelley's letters. His general appraisal of Keats certainly is mistaken in the light of modern opinion, simply because his realistic standards were not applicable in measuring the qualities of one of the supremely imaginative poets of our language. He saw that Keats was the sensual singer, the dreamer of luxuriant dreams that he was able to render into glorious verse through the sheer power and unpremeditated genius of his imagination—and Lewes should have let it go at that.

Another Romantic poet to whose reputation Lewes made even less of a contribution was Wordsworth. In 1850, the year of Wordworth's death, *The Prelude* made its first appearance in published form; and Lewes took the occasion to write an evaluation of the poet's works that is perceptive in some ways but overenthusiastic in its general disapprobation. *The Prelude* itself he dismisses as an "uninteresting performance" and as an "ambitious failure," meagre as autobiography and inadequate as philosophy, a collection of trivial anecdotes sometimes poetic but often "surcharged with a dense prosaism to be paralleled only by passages from his other works." It fails both as a poem and as a philosophical exposition of the genesis of a poet's mind—which is what Wordsworth originally intended that it should be. It has no orderly logic, governed as it is by childhood observations and casual associations rather than by any preconceived plan. To demonstrate his lack of personal bias, Lewes quotes from "Childhood" and "Schooltime," which he considers the best sections. Those on London and Cambridge he regards as far inferior to De Quincey's descriptions of Oxford and London in his *Autobiographic Sketches*—and here Lewes inserts the remark that De Quincey's prose is better by far than Wordsworth's "*very* blank" verse. In general, he concludes, the subjects Wordsworth treats in *The Prelude* are both too grand and too human for his "one-stringed lyre." Lewes's remarks have the virtues—perhaps doubtful—of being frank, sincere, and honest—if not always very tolerant or discerning. His judgments are comparable with his opinion of Wordsworth as a person—he has never heard of any instance to prove that Wordsworth was other than an intensely selfish man, or of any generous action that is recorded to "give warmth and vitality to a life of solitary self-worship." [144]

In his observations about Wordsworth as a philosophical poet, Lewes is no more complimentary. He feels that Wordsworth was meditative and contemplative, but not creative, like Sophocles or Shakespeare. Though his poetry contains some fine passages of natural description, it has no grandeur because he had no grasp of philosophical truth. He takes possession of his readers by means of his "diffusive egotism"; but, as a philosopher, he fails because he lacks human sympathy and because his conceptions are limited by "an incurable bias toward the trivial." This bias bothers Lewes most—the meanest flower, not the noblest life, stirs in Wordsworth "thoughts too deep for tears"; and he uses a pedlar to illustrate the greatness of philosophy; the mother of an idiot boy to exemplify maternal passion.[145]

As a nature poet, Wordsworth, Lewes concedes, has extraordinary depth of feeling and a brooding solemnity of thought; and he pays tribute to the lovely imagery and diction of the lyric poems by means of which Wordsworth communes with nature and his own soul. But Wordsworth's famous nature philosophy Lewes terms a "wretched absurdity." For a man to keep himself pious by seeking solitude, cataracts, and streams, and so impregnating his mind with the beauties of the landscape, is not a philosophical conception but "an ignoble, sensuous asceticism." Wordsworth's real tenderness and concern is toward Nature itself—but "not a heart-beat for Man!" Nature taught Wordsworth an intense selfishness, a taste for indolent enjoyment of his meditative moods; but it shut out his view of the nobility of human life and left him arrogant, narrow-minded, and selfish. His view of Nature actually is an inversion of the traditional order, by which most poets have assumed that Nature serves as a background for man, subservient to him in this respect. Wordsworth does the reverse, making man subservient to Nature; and thereby, in Lewes's opinion, he elevates "accessories" into "principals." By so doing, Wordsworth makes Nature supreme over man, violating what Lewes considers an esthetic principle: the "Human Soul must ever remain the chief object of Art, and Nature itself only becomes interesting in so far as it is associated with man." [146]

This view is that of the typical city man, or perhaps that of the scientific observer of natural phenomena—and Lewes was both. It shows, if not a lack of understanding on Lewes's part, at least a lack of that appreciation of Wordsworth's feelings and attitudes about nature that would seem necessary for a critic to have in order to regard the poet with anything but generally negative feelings. Yet much of what he said about Wordsworth anticipated currently respectable opinion. Most modern critics have no higher regard for *The Prelude* than Lewes did, though few of them deal with it in such scarifying terms. There are still doubts in many readers' minds about the substance of Wordsworth's nature philosophy, though none about the beauty of his early nature poems; and there are substantial reservations about the quality of the work he produced after the first decade of the nineteenth century. Lewes remained unimpressed by Wordsworth's exalted status as poet-laureate, and he judged him solely on the basis of his poetry. If his judgments seem harsh today, at least they have the virtue of being honest; and some have retained a remarkable degree of validity in the light of Wordsworth's present reputation.

In general, Lewes regarded most of the poetry of his contemporaries and immediate predecessors with considerable reservations. He was an observer and critic—not a creator and certainly not a poet. The scientific and realistic tendencies that characterized his thinking made him better equipped, as we have noted, for the criticism of fiction and drama than of poetry. His attitudes toward the Romantic poets in particular—except for Shelley, in whose favor he had a personal and not altogether consistent bias—are interesting manifestations of the typical stance of a Victorian observer who ostensibly remains unmoved by emotional excesses. His was an era—as he himself acknowledged—of observation and criticism, not inspired creation; and, as a typical man of his era, he was incapable of appreciating any but the poetry that was most appealing to it. There was no longer any question about such figures as Chaucer, Shakespeare, Spenser, and Milton, whose reputations already were firmly established. But there were considerable doubts about the English poets of the later eighteenth century and the first half of the nineteenth. Lewes's judgments may seem based on insufficient evidence and on a general lack of understanding, in comparison to modern opinion; but some of them, as we have seen, retain a unique vitality. At least he was completely candid, and he always attempted to base his judgments on esthetic principles rather than mere personal prejudice, on philosophical foundations rather than intuition or instinct—which explains to some extent why his criticism of drama and fiction was on the whole more reliable than his criticism of poetry.

V *American Literature*

We have considered aspects of Lewes's criticism of his contemporaries and predecessors both in England and on the Continent. We should also take note of his comments on American literature, which, though not extensive, are most interesting. He was a keen observer of literary developments across the Atlantic, and was one of the few British critics who were ready to admit in the 1850's that there was any indication of the rise of an indigenously American literature, or that the works being written by American authors actually were taking shape as the unique manifestations of a national culture.

Though Washington Irving, James Fenimore Cooper, and William E. Channing were well known in England during the 1820's and 1830's, most readers regarded their writings as imitations of British models. Most critics attacked later American authors as imitators as well—in spite of the use of native themes and subjects by such figures as Mrs. Harriet Beecher Stowe, Hawthorne, Melville, Longfellow, and Emerson, who at mid-century were becoming more and more popular with the British. But these critics adopted a patronizing tone toward the effusions of their New World brethren. As one literary historian, Clarence Gohdes, has shown, "the chief devotees of American literature among the critical classes . . . were likely to be extreme liberals or radicals in politics or Scotchmen by birth, sometimes both"—or occasional journalists, who were reflecting the tastes of middle-class readers.[147] No matter who they were, critics were inclined to be snobbish about anything having artistic pretensions that emanated from the United States.

Lewes—though not a Scot—was in the 1850's both an extreme liberal in politics and a journalist; and he was also a definite exception to the rule in his critical attitude toward American writing. He turned on it the same bright light of attentive and unbiased scrutiny that he did on the work of Englishmen, and there is little trace of British condescension in his comments about Americans that appeared in his *Leader* columns. Tolerant and perceptive, they mark him as one of the first English critics of any consequence to acknowledge the fact that an American literature was in process of being born. His feelings about this cultural phenomenon are indicated specifically in the introductory remarks to a criticism of Melville's *Moby Dick* that he wrote in 1851.[148]

He first concedes that lack of originality "has long been the just and standing reproach" to American writers—the best of them "were but second-hand Englishmen." But he now sees signs, not of "*absolute* originality," but of "such genuine outcoming of the American intellect as can be safely called national." Poe, Hawthorne, Melville, and Emerson are "assuredly no British offshoots." On the contrary—as an observer of what he calls "this commencement of an American literature, properly so called"—Lewes sees a characteristic in American writers that is "peculiarly their own." It is "a wild and mystic love of the supersensual," and he elaborates in glowing terms: "To move a horror skilfully, with something of the earnest faith in the Unseen, and with weird imagery to shape these Phantasms so vividly that the most incredulous mind is hushed, absorbed—to do this no European pen has apparently any longer the power—to do this American literature is without a rival." This power was not, however, of the very highest order, in Lewes's opinion—we must not forget that he was one of the first British exponents of critical realism. But, insofar as the ability to create vivid "Phantasms" is concerned, he insists that the Americans reign supreme. To concede the Americans supremacy in anything was a radical departure from the usual critical attitude in 1851, and even his use of the term "American literature" was an almost unheard-of innovation.

Moby Dick Lewes calls a "wild, weird book, full of poetry and full of interest." He sees "Nature" as its great asset, and hails "the sea breezes" and the "salt spray" as welcome alternations to the usual "old, wornout pathways of romance." Nature is never tiresome, and "there is Nature here, though the daring imagery often grows riotously extravagant." There is also a "strange fascination" in "the ghostly terrors" which Melville "so skilfully evokes." Reason rebels in vain. "Imagination is absolute." Though superstitions related by "vulgar pens" become simply incredible, "Imagination has a credulity of its own respondent to power. So it is with Melville's superstitions: we believe in them imaginatively" because of the sheer power of his prose.

Unhappily, Lewes did not continue with his comments on Melville in this criticism; he allowed himself to be sidetracked in order to introduce a long passage from De Quincey. Its only relevance is that it is a description of the superstitious nature of sailors, a topic that has a vague relationship to *Moby Dick*. Obviously, Lewes wanted an excuse to quote De Quincey, "our greatest prose writer"; and possibly he had said all he had to say about Melville—which was considerable, as the verdict of an English critic on an American writer. Too short as his criticism might have been, it still typifies a perceptive, intelligent attitude toward American letters that was shared by few of Lewes's contemporaries. It also demonstrates that Lewes had a keen and relatively early appreciation of Melville's powers as an imaginative artist.

Lewes continued his observations on American literature in a subsequent article on James Russell Lowell.[149] He first remarks on the recent popularity being enjoyed by writers from the United States, listing the "English editions of American authors" that "crowd our booksellers' windows." As a result, Emerson, Poe, Hawthorne, Dana, and Melville now "are well known"; and their works provide ample evidence that "a distinctly original literature" is appearing in America. Here Lewes re-emphasizes his previously stated opinion: he regards this new development as a welcome change from the recent past when "the literary aspect of America was melancholy enough." In an interesting digression, Lewes then speculates on American critical attitudes toward English writers. He wonders why the Yankees have been so eager to create a "national" literature completely divorced from the influence of England, while at the same time their devotion to the writings of the "good old mother country" has remained "passionate and intense." The highest praise for Cooper is to call him an "American Scott," and each promising young poet is happy to be known as an "American Tennyson." To Lewes, this conflict between dependence on England and pride in America seems feckless. Why should the Yankees, our relatives, be disgusted if "their intellectual faces should show a family likeness?" Rather, they should freely admit that they have created their literature in our image—as, indeed, he adds reasonably enough, "they could not but do" under the circumstances. Nationalism is noble, he concludes, but not "unjust pretence" to it. After this reminder of the "little weaknesses" that plague American letters, Lewes writes "with equal emphasis" about their "hopeful aspects," which include the works of Melville and Hawthorne as typical of the best that are emerging from the United States.

In his detailed criticism of Lowell, Lewes first introduces him as "a fine-minded, high-spirited, original man-of-letters, deserving to be better known here." But Lowell does not quite measure up to Lewes's high standards of poetic excellence. The key question is, "Can we introduce [Lowell] to our readers as an original Singer?" —and Lewes's reluctant answer is that he cannot. By the term "original Singer" he means a "poet proper," as distinct from "a literary artist of poetic mind and taste." The line between them is hard to draw, and the law that compels the critic to draw it is hard to explain. Among "high-minded, able men" there are only a few whose poems, though admirable, contain "the true delight, the peculiar joy, the something which, like true love, is one and one only. . . ." Lowell's poems, beautiful as they are, do not have this ephemeral quality, and Lewes goes into detail on a few of them to demonstrate the reasons for his opinion. His conclusion is that, though not imitative, they exhibit "a pervading air of imitation," so that they often seem to recall the work of other poets, particularly Keats and Tennyson, whose minds evidently have had a strong effect on one "so intensely appreciative" as Lowell. Consequently, "he gives you, every now and then, in the midst of poems original in treatment, a distinct glimpse of some poetic face, which, by force of sheer love, he has come to resemble in his own." To qualify this gentle and certainly inoffensive opinion about the ultimate derivation of Lowell's poems, Lewes quotes from the "Vision of Sir Launfal" and "Rosaline" to illustrate various aspects of "beauty and sadness" as well as a "characteristic oddness" in Lowell's works. But he assigns to the "highest place among his efforts" his humorous poetry. In *Biglow Papers* there are "touches of humour—flashes of sunny ridicule" that are all but "unmatched in the comic literature of our day."

In general, Lewes's appraisal of Lowell's poetry has stood the test of time. *Biglow Papers* remains as the most original if not the most exalted in style, and Lowell is remembered more for his satiric attacks on slavery and war than he is for the beauty and grace of his serious but more conventional effusions. Applying the same standards to these poems that he did to the works of other poets, Lewes found that Lowell was not an "original Singer," but that his poetry had undoubted qualities of sweetness and melody that distinguished it as being far superior to the ordinary run of contemporary verse. This fair and honest judgment is unprejudiced by the fact of Lowell's nationality.

Lewes had more reservations about another American, Nathaniel Hawthorne, who in the 1850's already was beginning to establish himself among British critics as an author who merited serious consideration. In his first extended criticism of Hawthorne, Lewes recognizes him as a romance writer of extraordinary talents—but as a romance writer only. He treates *The House of the Seven Gables* as a first-rate horror story, but he ignores its important symbolic aspects; consequently, his vision of Hawthorne is limited. He admires the novelty of the background and the vividness of the characterizations, which give the novel an unusual interest; and he sees in Hawthorne's work a "quaintness, a wildness, an imagination, and a sort of weird sombreness" that differentiates it from other romances of a similar type. Most of the long excerpts that take up much of the space in the review are descriptions of characters, which seem to have exerted a strange fascination over Lewes.[150]

He considers that the book's chief defect is its loose construction, particularly in the denouement, where Hawthorne shows lack of skill in handling the complex details that he has brought into the story. Lewes anticipates in this instance the opinion of one of the most reputable among recent historians of American literature, Professor Stanley Williams, who writes that the plot is "so artificial in its denouement as to invite a smile" at the author's "playthings"—the ghostly music, hidden panels, and old manuscripts making up the Gothic paraphernalia that also tried Lewes's patience and strained his credibility.[151] In Lewes's final conclusion, that the book has "unquestionable" originality and vividness, few successors have disputed him. In general, Lewes's criticism of *The House of the Seven Gables,* within the limits that he prescribed for himself, is sympathetic and discerning; and it is one of the first really serious, extended efforts by a British critic to arrive at any considered or adequate judgment of it.

Lewes is harsher in his criticism of *The Blithedale Romance* because he feels that Hawthorne has made improper use of his materials. Though the Brook Farm experiment formed part of the background, Hawthorne seemed to be afraid of "striking deep into realities" in his treatment of it; and, refusing to draw any social or moral lesson from the circumstances surrounding the experiment, he simply used it as the setting for a tragic love story. Lewes also feels that *Blithedale* is altogether too mournful, though the writing itself is of the highest quality. Dealing with the failure of a social scheme and the effects of this failure on the lives of the people involved in it, the situation offers no redeeming feature, no consolation for all its sadness. The book is better as an illustration of the tyranny that an Idea can exercise over a group of people, "coercing" them to martyrdom and cruelty, as exemplified in the behavior of Hollingsworth and his two victims, Zenobia and Priscilla. But sacrificing persons to a principle is worthwhile only if the sacrifice is not wasted, and in *The Blithedale Romance* it is. Hollingsworth, as the incarnation of an Idea, is unable to withstand the consequences of his acts, so that the book ends in utter frustration and failure—"nowhere triumph! nowhere hope!" [152]

Again we find that Lewes's insights anticipate subsequent opinion. Modern critics have not been so much interested in the moral and social implications of the setting as Lewes, a typical Victorian, was. But Professor Williams agrees with Lewes that Hawthorne used Brook Farm merely as a background for the "stormy emotional experiences" of the heroine, and he interprets Hollingsworth as typical of Hawthorne's other characters "who have surrendered themselves to an overruling purpose"—an interpretation that resembles Lewes's designation of Hollingsworth as the incarnation of an Idea and its consequent results.[153]

Lewes's reaction to the work of another American contemporary also is colored by his opinions about social issues. When *Uncle Tom's Cabin* was published in England in 1852, it was an immediate and sensational success, indicating that Harriet Beecher Stowe's poignant story had a strong appeal to mass readership and that there was a tremendous interest in the problem of slavery. Commenting on the book's popularity soon after its publication, Lewes wrote: "There is something fabulous in the success of that *Uncle Tom*"—the sale is "immense." Over twenty reprints already had appeared, and three hundred copies were being sold daily at the railroad stations. Soon, he concludes, it will be a "distinction" not to have read it.[154] But he had reservations about the book because of his attitude toward the subject it dealt with. He had seen the dramatic version when it was produced at the Olympic Theatre in September, 1852; and he had also reacted against it. In his review of the play he conceded that *Uncle Tom* had the attributes of popular drama, but he felt at the same time that slavery and the privations of "niggers" were unfit subjects for mirth—even though the piece aroused the sympathies of the audience in favor of the "miserable slave" who was involved.[155] Lewes's main objection was that the essential tragedy of the situation is forgotten in the details of the drama, and it is this tragedy that prevents him from being able to read the book. There is no pleasure in the pain of learning about such a "gigantic and *immediate*" reality as slavery, particularly in view of the fact that there is nothing that he personally can do to alleviate the situation. The living horror of slavery is too vivid to allow him to enjoy a book about it, just as the thought that slavery still exists in the United States makes it impossible for him to enjoy the play.

As an extreme realist, Lewes was incapable of contemplating *Uncle Tom* as anything except a pitiful, harrowing depiction of the truth. He could not divorce the circumstances of Tom's fictional life from the real lives of countless wretches just like Tom of whom the book constantly reminded him. The objective critic of fiction was overwhelmed by the passionate lover of liberal causes —which perhaps was just as well. Lewes almost certainly would not have appreciated Mrs. Stowe's novel purely as a work of art, and he would not have approved of it as propaganda, worthy as the cause was for which it struck a blow. His refusal to read it—or at least to comment on it—reflects his unwillingness to praise an author's attempt to capitalize on a humanly tragic situation, regardless of how good the reasons for doing so might be.

No other extensive criticism of American authors by Lewes has come to my attention, besides those we have just considered, though he made brief comments on several. He reviewed Margaret Fuller's *Memoirs* in 1852 and found it the "most acceptable" book to come from the United States in a long time, though he felt that Miss Fuller was a better talker than a writer, one of those whom he designated as having "more aspiration than inspiration." [156] Concerning a reprint of Washington Irving's *Life of Mahomet,* Lewes observed that, though charmingly written, it was "not equal to the magnificence of its subject." Likewise he was not impressed by a new edition of Franklin's *Autobiography.*[157] The fiction that came from the United States invariably interested Lewes more than biography or other types of non-fiction. Certainly he would have approved of the trend toward Realism in the novels of such writers as Stephen Crane, William Dean Howells, and Theodore Dreiser if he had lived to read them. Those writers whom he did have an opportunity to evaluate, he saw for what they were; and he recognized Hawthorne, Melville, and Lowell as important manifestations of a new American literary vitality.

CHAPTER 4

The Playwright

I *The Acted Plays*

LEWES'S dramatic criticism is much more widely known than his criticism of other forms of literature, probably because its quality is in general more consistently high. Though his interests were almost universal, he was deeply involved in the world of the theater during the years he wrote the bulk of his criticism; and this involvement is reflected in the relatively greater amount of attention that he gave to the drama in comparison with fiction and poetry. The theater always fascinated him, as we have seen, and his early experiences as an actor made him a better drama critic than he would have been if he had never had them.

Yet another—and more influential—facet of his background was his experience as a playwright. It was extensive and extremely practical. In all, he wrote—or had his hand in the writing of—some twenty plays that we can identify. Most of them were direct adaptations from popular French comedies that Lewes converted for production in London theaters between 1850 and 1856, while he was drama editor of the *Leader.* One of his few original plays, *The Noble Heart,* was first staged in 1849, with Lewes himself in the lead part. Another, *Captain Bland,* written in 1857, was never performed in England but turned up in Wallack's Theatre, in New York, in 1864. At least two did not appear as dramas at all and were changed into short stories; and several never saw the light of day in any form and remain in manuscript.

These plays do not reveal Lewes as an original or outstanding dramatist, but they do demonstrate that he was acquainted with the inner workings of the theater as well as with the demands of public taste. As a drama critic, he was not merely another spectator in the audience but was in the unique position of being a part of the theater that he was observing; and on several occasions he wrote criticisms of his own plays. This direct participation not only contributed materially to his knowledge of the practical problems of stagecraft but also gave him insights into the techniques of the acting drama that he never could have gained otherwise.

The first of his plays to be produced on the professional stage, as far as I have been able to determine, was *The Noble Heart,* a five-act tragedy in blank verse modeled after the Elizabethans. He probably wrote it as early as 1841, but it did not appear until 1849, when it was shown seven times during April and May in Manchester and Liverpool, with Lewes himself playing Don Gomez, the leading role. When it opened in London on February 18, 1850, at the Olympic Theatre, several changes had been made. G. V. Brooke, a professional actor, not Lewes, was Don Gomez. The five acts had been cut to three, and several lines were deleted at the request of the government censor, to Lewes's disgust. In his Prefatory Letter to the published edition, Lewes accuses the "prudery" of "theatrical aesthetics" of forcing him to change the word "God" to "Heaven" in a line that originally read "The Heart hath but one resting place—in God." Soon, he fears, it will be altered to "sky" and then to "that place"—with disastrous effects on the drama. But the deletions remained, and Lewes still was featured on the playbills as the author—the first and last time that he ever allowed his real name to be used in connection with the writing of a play.[1]

The opening London performance seems to have been well received by the audience. Henry Morley, the reviewer for the *Examiner,* relates that Lewes was "called for" after the final curtain and "passed smiling across the stage."[2] But the critics were not overly enthusiastic. John Oxenford, in the *Times,* expresses his admiration for the clearness of Lewes's plan and for his sharp delineation of character, but he decries his "overpredilection for controversial dialogue," which impairs the construction of the play and results in lagging action and unnatural behavior on the part of the actors.[3] The *Spectator* critic finds yet another defect in Lewes's choice of subject, which, he feels, "will displease many whose taste has been nurtured by food of a different species."[4] The *Literary Gazette* reviewer is less oblique, and perhaps reflects the conventional Victorian view of a play dealing with the theme of a father and son in love with the same woman. "However skilfully it may be treated," he writes, it is "altogether revolting."[5] The consensus concerning Lewes's ability as a dramatist, as demonstrated by his composition of *The Noble Heart,* was that he had not yet proved himself, but that he showed promise for the future. Regarding Lewes as one of themselves, the critics probably were kinder to him than they would have been to an unknown author.

The tragedy, which ran for seven more nights after the opening, closed on March 1, 1850. A week later the Olympic Theatre also closed—rather abruptly, when the discovery was made that Walter Watts, the manager, was operating it with the substantial help of funds that he had embezzled from the Globe Insurance Company, where he had been employed as a clerk. Interestingly enough, Lewes had commented on his unusual generosity, attributing to him a "liberality, courtesy, and promptitude, rare indeed among managers."[6] According to his Literary Receipt Book Lewes was paid the unusually generous sum of one hundred pounds for the production rights, in February, 1950, a month before Watts went bankrupt. In the light of what happened, Lewes was fortunate. Whether or not his play would have had a longer run if Watts's financial habits had not been so erratic is, of course, difficult to determine. Watts may have intended to produce it again, but no other manager revived it, and it never reappeared in England. But it was presented in New York, about a year after the debacle of the Olympic, at the Bowery Theatre, on February 5, 1851, for a three-night run. Four years later, on January 29, 1855, it was billed as a "New Romantic Play" being presented for "the first time in the United States" at the Boston Museum with the famous tragedian E. L. Davenport as Don Gomez. Despite the featured—if mistaken—billing, it survived only a few performances during the cold Boston winter; and except for a single amateur presentation by the Garrick Club of New York at the French Theatre on April 15, 1858,[7] the play has not appeared again.

The style and content of *The Noble Heart* indicate that Lewes wrote it under a combination of influences. As the *Spectator* reviewer commented, the arrangement is from Corneille, the personages from Calderon, and the "love for abstract debate" either from France or Spain. Much of the dialogue has an Elizabethan ring. The action concerns Don Gomez, a rich nobleman, whose son, Don Leon, falls in love with Juanna, a commoner. The complications arise when Don Gomez also falls in love with Juanna, who, ignorant of Don Leon's identity, marries Don Gomez in order to save her family from ruin. When the son returns from the wars on his father's wedding day, catastrophe appears imminent. Don Gomez finally renounces all worldly pleasures after he discovers the facts, and goes off to the desert.

The play as a whole is neither Classic, Elizabethan, nor Romantic; but it has elements of all three genres. Though there is some fine poetry, its literary value is considerably reduced by a lack of dramatic consistency. Whatever model or convention Lewes was trying to imitate, his chief objective was to write a successful play. He chose the form of a verse tragedy at a time when it was acceptable in the acting theater, though he actually disapproved of it himself; and he had written a series of diatribes against the "antiquated phraseology" and "obsolete ethics" of the Elizabethans, demonstrating that their works were completely inappropriate as models for contemporary playwrights.[8] As a critic, he was right; but he ignored his own precepts in his eagerness to score a dramatic hit. *The Noble Heart* was not a very noble failure, though the experience of writing and acting in it—even if briefly—certainly added to Lewes's knowledge of the working theater.

Lewes's next effort as a playwright was more successful. It was a comedy called *The Game of Speculation*, the first of his translations from French originals written under the peculiar pseudonym of "Slingsby Lawrence." One of a number of British play-makers—or plagiarizers, strictly speaking—who followed the same procedure, Lewes was not violating any copyright laws since none existed when he "borrowed" French scripts and adapted them for use on the English stage. Of the dozen or so that he wrote, *The Game of Speculation* was the best, principally because he translated it from a first-rate play that eventually became a stock piece in the Comédie Française. Originally a five-act comedy, *Le Faiseur*, it was written between 1838 and 1840 by Honoré de Balzac, but never performed. Later it was revised and reduced to three acts by Adolphe D'Ennery. With another title, *Mercadet*, it opened on August 24, 1851, at the Théâtre Gymnase and scored a considerable success. Lewes used this version for his English adaptation, which appeared a scant six weeks later, on October 2, at the Lyceum Theatre in London, where it had an equally enthusiastic reception.

During the next four years *The Game of Speculation* had well over a hundred performances, and it was revived as late as 1877.

Charles Mathews, the famous English comedian who originated the lead role of Affable Hawk, regarded it as one of his best "vehicles." Charles Dickens wrote that Mathews considered it "perhaps his favorite part," and Lewes himself felt that the "artistic merit" of his acting "was so great that it almost became an offense against morality, by investing a swindler with irresistable charms. . . ."[9] The success of the play seems remarkable in view of the circumstances under which Lewes adapted it. According to a note of the flyleaf of the acting edition, signed "S.L.", it "was written in less than thirteen hours and produced after only two rehearsals."[10]

Whether or not "S. L." was exaggerating, the interesting question remains: What did Lewes do to this somewhat sleazy bit of French fluff, to convert it into a comedy fit for the amusement of the average, respectable, Victorian theatergoer? Opinions differed about its quality and appropriateness. Thornton Hunt, in his review of the opening performance, called it "an original translation," a comedy with the same plot as Balzac's, but with "little trace of the French" in its details and dialogue.[11] A few months later Edward F. S. Pigott, describing his impressions of the French version, wrote that he "was more impressed by Lewes's wonderful adaptation to English society" when he saw the original acted in Paris than he had been when he first read the play in English.[12] On the other hand, John Hollingshead called *The Game of Speculation* a "phonographic echo of Balzac," and William Archer felt that Lewes followed *Mercadet* "very faithfully" in most ways; he showed originality "solely in the more or less inappropriate interpolation of some of that 'wit' which belongs to the tradition of English comedy." But the attempt to Anglicize the picture of manners, in Archer's view, "was certainly not successful."[13]

Although Lewes's version is far more than a mere "phonographic echo" of Balzac's comedy, Hunt was hardly justified in implying that Lewes created a new play from old materials. He made few changes in dramatic structure, and the characters in both plays perform almost the same functions. In many instances entire conversations are simply translated word for word. But he was careful to "Anglicize" the background and much of the dialogue in order to satisfy the taste of London audiences; in doing so, he was more successful than Archer said he was. In addition to the obvious alterations in the names of characters and places, he changed the entire atmosphere of the play so as to make it typically English.

Lewes employed several interesting devices to bring about this change. One was his use of local or topical references to make his characters unmistakably English. For example, the butler calls Affable Hawk—the Mercadet of Lewes's version—"the Van Amburgh of the city," comparing him to a popular London animal trainer.[14] Lewes also was very liberal about converting idiomatic and technical expressions from French to English so that they sounded like original versions rather than translations. In the French, Pierquin, one of Mercadet's creditors, is called "un tigre qui se nourrit de billets de mille francs" (a tiger that feeds on thousand-franc notes).[15] Grossmark, his opposite number in *The Game of Speculation,* is described in a more typically Anglo-Saxon idiom as "A shark that feeds on post obits" (Act I, Sc. 1, p. 4).

A lengthier illustration of this kind of extensive alteration in the language can be seen by comparing the following passages from the two versions, which are dilations on the advantage of credit. In the French original, Mercadet, talking to his servant, Virginie, says, among other things, that ". . . . aujourd'hui le crédit est toute la richesse des gouvernements, mes fournisseurs méconnaîtraient les lois de leur pays, ils seraient inconstitutionnels et radicaux s'ils ne me laissaient pas tranquille . . ." (Act I, Sc.4, p. 160). (. . . today credit is all the wealth of governments, my creditors would not recognize the law of the land, they would be unconstitutional and radical, if they did not leave me alone).

Affable Hawke expresses these sentiments in the following characteristically British phraseology: "Mrs. Mason, in these days credit is everything—credit is the wealth of commerce, the foundation of the State. If my tradesmen refuse credit, it is a proof that they have no respect for the British Constitution, our safeguard and our pride! They are radicals and chartists of the worst description!" (Act I, Sc. 1, p. 5).

Lewes's introduction of what Archer deplored as inappropriate British stage "wit" was yet another device to Anglicize the comedy. Labored as this brand of humor seems to us, it was what London audiences wanted. "Affable Hawk," of course, contains implications about the main character that are not in the original

French name of Mercadet. Lewes carried the word play further by inserting such lines as the remark that the name Hawk "suggests uncomfortable ideas to the pigeons!" (Act II, Sc. 1, p. 24). On the same level of British stage "wit" is Hawk's question about Sparrow, his long-departed partner. "What Sparrow?" he asks. "Cock Sparrow? Am I, Hawk, to be the victim of such a Sparrow as that?" (Act III, Sc. 1, p. 43). Again—and how British audiences sustained this pun for a hundred performances is a mystery —he plays on the word "Calcutta" when he quips that Sparrow has returned from India with "an incalcuttable fortune" (Act III, Sc. 1, p. 37).

Lewes also makes extensive vocabulary changes in order to convert *The Game of Speculation* into something more acceptable to Victorian tastes than the French version. For example, De la Brive, the destitute dandy, describes himself as "Un homme . . . capable d'inspirer des passions et de les justifier . . ." (A man . . . capable of inspiring the passions and of vindicating them) (Act II, Sc. 4, p. 208). His British counterpart, Sir Harry Lester, steers clear of any mention of "des passions," substituting a simpler and more innocuous self-characterization: "A man with such whiskers as mine . . ." (Act II Sc. 1, p. 24). Lewes omits entirely most of Balzac's cynical references to the life of a Parisian man-about-town. To the remark that "le mariage est le suicide des dandys, après en avoir été la plus belle gloire" (marriage is the suicide of the dandy, after having been his greatest glory), De le Brive replies, "Les femmes et moi . . . nous nous sommes ruinés réciproquement, et, par les moeurs qui courent, rencontrer une Anglaise, une aimable douairière. . . ." (The women and I . . . we have reciprocally ruined each other and, according to current mores, I should get acquainted with an English lady, a lovable heiress) (Act II, Sc. 4, p. 208). There are no shady references in *The Game of Speculation* to reciprocal ruin or to the glories of marriage for the dandy before he becomes a husband. All Sir Harry Lester says in the corresponding episode is a rendition of the final lines: "The only chance I have lived upon for some time, has been that of meeting with an heiress or a rich widow . . ." (Act. II, Sc. 1, p. 23). Many other passages in the original play are brilliantly satiric, but Lewes left them out, apparently because he felt that they were unfit for British ears. Charles Mathews was not completely accurate, therefore, when he wrote that "not a word of the piece as acted at the Gymnase has been lost" in Lewes's version; but he was right in concluding that "Much has been added to fit it to the British stage." [16]

Lewes also made some changes in the play because he wanted to achieve dramatic effects that were not in the original. For example, he concludes Act I with a scene in which Prospectus, one of the creditors, lends Hawk three hundred pounds after Julia, Hawk's daughter, has made an impassioned appeal. In the French version another scene follows, picturing Mercadet's unholy glee at this stroke of luck. Lewes left it out, probably because it makes Hawk appear to be a much more contemptible character than Lewes wanted him to be.

The variant endings of the two versions illustrate another kind of alteration, one dictated by differences in English and French stage conventions. In the original, Mercadet offers to loan his daughter's rejected suitor ten thousand francs, and finally congratulates himself upon at last becoming a creditor. To a similar closing scene Lewes added a long, moralistic speech by Hawk that has no equivalent in the French. But in London it was customary to tack some kind of a moral onto a play, no matter how farfetched, and so Lewes gave his version this extra English touch —which of course would have been completely out of place in *Mercadet.*

The changes Lewes made did not wholly convert *Mercadet* into an English comedy of manners. *The Game of Speculation* is not a reflection of English society in the 1850's; it is simply a clever, thorough Anglicization of a French satire on a limited segment of contemporary life. It attempts to do no more in English than the original does in French. Lewes added or substituted enough to convert Balzac's play into an approximation of an English one, so that it is more than a French comedy written in English; but he made no fundamental alterations in the original conception of the play or the characters. Mercadet and Affable Hawk are one and the same man, whose background may shift and whose activities may have different designations, but whose nature and function remain constant. The plays are essentially similar as social commentaries. *The Game of Speculation* owes its success to its appeal to British audiences—essentially the same kind of an appeal that *Mercadet* had to the audiences in the Théâtre Gymnase and later at the Comédie Français.

Probably because his first attempt was so successful, Lewes was asked to supply more plays for Charles Mathews' repertory. According to the terms of an agreement made in January, 1852, Lewes was to receive a salary of ten pounds a week, although the payments were irregular after the first two months the agreement was in force. During the next four seasons eight of Lewes's plays were produced at the Lyceum, for which he received well over three hundred pounds, plus the printing rights. All of them were adaptations from French originals; and, although they were received with varying degrees of enthusiasm, none was so consistently successful as *The Game of Speculation.*

The first to appear in 1852 was *A Chain of Events,* written under his usual pseudonym, Slingsby Lawrence, in collaboration with Mathews. Adapted from *La Dame de la Halle,* first presented in Paris at the Théâtre de l'Ambigu Comique on February 7,[17] *A Chain of Events* opened in London a little over two months later on April 12. It follows the original story line closely, although there are some additions, including an elaborate ballet, several songs, and a shipwreck. The scene is laid in Paris in both versions, and the characters in the English have French names, though not the same ones.

Usually French plays were condensed for presentation in England, but *A Chain of Events* was lengthened. Lewes and Mathews added another act to the original seven, and the whole production took about four hours to stage. In the eyes of one critic, the result of this elaboration was "a succession of some of the most remarkable stage effects ever witnessed in a drama not belonging to the region of fairy land." Particularly impressive was the "real ship" in the storm in Act II, with "real actors" aboard, which "really sinks through the bottom of the stage." Though not quite so rhapsodic, the reviewer for the *Examiner,* Henry Morley, admitted that "the shipwreck of the rogue and his victim . . . is a marvellous scene." [18]

A Chain of Events is complex, rambling, and loosely constructed, a succession of more or less related scenes rather than a play. The principal characters are Gaspard, the villain; Michel, a commoner; and Michel's faithful wife, Thérèse, a beautiful but humble market woman of Paris. Gaspard, in the English version, is finally shot by a volley of musketry from a squad of soldiers "who have been secreted behind the counter," and he plunges "over the parapet"—giving the conclusion of the Lyceum performance a spectacular fillip that was absent from the French original. Such touches as this one—plus the storm at sea, the picturesque scenery painted by William Beverley, and the songs and dances—must have satisfied the spectators in spite of the feebleness of the story. According to Mathews' record, *A Chain of Events* ran for fifty-nine performances and was revived for eight more during the following season.[19]

Lewes's next effort for the Lyceum was a one-act farce, *Taking by Storm!* that was first presented on June 3, 1852. For some reason or other "Frank Churchill" was used as a pseudonym, and as far as I have been able to discover this was the only time Lewes varied from the usual "Slingsby Lawrence." Adapted from *Tambour Battant,* a comédie-vaudeville which opened in Paris on October 30, 1851, *Taking by Storm!* ran for twenty-three nights and had the same number of performances when it was produced a year later. It differs from the French version only in the opening scenes. Most of the remainder is a direct translation, with a few insertions and changes, including one new character whose added lines resemble the interpolations of stage "wit" that enliven *The Game of Speculation.*

Tambour Battant has an extremely unsubstantial plot; and, as the name suggests, it is a parody on French army life. *Taking by Storm!* which makes fun of the British Navy, makes use of the same kind of stage paraphernalia that had endeared the enormously popular *Black Eyed Susan* and other nautical melodramas to British audiences for decades. The heroine of *Tambour Battant* is Constantine Cavalier, whose brother, an army captain, has been killed in the French campaign in Africa. Fanny Seabright, her counterpart in *Taking by Storm!,* has lost her father in the naval bombardment of Acre. Rose Briquette and Betsy Mizen, Constantine's and Fanny's companions, have been widowed by the loss of their husbands in the same battles. Both pairs of girls yearn for the excitements of the past, and Lewes makes some rather amusing changes in the dialogue from army to navy terminology.

For example, when Constantine says, "Eh bien, rejouis-toi, ma fille! car bientôt, peut-être, nous rentrerons sous les drapeaux" (Well, rejoice, my girl! for soon, perhaps, we will return to the colors), Rose shouts, "Mille Tonnerres!" (A thousand thunderclaps). In Lewes's translation, Fanny asks, "What should you say to another cruise, Betsy?" and the enthusiastic reply is "Shiver my timbers! You're not in earnest!" [20] The "talking by storm" applies to the wooing of Fanny by Backhuysen Buff, a painter, called Antenor Duroseau in the French version; but both names are appropriate. Lewes alters all the references so as to localize the action in England, as he does in *The Game of Speculation;* and he also adds a typically British stage ending. *Tambour Battant* closes with a song by the three principals and a final chorus, but *Taking by Storm!* concludes with an appeal for applause by Backhuysen Buff.

Lewes himself, writing as drama critic for the *Leader* with the dubious privilege of sitting in judgment on his own play, called *Taking by Storm!* "an extravagance rendered amusing by good acting," though "outrageously improbable." The *Spectator* reviewer, who agreed, asserted that Mathews proves by his "vivacity" that "the slightest piece in the world may receive substance from excellent acting." The same critic remarks that the "smart dialogue" indicates that John Morton probably is the author—a compliment to Lewes since Morton then enjoyed a considerable reputation as a writer of successful comedies.[21] Though not so popular as *The Game of Speculation, Taking by Storm!* served its purpose in supplying Mathews with a good farce that was as well received by Lyceum audiences as most French adaptations of the same type and quality.

During the following season, two more of Lewes's plays were staged at the Lyceum, *A Strange History* and *The Lawyers.* Written in collaboration with Mathews and first presented on March 29, 1853, *A Strange History* was adapted from a long French *drame* called *Marianne,* and resembles in many details *A Chain of Events.* Despite the beautiful Beverley landscapes, the remarkable stage effects, and considerable cutting, *A Strange History* was a failure. It ran for eleven nights and was never revived at the Lyceum, though it appeared two months later in New York, where it was described as "too strange for utterance in terms of success." [22] The play lacks dramatic interest because it tells too many rambling stories at the same time. Commenting on it as drama reviewer for the *Leader* and using "Vivian" as his pseudonym, Lewes was again critical of his own creation. Addressing the author directly—which adds an ironic touch, under the circumstances—he writes, "As soon as you have excited a strong interest in *Christine* . . . you withdraw her from the scene . . . introducing a new set of persons and a new story to our attention! But I want to know what has become of *Christine.* I haven't the slightest regard for that young count in love with *Estelle—Christine* is the person whose fortunes I am following. . . . Then again, no sooner have you opened a new story—nay, two new stories . . . than you bring back *Christine,* and bring in another love story. . . ."[23]

In the original French play Marianne—whose name is changed to Christine in the English version—is united to Bernard, a soldier, by the bonds of affection. They are separated, and Marianne is falsely accused of theft and disgraced. Meanwhile, Bernard becomes a general and rears their son as a gentleman. Years afterwards Marianne returns, reconciliation follows, and her innocence is finally established. To this already complicated story Lewes added several new characters and events, so that—as "Vivian" so effectively put it—*A Strange History* becomes a hopelessly confused mixture of unrelated romantic episodes with no cohesive plot to unify them; its failure as drama was inevitable.[24]

Lewes's next Lyceum effort, *The Lawyers,* is a three-act comedy about the British legal system based on a French play called *Les Avocats.*[25] It was first produced on May 19, 1853—the same year, incidentally, that Dickens completed his immensely popular *Bleak House,* a fictional satire on the same subject. *The Lawyers,* which scored a considerable success, ran for thirty-nine nights. It also appeared in New York, opening at Burton's Theatre on August 19, and had several repeat performances. Its reception in London was cordial, and Slingsby Lawrence was warmly praised by the critics. John Oxenford wrote in the *Times* that he would almost give the playwright credit for an "original production," for it is "a thoroughly English piece; the dialogue is written with English vigour and the abuses of the bar are satirized with a perfect feeling for the professional peculiarities of this country. Although the course of action borders on caricature, nothing can be more life-like than the deportment of the barristers as they lounge through the hall. . . . And it is not the colouring alone that is original. The adaptor has altered the plot of the Gymnase piece in several essential particulars. . . ."[26]

The critic in the *Spectator* also praised Lewes's originality, and wrote that the plot was "the least important part of the whole affair. Mr. Slingsby Lawrence, by giving us such adaptations as *A Game of Speculation* and *The Lawyers,* and Mr. Charles Mathews . . . are doing more real service to the drama, and are presenting us with better pictures even of English life, than a host of 'original' writers, who show their nationality by incoherence and absence of constructive art." [27] Comparison of *The Lawyers* with some of the badly written native plays that were being produced at this time in England demonstrates that Lewes deserved the compliment.

But notwithstanding the acclaim, the real credit for the construction of *The Lawyers* must go to the authors of *Les Avocats,* not to Lewes. He adds or substitutes material that serves to localize the story in London, but he follows the original plot and makes no fundamental changes in dramatic structure. He creates one new role, the meddlesome mother-in-law, Mrs. Almonia Naggins, which he wrote in for Madame Vestris, the famous character actress, who was a member of Mathews' company. In both plays the plot revolves around the troubles of a young couple who go to court over a quarrel, and lawyers and their methods of doing business are broadly satirized. For the numerous songs in the French comédie-vaudeville, Lewes substitutes speeches poking fun at British legal procedure and inserting his usual quota of stage "wit."

In the original, for example, when a new client calls on Grandier, a veteran lawyer, his nephew, Blesinet "un avocate sans causes" (a lawyer without cases), exclaims enviously, "Encore un client! . . . est il heureux!" (Another client! . . . he is a happy man!). In the translation, Quality Court, Blesinet's counterpart, makes a similar remark, then continues with an added description of his uncle, Sextus Settle, that has no French equivalent: "—predestined for success in the legal career. Born on the first day of term—born with a caul—a call to the bar—swaddled in parchment—weaned on pounce and stamped for a lawyer by your very godfather when he christened you Sextus Octavius—for isn't that Latin for six and eightpence?" [28] Court's conduct of a hypothetical murder case, also original with Lewes, includes a humorous reference to the possible disastrous effects of spontaneous combustion on a lady with "a tendency to alcohol." [29]

In Act II, the action of *The Lawyers* is transferred from the

Palace of Justice in Paris to the London Guildhall. Lewes makes the usual appropriate changes in the conversations, but follows the plot of the original, except for the insertion of a scene showing his added character, Mrs. Almonia Naggins, in the act of bolstering her daughter's fading resentment against her husband. Quality Court's acquisition of his first two clients, a poetry-writing murderer and a country bumpkin, are taken directly from the French; but Lewes inserts some characteristically British comic elements. The changes in Act III are along the same lines: he adds an encounter between Mrs. Naggins and her daughter, Mrs. Brown, in which Mrs. Naggins causes trouble by calling attention to a scurrilous article in the *Times* about the lawsuit and making remarks (not present in the French) about Mr. Brown's perfidy. The *Times* story is a translation from one in *La Gazette des tribuneaux* in the original play. As a result of the scandal, Armand, the wronged husband in the French version, challenges the offending lawyer, Brisard, who urges him to desist by appealing to his "sens commun" (Act III, Sc. 8, p. 56). In *The Lawyers* (Act III, Sc. 1, p. 26), Brown challenges Bullyrag, who threatens to "file an information" against him in the Queen's Bench—apparently Lewes thought this was a more characteristically British reaction than an appeal to common sense. He also gave the play a typical English stage ending by converting Blesinet's final song into a speech by Quality Court, asking the audience for a "favorable verdict."

The changes Lewes made in the plot and structure of the play are minor. His originality lies in the complete and thorough anglicization of the background of *Les Avocats* and in his adaptation of the dialogue and situations to the exigencies of British stage usage and convention. The addition of Mrs. Naggins to the cast does not change the play, but the role must have provided Madame Vestris with some good opportunities to caricature the traditional mother-in-law. Although *The Lawyers* does not quite justify Oxenford's designation of it as an "original production" because too much of the French remains in it, it does demonstrate Lewes's remarkable skill and facility in converting an indigenously French comedy into an acceptable British farce.

His next contributions to the Lyceum repertory appeared in 1854: *Give a Dog a Bad Name,* a one-act farce, and *Sunshine Through the Clouds,* a full-length comedy. Another farce, *Wanted a She-Wolf,* which opened at the Lyceum on March 23, was probably also written by Lewes, although it is not listed in his Literary Receipt Book and I have not been able to discover any copy of it. In his review of it in the *Leader,* Lewes refers to the author as "some admirable unknown," and Slingsby Lawrence is not mentioned in the Lyceum notices.[30] In any event, *Wanted a She-Wolf,* which was adapted from a piece by Alexandre Dumas called *Romulus,* was not a success; it was permanently withdrawn from the Lyceum bills after seven lackluster performances.

Lewes had better luck with *Give a Dog a Bad Name.* First presented on April 18, it ran for thirty-nine nights. It was adapted from a "proverbe en un Acte" produced the preceding year in Paris, called *Quand on Veut Tuer Son Chien . . . ,* apparently the first part of a variant version of the familiar French proverb, "Qui veut noyer son chien, l'accuse de rage" (He who wants to drown his dog, accuses him of having rabies).[31] Lewes took his title from the English equivalent, "Give a dog a bad name and hang him." The farce follows the French closely, with the usual name changes and some added "wit," except for the ending, which has a characteristically Victorian twist. In the original, a young and innocent wife is almost seduced by an unscrupulous friend of her good-hearted but unromantic husband. In the end, the husband wins out and there is a reconciliation scene in which he says, "You shall see the right way to serve these mischievous bachelors who come prowling around domestic hearths." The thwarted home-wrecker admits that husbands "always get the best of it" and foresees his own marriage, "if only in self-defense." There are no such pronouncements about marital felicity in the French version. The first-night audience at the Lyceum was pleasantly surprised at the end to discover "what an intensely virtuous work" it was, though "*ultra*-French in its tone" and appearing "dreadfully immoral" at the outset, according to the *Times.* The reviewer for the *Leader* —probably not Lewes—also congratulated the author for avoiding the French conclusion and ending "with an appeal to English sentiment."[32]

Sunshine Through the Clouds was first presented at the Lyceum on June 15, 1854, and had considerable success although it played in competition with the French version, *La Joie Fait Peur,* by Madame Emile de Girardin, which had opened at the St. James's Theatre a few weeks before. Vivian, who had given *La*

Joie an enthusiastic review in the *Leader,* expressed his admiration for Madame Girardin's evocation of emotions that are "true to almost universal experience"; and Lewes's adaptation shows that he tried to retain the realistic elements of the original.[33] He anglicized the background but varied from the French text only in necessary details. *Sunshine Through the Clouds* has a simple plot about breaking the news of a son's safety to his mother, who thinks he has been killed in battle. The delicate handling of her emotions by the rest of the family provides a pathetic and suspenseful situation. Madame Vestris played her part with apparently considerable effect. Oxenford, in the *Times,* praised the "depth and pathos of her delivery," and the *Spectator* reviewer admired her adherence to "domestic pathos." [34]

There is less British stage "wit" than usual in *Sunshine Through the Clouds*—an omission which may have contributed to its success. Lewes's translation varies from the French only enough to localize the events in England, and most of the changes he makes are idiomatic. For example, when the supposedly dead hero suddenly returns he says to his old servant, "Me voilà! Mon vieux Noël, je n'ai rien mangé depuis vingt-quatre heures, vite une omelette!" (Here I am! My old Noel, I haven't eaten for twenty-four hours, quick—an omelet!). In the English version he exclaims, "Now then, Sandford, here I am, hungry as a hunter!"—and he does not ask for an omelet.[35] The change is not significant despite a complete departure in tone from the French, and it is typical of Lewes's mode of translation. The piece was appropriately termed "a careful imitation of the excellence" of the original, even though Lewes made an essentially British comedy out of it.[36] His close adherence to the French dialogue demonstrates his sense of dramatic propriety. He knew that any considerable alterations would impair the effect of the whole play, and so in his treatment of *La Joie Fait Peur* he deviated from the original much less extensively than in his other adaptations.

Less than a month after *Sunshine Through the Clouds* opened, Lewes and George Eliot went to Europe together, where they remained until March, 1855; and, during this time, no new play by him was produced at the Lyceum. But on March 15, a few days after their return, the last of Lewes's comedies for Mathews appeared. It was called *A Cozy Couple*—certainly an opportune name for a play written at this juncture in his life. Unfortunately it was withdrawn after four performances when Mathews' management of the Lyceum terminated abruptly because of financial difficulties. The play was well received by the critics, and it probably would have had a longer run under more favorable circumstances. John Heraud in the *Athenaeum* called it a "well written and well acted" original piece. The *Spectator* reviewer picturesquely noted that the Lyceum had closed after "flaming up for a moment with a short original drama, which, excellent in idea, and performed with a degree of finish that could scarcely be surpassed, might have gained a solid reputation at a less flickering establishment." [37]

But *A Cozy Couple* was not original. Lewes had adapted it from Octave Feuillet's *Le Village,* which was first presented at the Théâtre Français in June, 1856. It came out in a published edition in 1854, and Lewes translated it into *A Cozy Couple* for production in London the following year. The fact that the French version had not yet appeared in Paris led the English critics to believe that it was an original play. It resembles Lewes's other adaptations, with the usual careful and ingenious anglicizations, although the opening scene is new. It pictures the hero, Mr. Dormouse, sitting snugly at home by the fire, reading to his contentedly nodding wife, a depiction of conjugal felicity that had no place in the French version. Lewes made only one other major change. In the original, Rouvière, an old bachelor, almost lures the happily married Dupuis away from his peaceful hearth by comparing his carefree, nomadic life with Dupuis' humdrum existence as a provincial husband. In the end, Rouvière, caught in his own trap, decides to stay with the contented couple, concluding the comedy by asking Madame Dupuis to call in her cat—to which he had objected previously—because he is so well acquainted with "les miseres de l'exil" (the miseries of exile).

The English version ends in a much more serious and sentimental vein. There is no talk about such a frivolous subject as a cat. Mrs. Dormouse, the wife, makes an impassioned closing speech, saying that now the past can be forgotten. She and her husband resolve to give the errant bachelor "a cheerful home" and to soothe his declining years "by affectionate solicitude." They will prove to him that, "whatever travellers may say in favour of a wandering life, the true, the lasting happiness, after all, is easily to be found by the snug fireside of every COZY COUPLE." This ending no doubt was calculated to please the solid British audiences before whom the play was performed, and apparently it did. But nothing like it would have been tolerated in the Théâtre Français.[38]

Lewes's connection with the Lyceum ended after the short but happy life of *A Cozy Couple,* though the piece remained one of Mathews' favorites. A few months after it closed, another of Lewes's contributions to the London stage appeared at the Haymarket Theatre, a farce called *Buckstone's Adventures with a Polish Princess.* First produced on June 29, 1855, it was an "afterpiece" at a benefit performance for the popular actor, J. B. Buckstone, who was then manager of the Haymarket. Billed as "entirely new and original," it is so slight that no source was necessary; and, although it appears frequently on the bills during July and August, it was not a sensation. Oxenford's verdict in the *Times* was that it "did very well for a benefit" but was "rather absurd." [39] Lewes had written it in 1854 for Mathews, but it was just as appropriate for Buckstone, also a comedian. The flimsy plot concerns the hero's dream about an involvement with a rich but ugly Polish princess. His troubles start when he drinks a toast at a dinner in Moscow "to England and confusion to her enemies"—as tactless then as it would be today, though a "hot" war actually was going on during the summer of 1855 between England and Russia.[40] In any event, the farce's popularity, such as it was, probably depended heavily on its slurs against the Russian nobility and upon the usual examples of British stage "wit" with which Buckstone's speeches are plentifully interlarded.

The last of Lewes's plays to be presented in London that I have been able to discover was *Stay at Home,* a "comedietta" that opened at the Olympic Theatre on February 11, 1856. Interestingly enough, two more of his comedies were appearing in London during the same season: *Taking by Storm!* and *The Game of Speculation,* both at Drury Lane. Lewes had written *Stay at Home* in 1853, but production of it was delayed because *Ranelagh,* an adaptation of the same French original, *Un Mari qui se Derange,* had been produced in London in 1854. Lewes, who had reviewed *Ranelagh* in the *Leader,* had objected to the weakness of the author's "grasp of realities." The play would have been much more amusing if "a picture of life" were presented "in lieu of . . . mere stage intrigue." Specifically, he finds "only a hint" of a scene in the episode in which the young husband, Sir Robert Rovely, stays home for a "cozy conjugal evening" with his wife instead of going out as he usually does—and finds he is painfully bored. In *Stay at Home,* this scene is built up considerably. Mrs. Lauriston, the errant hero's lovely wife, tries to entertain her husband "by playing and singing . . . and continues the song after she finds he is asleep, until, the voice getting more and more tremulous, she falls forward in a fit of sobbing." [41] This touch of pathos is absent from the French original and from *Ranelagh.* Apparently Lewes inserted it with good effect since Fanny Ternan, the actress who played the broken-hearted wife, received warm praise from the critics.

Comments on *Stay at Home* indicate that Lewes anglicized the original with his usual thoroughness. He shifted the background from the Maison d'Or to Cremorne Gardens, a popular London amusement center; and he changed his hero from a Parisian man-about-town to a young English author. The *Spectator* reviewer observed that the dialogue had been "completely rewritten" and that the piece "is made to look as English as any piece can look that has a bal masqué and a duellist among the essential elements of its plot." John Oxenford in the *Times* wrote that the "modification of the dialogue is skilfully performed, so as to bring the work as near to the sympathies of the London we live in as the nature of the subject will admit." Oxenford also approved of the wandering husband because he utters a "moral" at the end, and praised the play's author because the title is an "ethical admonition"—Victorian embellishments that were again absent from the French.[42] But, in spite of this critical acclaim, *Stay at Home* scored only a moderate success and was removed from the Olympic bills on March 1 after a run of seventeen performances.

At about the same time that *Stay at Home* was being performed, Lewes was working on a melodrama called *Captain Bland,* one of the few original plays he ever wrote. He probably started it late in 1855, intending it for production at the Olympic, although he did not submit it to Wigan, the manager, until early in 1857. Wigan, who found the play unsatisfactory at this time, returned it to Lewes after a few rehearsals. Three years later, in January, 1860, he wrote to Lewes, asking to see the play again. Deeply involved by this time in scientific research, Lewes was "altogether indisposed to enter once more into theatrical matters."

He offered *Captain Bland* to Wigan for one hundred pounds "as it stands" but refused to "do anything to it" or to allow his name "to appear with it." After long and complicated negotiations—during which Lewes did alter the play extensively—he finally got his price in May, 1861.[43] Wigan still did not produce it; and, as far as I have been able to determine, it was never performed in England.

But what was not good enough for England apparently was adequate for the United States. *Captain Bland* appeared for the first time on any stage at Wallack's Theatre in New York on May 30, 1864, and it was billed in the New York *Times* as "an entirely original drama, of novel construction and peculiar effects," by "Mr. G. H. Lewes—an English writer, of unusual culture, whose labors have graced almost every branch of letters." James W. Wallack, the owner and manager of the theater, either was unaware of Lewes's stipulation that his name should not be associated with the piece, or he simply ignored it. In any event, he did not hesitate to capitalize on Lewes's reputation, and the *Times* notice is obviously calculated to rouse interest in the play because of its author's fame. There was also a special notice in the *Times* concerning a "singular feature about this piece," the fact that "it has not yet been played in England. Mr. Lewes will receive his first verdict from New York." [44]

Evidently *Captain Bland* had an adequate cast and was well staged. Lester Wallack played the title role, and Mary Gannon was Mrs. Bluster, the feminine lead. Both were first-class actors, according to American standards; but, in spite of the efforts of the players and the management, and notwithstanding whatever favorable publicity may have resulted from the use of Lewes's name, *Captain Bland* was not a success. It had four performances during the opening week, and was withdrawn until June 13, when it appeared once more, for the last time. To my knowledge it never was revived, either in America or England.

The comments of the New York *Times* reviewer probably reflect the critical consensus on *Captain Bland* at the time of its production: "It was excellently played in all respects and had it been produced earlier in the season, would, we fancy, have earned a better fate. The language of the piece is extremely good, and Mr. Lewes displays tact in drawing characters, although the Captain himself is odious. Mr. Lester Wallack played with admirable discretion; in coarse hands the part would have been intolerable. Nothing could well be better than the death scene of the unfortunate scoundrel."[45] The observations in *Frank Leslie's Illustrated Newspaper*, one of the most popular American weeklies of the day, are far different in tone, and at times border on insult. The writer asserts that the play

> was written for a Bowery locality, and pruned down to suit Broadway. This pruning, while it has not helped the morality or respectability of the piece, has cut away all the merit of it, supposing it ever had any, which is doubtful. The hero captain, done in his usual style by Lester Wallack, seems to have devoted the best years of his life to the pursuit of matrimony under difficulties. He has also succeeded in his infantile years in contracting alliances with some 70 or 100 females—more or less—and is still ardently pursuing other chances to perpetrate the same violation of the statutes. On this fact hinges all the action of the play. . . .[46]

This review is unjust, as well as exaggerated; for *Captain Bland*, though not a good play, is better than an ordinary Bowery melodrama. As its unenthusiastic reception attests, it did not appeal to wartime New York audiences because they were interested in other fare; but the play is not particularly immoral, and the reviewer's exaggeration of the hero's romantic inclinations is completely unwarranted.

The favorable reaction of another critic indicates that there was at least some difference of opinion. The *Albion*, a magazine devoted chiefly to reprinting articles from English periodicals, carried a long, glowing account of *Captain Bland* which showed considerable contempt for American dramatic taste. The writer first indulges in a detailed panegyric on Lewes's brilliant literary career; then, with a singular lack of critical acumen, he embarks on a rhapsodic appraisal of the play. It cannot achieve wide popularity in the United States because it lacks "variety of sharp contrasts, striking stage effects, and commonplace ideas," he begins, rather snidely. But, in an appeal to the intelligent few who have the mentality to appreciate it, the critic maintains that it

> must always delight students of character, who prefer delicate tints to glaring daubs, and relish the eccentric more than the conventional. And for this brief reason: it presents, in bold relief, and in perfectly blended colours, a vivid picture of the diabolical aspect of man. This has been

attempted by many writers, since Shakespeare drew Iago and Richard III; but, in no subsequent instance, has it been achieved with more entire truthfulness to nature than in Mr. Lewes's graphic picture of *Captain Bland*. . . . In the development of this story Mr. Lewes has exercised the tact of the artist. Concentrating interest upon those vivid situations wherein conduct illustrates character, he avoids the defect of tediousness, by merely suggesting details. But . . . precisely because his plot is not wrought out to the extremest point of prolixity, it is liable to misapprehension. . . . The fact is that its persons are strictly real, that its plot is perfect, and that its construction is without a flaw. This may not be evident on the surface; but there are works which require thought for their appreciation, and this is one of them. To the student of history, to the analyst of manners and character, there will always be pleasure in the drama of "Captain Bland." [47]

Captain Bland is no more deserving of this encomium than it is of the scarifying abuse it received in *Frank Leslie's Illustrated Newspaper*. The captain himself is a perfectly ordinary villain, of the type which appears in many other nineteenth-century dramas; and to compare Lewes's characterization of him with anything by Shakespeare is ridiculous, as is the critic's claim that the plot is "perfect," that the play's construction is flawless, or that the characters are "strictly real."

The story, which may or may not be original, concerns Bland's efforts to recoup his fortunes by taking advantage of the fact that he has been married previously to two different women, Margaret Leigh and Mrs. Bluster. Both think that he has long since been dead; and, at the start of the play, they are respectively engaged to Lord Chillingham and Mr. Perkins. Under these circumstances, Bland's sudden appearance causes considerable embarrassment. The unraveling of the plot after he arrives on the scene depends heavily upon events that have occurred in the distant past. There are constant references to them, but exactly what has happened previously never comes out very clearly. The *Albion* critic's remark that the story "is not wrought out to the extremest point of prolixity" is an understatement. The delineation of plot and background is so vague that the whole play conveys the impression that it was loosely thrown together at various times and under varying circumstances. The condition of the prompter's copy, which probably is the only version of the play now in existence, indicates that the play was subjected to many revisions, which account to a considerable extent for its structural weaknesses. These are particularly evident in the last act, when the captain's precipitous fall from his advantageous position is accomplished altogether too easily. Just as the truth is about to come out, a squad of soldiers, who arrive at just the right moment, conveniently shoot him; and Margaret and Mrs. Bluster can marry the men of their choice without further ado. The final scene rushes forward with breathless rapidity to an abrupt and highly improbable conclusion, and so much happens in so little time, with so many gaps in construction, that the entire action seems disconnected and far-fetched.[48]

The characters in *Captain Bland* are drawn straight from the repertory of the nineteenth-century British theater. Bland himself is the suave, unscrupulous villain; Margaret Leigh, the typical beautiful but wronged heroine; Lord Chillingham, the brave and faithful lover; Mrs. Bluster, the widow with a past; Perkins, the officious elderly suitor. All were familiar figures, in various versions, to New York and London audiences. The lines Lewes gives them are occasionally very clever. The opening scene between Surly Joe and Mary, the maid, is charming; and some of Mrs. Bluster's dialogues with her rival lovers are witty and humorous. For example, she opens her first conversation with Captain Bland, after recognizing him, by asking, "Sir, *did* you ever die?" His reply is, "Never, did you?" [49]

But many of the speeches are melodramatic and unnatural, particularly in the scenes involving Margaret, Captain Bland, and Lord Chillingham. The changes made in the prompter's copy, apparently for reasons of propriety, do not help matters. When Bland attempts to make violent love to one of his former wives, he says that he is convinced that "in the fever of hunger and desire a thousand schemes have been combined to make you mine." [50] The word "desire" later was crossed out, and "passion" written in above it, probably by Lewes himself; perhaps he felt that the genreal implications of the term "passion" were more acceptable to contemporary audiences that the more specific ones of "desire." There are many similar alterations, some by Lewes, some by others. They indicate that Queen Victoria's influence had spread across the Atlantic even into the corrupted purlieus of Broadway.

Though by no means a good play, *Captain Bland* is comparable with the average drama of the same type that was popular in the mid-nineteenth-century theater. After all, Alfred Wigan had thought well enough of it to pay Lewes one hundred pounds for it; and he had actually put it into rehearsal. It failed in New York not necessarily because it was inferior as entertainment to other plays, but because it was introduced at the end of the theatrical season and at a time when the events of the Civil War were very much in the public eye. The theaters were well patronized, but at this particular juncture audiences wanted sensation pieces and old-time favorites, not gentlemanly melodrama. Under more favorable circumstances, *Captain Bland* might have had a modest run, although in its present form it never could have achieved any substantial success because of its serious defects in plot and construction.

II *The Unacted Plays*

Lewes wrote or adapted several other plays besides those which actually appeared on the stage; like many a better playwright, he was not always successful in his attempts to sell his dramatic wares. His unacted pieces evidently were written with the purpose of pleasing contemporary British audiences. Those that are available in manuscript are, with one exception, direct adaptations from French originals. Whether or not they would have been successful in the theater is of course difficult to judge; in Lewes's own opinion, "Nothing but the positive test of acting can decide the merit of a play. Critics may judge of its wit, truth, and depth of character displayed; critics may tell how near it approaches to Molière or Farquhar; actors can tell whether the 'parts' will suit them . . . but no one can tell whether the play will succeed." [51] These reservations certainly apply to Lewes's unacted plays, intended as they were for stage representation.

The best of them, and perhaps the best one Lewes ever wrote, is *Pretension,* or *The School for Parvenus,* a five-act prose comedy written in 1843 or before.[52] As far as I have been able to ascertain, it was not adapted from any other play. The fact that it was never produced does not reflect on its quality, and there were many circumstantial factors in the way of its acceptance by one of the London theaters. As Lewes wrote in some of his critical articles on the drama, the period was most unpropitious for young playwrights who aspired to introduce their works to the stage. The Covent Garden and Drury Lane monopolies were abolished in

1843, but other theaters did not produce legitimate plays in any quantity until several years later. Because of the limited number of theaters available, and the conditions under which writers were forced to work, it was extremely difficult for an unknown author to market even a good five-act drama; and Lewes was no exception.[53]

Pretension could be compared with the average popular comedy being presented in London during the period from about 1840 to 1865. Typical examples are Dion Boucicault's *London Assurance*, Bulwer-Lytton's *Money*, and Douglas Jerrold's *Bubbles of the Day*. Like them, *Pretension* is constructed from elements that were familiar to every London playgoer: a flimsy plot, clever dialogue plentifully interspersed with British stage "wit," and characters that are for the most part modeled after traditional theater stereotypes. But there is a difference. The usual comedy made no attempt to deal with social phenomena that actually were taking place in England at the time. One was the gradual infiltration of the blooded aristocracy by members of the middle class, who were assuming control of most of the nation's wealth. Their adoption of the manners, titles, and affectations of the nobility—along with the nobility's willing acceptance of their presence as long as it was accompanied by money—was a rich source of social satire. But this kind of satire had no great appeal for contemporary theatrical audiences because it struck too close to home for many of the people who comprised them—social climbing simply was too respectable an occupation to be a fit subject for ridicule.

Pretension, which deals directly with the efforts of the moneyed middle class to move into high society, has, therefore, a definite bearing on what was happening in the lives of real people. Although the plot is weak, it is not utterly outlandish; and some of the main characters resemble human beings as they actually were. In particular, Mr. Thompson, a tallow merchant, and Mr. DeCourcy Phipps, a stock broker, are characterizations that have the ring of truth, even though Lewes manufactured them to illustrate different kinds of pretension. Both are what he calls parvenus of station, who have the same objective in view: a place in fashionable society for themselves and their families.

Thompson's pretension lies in his inordinate pride in his low birth. He continually boasts that he "sprang from nothing." The respect that's due him, he says, "is my own hard earning. . . . Let them who like be proud of empty titles and parchment conventions. I stand upon Tallow!" But it is unthinkable that his daughter, Arabella, should marry a grocer; for "a grocer is very *low.* Not that I care for that. I've no humbug about me, as you know. I don't care a snap for titles. But still, my dear, one's respectability . . . one's position in the Tallow line! A grocer? No, no, we must not forget what is due to society. . . ." When he learns that Arabella is to become engaged to a lord, Thompson is overjoyed. "This is certainly glorious," he exclaims, in rapture. "A nobleman . . . with nobility stamped upon his brow! Not that I admire him the more on that account. No, no, I am an English Merchant and am content to be one." Still, he concludes later, "all things considered I must say this is the proudest day of my life!" Thompson's eagerness to join the ranks of the aristocracy, despite his pride in his humble antecedents, illustrates a kind of pretension that Lewes held in particular contempt.[54]

DeCourcy Phipps, who is even more of a hypocrite than Thompson, cuts himself off from his middle-class background. He assumes a new name, adopts a new set of ancestors, and claims to be an aristocrat because of "certain ineffaceable distinctions" which differentiate him from other people. For there is a difference, he explains to Thompson, "Just the difference, my dear sir, between mutton and venison, a hack and a hunter, Brummagem and St. James." [55] Voiced by Phipps, whose origins are the same as Thompson's, this affectation of superiority on the basis of ancestry is especially offensive.

Both Phipps and Thompson are exposed for what they are at the end of the play: a bogus aristocrat and a social climber. Lewes's treatment of them is broad and exaggerated, but there are touches of humor and true satire in the characterizations. It seems evident that Lewes was trying to delineate real people, not merely conventional stage types. He was ridiculing the actual weaknesses and foibles of members of the new aristocracy of wealth. In his attempt to make use of lifelike characters, within a framework consistent at least to some extent with actuality, Lewes was carrying out his own critical ideas concerning dramatic realism. The writer of a domestic comedy, he felt, "has a serious and laborious, no less than a noble task, that of *observation* of life" as it really is.[56]

The minor characters in *Pretension* are not so accurately drawn as Phipps and Thompson. Their chief function is to personify some of Lewes's other ideas on the subject of pretension. Lady Anastasia Needylove, an indigent aristocrat, professes a deep attachment to poverty, although she agrees to marry Phipps in spite of his wealth. Her affection is forced, and she is too ostentatious about her love for the poor, but Lewes's treatment of her in the scene in which she is exposed in her true colors is keenly humorous. After she has heard that Phipps is about to go bankrupt, she says to him, "I venerate poverty . . . but . . . it may seem superstitious . . . yet the idea of bankruptcy makes me *shudder!* You will laugh at my womanly weakness, but I could not marry a bankrupt." She reconsiders—after it becomes evident that Phipps is not going to lose his money after all; and she generously offers to restore him to his former place in her affections. His reply is heavily ironic but very appropriate: "It may be superstition. . . . You will laugh at my vulgar weakness . . . but I could *not* marry a lady of your consequence!" [57]

Like Lady Anastasia, the other minor characters in *Pretension* are sketches rather than people. Tibbs and Flapper, Lady Anastasia's aristocratic friends, are typical stage fops, drawn straight from the Restoration theater. Their function is to demonstrate the emptiness and superficiality of the world of fashion into which Phipps and Thompson are so anxious to be admitted. Mrs. Thompson, the wife of the tallow merchant, is refreshingly unaffected in her pretensions. She is frankly delighted at any prospect of association with the aristocracy; and, when her husband expresses his contempt for rank, she disagrees with him heartily. "There is no denying it," she declares. "Rank is delicious!" [58] Her daughter, Arabella, who likewise venerates nobility, anticipates with rapture an engagement to an aristocrat. "To be a Baronet's wife!" she exclaims. "To by my lady! To escape from the murky atmosphere of the city into the pure refined intoxicating air of the west end!" [59] The attitudes of Mrs. Thompson and Arabella typify, with a reasonable degree of accuracy, the deep respect in which rank was held by the members of their class; here again Lewes was trying to portray the actual feelings of real people.

Although these characters were more or less familiar stage figures, Lewes's consistent employment of them as personifications of human foibles contributes to the weakness of the comedy itself.

In their speeches and actions, Lewes seems to be more interested in how well they illustrate the points he is trying to make about pretension than he is about how effective they are as characters in a play. What they have to say becomes more important than what happens to them, and *Pretension* develops into a series of clever conversations that do not hold together very well as drama. The weakness of the plot, coupled with the truth of the characterizations, could account for the fact that no theater manager thought enough of the play to produce it. As an attempt to mirror an aspect of actual life, it is better as an essay in satire than as a comedy.

In writing it, Lewes was carrying out his own critical precepts about realism in the drama, but at the same time he was violating the conventions of contemporary British stage usage. Most of his fellow dramatists depicted, according to Lewes, "not what is daily enacted in our drawing rooms and streets, but what the stage has traditionally handed down to us as the customs of certain classes." [60] Ironically enough, that is what most of his successful acted plays depicted; but *Pretension,* his one attempt to portray "what is daily enacted in our drawing rooms and streets," never was produced. Apparently Lewes's ideas about realism, as demonstrated in this play, were too far ahead of his time to be put to the test of actual use in the theater.

The only original unacted play in the collection of Lewes's manuscripts in the Beineke Library at Yale is *Pretension.* The others, adaptations from the French, are done in more or less the same manner as those that were staged. Two of them, *Marguerite* and *The Miser's Niece,* were left unfinished, and are of such poor quality that we can assume that Lewes abandoned them. I have been unable to discover the original French pieces from which he attempted to adapt them. *The Miser's Niece* is signed "G. H. Lewes," probably indicating that he wrote it before 1851, when he started using Slingsby Lawrence as a pseudonym. *Marguerite* is unsigned, but there is not much doubt that it too was an early—and abortive—effort.

On the cover of the manuscript, Lewes labeled *The Miser's Niece* a "comedy in two acts," but it has few comic elements. The humor, which is extremely broad, consists chiefly of remarks about the habits, morals, and intelligence of the French and apparently are Lewes's additions of British stage "wit." The action concerns the love affair between a humble but respectable niece of a French miser and the scion of a "rich but proud" family, who disguises himself as a poor music-master in order to gain access to her. The deception is discovered at the end of the first act; and, even though this act is all that has survived in the manuscript, the subsequent complications and their resolution are obvious. The situation is threadbare, the characters are stereotypes, and the dialogue is completely unnatural. The play does not compare either in interest or in style to any of Lewes's successful adaptations, and the assumption that he never bothered to complete it seems a safe one.

Marguerite likewise is inferior to Lewes's other plays. He labored under the initial disadvantage of the fact that the French original seems to have been an unusually poor five-act melodrama. He adapted the first three acts, but omitted to translate those portions of the dialogue which required no substantial changes. In many instances, instead of filling in the complete conversations, he inserted a brief note, such as "here follows a scene, as in the original, in which Andre. . . ." Lewes did not translate the last two acts, but merely outlined them, perhaps with the intention of submitting the unfinished play to a producer before going ahead with it. The note at the beginning of his sketch of Act IV indicates that he knew enough about audience reaction to realize that the spectators, at least in an English theater, would tolerate just so much tragic action without "a little respite" and no more: "After so much grief and tears a little respite of comedy will be necessary, and this act in the early portion must be gay. The following is an outline of what is proposed." The piling up of grief upon grief on the heroine's innocent head presents a picture of unmitigated sadness that is too pitiful to be enjoyable, and Lewes's decision to insert some comic relief was well taken. But he did not undertake the alterations he proposed, perhaps because he found that the task of making the last two acts presentable was too difficult. In any event, the relegation of *Marguerite* to the limbo of unacted and unactable plays was no great loss to the British stage.

The two other unacted plays by Lewes that are available in manuscript are one-act farces, *Drat that Dick!* and *The Fox Who Got the Grapes*. These adaptations, complete and ready for staging, are much better written than either *Marguerite* or *The*

Miser's Niece. As we already have discovered, Lewes wrote *The Fox Who Got the Grapes* in 1854, originally submitted it to Charles Mathews for production at the Lyceum Theatre, failed in his efforts to get it staged, and finally converted it to a short story, "Mrs. Beauchamp's Vengeance," which appeared in *Blackwood's Magazine* in 1861. Like *The Fox, Drat that Dick!* was also intended for the Lyceum. Lewes adapted it from a French comedy, *Le Misanthrope et L'Auvergnat,* which opened in Paris on August 19, 1852. Unfortunately, another playwright, William Brough, also wrote a version of the same piece called *A Phenomenon in a Smock Frock;* and it appeared at the Lyceum on December 13. Just why Mathews preferred Brough's translation to Lewes's is difficult to explain. One possible reason is that Brough's is shorter and more suitable for use as an afterpiece, or perhaps he finished writing it before Lewes did his; and Mathews, always eager for a new farce, took the first one that was available.

Lewes's elaborations on the original are more extensive than Brough's, although both writers adhered to the French plot and characterizations. Both also substituted, in most instances, prose dialogue for the French song. The principal characters are Chiffonnet, who is called Mr. Sowerberry in Brough's play, and Grimball in Lewes's; and Machavoine, the water-carrier from Auvergne, who is Buttercup, a milkman from Somersetshire, in Brough's version, and Dirty Dick, an ostler, in Lewes's. The farce concerns the embarrassing situations that arise when a disillusioned old hypocrite hires an honest man as his servant for the sake of having someone in his house who always will tell the truth.

Lewes's version differs from the other two principally in his characterizations of Dirty Dick and Grimball. In the original and in Brough's play, Dick's counterparts are country bumpkins who are too unsophisticated to tell lies, even when to do so is to their great advantage. Lewes's ostler, on the other hand, has a positive motive for telling the truth: he is a disciple of Rousseau, and so feels that "in the present degraded condition of mankind there is no sense of truth left, nor won't be till men return to a State of Nature." [61] He, for one, is going to help mankind back to this idyllic state by always telling the absolute truth. There is no reference to Rousseau or his doctrines in either the original French play or *A Phenomenon in a Smock Frock.* Grimball also is more of a philosopher than his counterparts in the other two versions of the play. When he discovers Dick's peculiarity, he says, "In my anxiety for Truth I have nourished a scorpion in my flannel waistcoat. . . . Who can wonder that I am a misanthrope when human nature is so base that it turns even virtues into vices, and makes Truth itself detestable!" [62] And in his concluding speech—which is not in either of the two other versions—Grimball speculates: "O human nature! Everywhere alike! . . . Who is there that really cares for truth? Don't we all think it precious—*too* precious for everyday use?" [63] Whether or not such philosophical insertions influenced Mathews' decision not to stage *Drat that Dick!*, the fact remains that it was never produced, as far as I have been able to discover, and Lewes made no further use of it.

We may conclude that Lewes's considerable experience as a playwright as well as an actor—both successful and unsuccessful —gave him a thorough familiarity with the demands and conventions of the contemporary theater, and a personal insight into the practical problems of production and staging. He was no mere bystander, but an active participant in the life of the working theater. He was one of the few critics who united a firsthand knowledge of the mechanics of the stage with the intellectual capacity to comprehend the esthetics of the drama itself. As a consequence, his dramatic criticism, to which we now turn our attention, had as its basis a rare combination of actual experience, profound philosophical theory, and a thorough understanding of the theatrical and literary aspects of dramatic form.

CHAPTER 5

Lewes's Criticism of Drama in the Contemporary Theater

I *The Working Critic*

BERNARD SHAW once called Lewes "the most able and brilliant critic between Hazlitt and our own contemporaries." [1] In 1896, he wrote a review of Lewes's and Forster's newly published *Dramatic Essays*, in which several of Lewes's articles in the *Leader* are reprinted; and his remarks on this occasion explain why he thought so highly of Lewes's dramatic criticism and provide an accurate, revealing insight into his techniques and capabilities. Shaw considers that both Lewes and Forster possessed "the cardinal faculty of the critic: they could really and objectively see the stage; and they could analyze what they saw there." But Forster lacked Lewes's "variety of culture, flexibility, and fun." What Shaw admires most in Lewes is his "rare gift of integrity" as a critic:

> When he was at his business, he seldom remembered that he was a gentleman or a scholar. In this he shewed himself a true craftsman, intent on making the measurements and analyses of his criticism as accurate, and their expression as clear and vivid, as possible, instead of allowing himself to be distracted by the vanity of playing the elegant man of letters, or writing with perfect good taste, or hinting in every line that he was above his work. In exacting all this from himself, [he took] his revenge by expressing his most labored conclusions with a levity that gave them the air of being the unpremeditated whimsicalities of a man who had perversely taken to writing about the theatre for the sake of the jest latent in his own outrageous unfitness for it. . . .

Shaw sees integrity, frankness, and intelligence as the distinguishing features of Lewes's criticism of the contemporary theater. In particular, Shaw also appreciated Lewes's style and went so far as to compare it favorably with his own, observing that Lewes's articles are "miles beyond" the "crudities" of Corno di Bassetto—who was Shaw himself—and admiring his method as "the combination of a laborious criticism with a recklessly flippant manner." [2]

A typical example of this "combination" is Lewes's expression of his own view on the importance of the journalistic critic's function—one that he discharged himself during his nearly five years as "Vivian," the drama critic for the *Leader*, from 1850 to 1854. Profound as the pronouncements may be of the "grand seigneurs" of criticism, writes Lewes, yet some respect is due to those who, like himself, must label plays and actors good or bad "*before* the world has decided," who must pass judgment immediately, guided only by their own taste and intelligence. The writings of Plato, Aristotle, and the great Latin critics are highly serious, but "I should like to send Quintilian to a 'first representation' with the necessity of his proceeding straight from the theatre to the printing office, and there sitting in judgment on the new work, his article to be read by thousands before he is awake on the morrow!" [3]

No matter how flippant Lewes seems to be in the expression of an opinion, there is always an undercurrent of gravity in his criticism if he feels that the topic he is considering is at all important. He also writes with an absolute fearlessness and frankness, and sometimes the engaging brilliance of his style is all that prevents him from being insulting. He is often sarcastic, but never willfully abusive or destructive. He almost always cites his reasons for what he thinks, whether his criticism is favorable or unfavorable; and, perhaps most important in a critic, he is invariably and sometimes mercilessly sincere. As we have seen, this quality of absolute sincerity permeates his literary criticism as well. It often got him into deep trouble with theater people, who are often inclined to be more sensitive, or perhaps more vocal, than mere authors.

For example, Lewes had several run-ins with Charles Kean, who was then at the height of his success as an actor. He was also manager of the Princess's Theatre from 1851 to 1859; and, on one occasion, when Lewes failed to wax enthusiastic enough about him, he retaliated by canceling Lewes's free admission pass. This action prompted a mock-heroic tirade in the *Leader*, headed "Vivian in Tears! (All along of Mr. Kean)," a masterpiece of witty and satiric invective, and a typical example of Lewes's handling of a serious subject in a frivolous but extremely effective way: "What a thing is Life! Yesterday I was the gayest of the gay . . . today you see me struck . . . into the gloom of immeasurable despondency! . . . Weep! weep with me ye that have any tears! Let me, like a Prometheus of private life, fling my clamorous agonies upon the winds, and call upon every feeling heart to listen to my 'billowy ecstacy of woe!' Hear it, ye winds—Charles Kean has cut me off the Free List!"

After this introduction, Lewes continues to mourn his fate in the same epic vein, but his plaintive regrets have a sharp edge of sarcasm: "Oh, *why* didn't I write more glowingly about his genius; *why* did I not, by some critical alchemy, convert his peculiarities into talents; *why* did I not discover eloquence in his pauses, variety and expression in his gestures, and intelligence in his conceptions?" [4]

But Lewes is careful to qualify his abuse of Kean's vanity and incapacity. He asks permission "to stop the flood of grief" in order to explain his attitude and his actions. When he had promised to lend Kean his support in undertaking the management of the Princess's Theatre, Lewes had insisted that "it was one thing to support a theater by all friendly offices, and another to praise actors or pieces which I did not approve." Because his articles were not "fulsome eulogies," Kean regarded him as an enemy. "Can Mr. Kean suppose that by suppressing *free admissions* he suppresses *free speech?*" Lewes asks. "Let him undeceive himself. I shall be there on first nights as of old," but "I shall remember that kindly silence is interpreted as insult, and shall speak out just what I think." In spite of Kean's action, Lewes concludes, he will not be unjust in his future criticism, just as he has not allowed himself to be "eulogistic" in the past.[5] Here Lewes asserts his independence as a critic and stands upon his right to express himself freely, no matter what his opinions are and notwithstanding the pressures that may be exerted upon him to express himself otherwise, and the attitude he adopts in this article typifies most of his critical writings.

II *On Tragedy*

Perhaps the most interesting aspect of Lewes's view of tragedy is his opinion about the Elizabethan drama. His basic premise is that it should not be used as a model for imitation on the modern stage because it depends upon an antiquated tradition based on outworn artistic standards. Even Shakespeare's plays, Lewes felt, are essentially inappropriate in form for production in the nineteenth century. Such an opinion was a radical departure from the generally accepted view of Shakespeare and his contemporaries, expressed at a time when, as Lewes once remarked, "anything less than five acts and blank verse" was scarcely considered a tragedy fit for presentation in the British theater.[6]

But his depreciation of the form of the Elizabethan drama was consistent with his theories on esthetic relativism that we already have seen applied in his criticism of poetry. An example of their application is his opinion of *The Patrician's Daughter,* a typical five-act tragedy in blank verse written in the Elizabethan mode by J. Westland Marston, first performed in London in 1842. Lewes considers it the product of a literature of imitation that is "essentially vicious" and "incompetent to the demands of the age, and to the end of art." The adoption of the "antiquated phraseology" and "obsolete ethics" of the Elizabethan dramatists is altogether erroneous; in order to "warm the mind to exaltation, or to stir the heart to tears, the poet must use the sentiments of [his own] age and the simple language of truth." Lewes foresees a reaction against the old dramatists as models, a reaction that "no one intimately acquainted with their writings can fail to acknowledge as just." [7]

Several years later he wrote an even more emphatic condemnation of the Elizabethans, maintaining that "*the greatest injury yet sustained by the English drama was the revival of admiration for the Old English Dramatists,*" who were justly forgotten until Charles Lamb and his friends "exhumed" them. In Lewes's opinion, the works of Kyd, Peele, Marlowe, Dekker, and the others are "detestable": their plays are poorly constructed, their characters are "*sketched* rather than developed," and their situations "for the most part are violent, horrible, and clumsily prepared." In short, the dramas of Shakespeare's contemporaries and immediate successors, "besides being wearisome in reading . . . are essentially unfit for the modern stage and therefore are not good models for our living dramatists." [8]

Lewes's subsequent criticism of *The Duchess of Malfi* elaborates effectively on these observations. Webster's play is a "motiveless and false exhibition of human nature," not the work of a true dramatist. Conceived with "clumsy ignorance," the dramatic evolution of passion is "mediocre"; the horrors are "childish because they grow out of no proper ground" and are not "the culmination of tragic motives." All that is praiseworthy about *The Duchess of Malfi,* in Lewes's opinion, is the poetry; but even it fails to arrest the spectator, though it may charm the reader. The "resuscitation" of the old dramatists actually has obstructed the progress of the drama by encouraging poets to believe that "imagery will supply the place of incidents, and that tragic *intentions* which boldly appeal to the imagination" are sufficient. The successful dramatists of his day, Lewes concludes, are those who do not imitate the Elizabethan form, despite the fact that it is considered the best model by so many playwrights and critics.[9]

These sentiments still would be considered heretical in some quarters; but, in 1850, most critics regarded the Elizabethan drama with the deepest respect. In the review in *The Play-Goer* of the same performance of *The Duchess of Malfi* that Lewis excoriated, Webster was called "*per se,* the greatest tragedic author that we have; in fact, in the solemn, mysterious power, in the cloistial style of tragedy, distinguished from the awful fatality of Aeschylus, and the passionate appeals of Shakespeare he is unsurpassed: in that sense, he is greater than Shakespeare. . . ."[10] The same critic quarrels with R. H. Horne, who adapted *The Duchess of Malfi* for its modern production, because he has made too many changes in Webster's original. The great esteem for the Elizabethans that is implied in these remarks is typical of the general attitude toward the old dramatists.

Yet Lewes's judgment that the Elizabethans are completely inappropriate as models for contemporary dramatists has proved to be a valid one. The great nineteenth-century poets composed their dramas in the Shakespearian tradition, but made no constructive contribution to the development of the theater. Shelley's *Cenci,* Byron's *Sardanapalus,* and Browning's *Strafford* are examples of the sort of drama Lewes was referring to when he wrote about the injurious effects of "the revival of admiration for the Old English Dramatists." These plays contain great poetry, but they are not suitable for production on the modern stage, and were failures as dramatic presentations.[11] The efforts of lesser men of letters to write Elizabethan plays for the Victorian theater also were not successful. Thomas Noon Talfourd's *Ion* called forth much favorable comment when it was first produced in 1836, but it has long since been dead as drama either for the stage or for the study. The same can be said of R. H. Horne's *Gregory VII,* which appeared in 1840, and of J. W. Marston's *Patrician's Daughter,* the subject of Lewes's adverse criticism in 1842.

In 1850, Lewes's counsel to "all aspiring dramatists" was "to forget, if possible, that Shakespeare had contemporaries" and "to shun the old writers as they would the plague"; for the drama "should be a reflex of our life, idealized of course, but issuing out of the atmosphere we breathe." Lewes's advice has been prophetic. The development of tragedy in particular is attributable to a considerable extent to the decreasing influence exerted by Elizabethan forms and conventions upon dramatic writing. Since the days of Robertson, playwrights have placed their faith in realism, in both style and content; conversations, situations, and characters have been modeled after the actualities of everyday life. Shakespeare's reputation has remained very much as it was, but dramatists no longer strive to emulate him. Referring to him and Racine, Lewes was right when he declared, "Not *because* of their form—of what is temporal and peculiar to their epochs in them—do these masters hold us in their spell, but *in spite of it.*" In order to appeal to the public taste and move men's hearts, the modern dramatist "must quit the study, and try to image forth some reflex of the world that all men know, speaking their language, uttering their thoughts, espousing their idealisms." [12]

These sentiments foresee with an almost uncanny accuracy the opinions expressed nearly a century later by a historian of the drama, Allardyce Nicoll, who wrote, with the wisdom of hindsight, that what the nineteenth-century theater wanted was "the impulse that comes from reality." If it had welcomed the poets to its stage who wrote in the tradition of the Elizabethans, it "might well have hindered rather than furthered the remarkable revival of dramatic work that characterizes our own period." [13] Certainly Lewes, if he had lived, would have been satisfied with Nicoll's estimate of the results of shedding the influence of Shakespeare. And Lewes's injunction to the dramatists to "image forth some reflex of the world that all men know" is of a piece, as we have seen, with his constant insistence that the novelists should try to do the same thing if they hoped to achieve any degree of lasting fame.

Another important aspect of Lewes's criticism of tragedy in the Victorian theater is his attitude toward the French drama. Like his opinion of the Elizabethans, it did not accord with the views of his contemporaries. Most people who were interested in French drama were more impressed with the plays of Eugène Scribe than with those of Racine and Corneille. Lewes's criticism of Rachel's performance in Scribe's extremely successful tragic melodrama, *Adrienne Lecouvreur,* is a typical expression of his attitude.[14] The fact that *Adrienne Lecouvreur* has been more favorably received than Racine's *Phèdre* or *Andromaque* indicates to Lewes that the "public d'élite" who patronize the French plays actually have no appreciation of art because they do not comprehend it. They would rather be amused than perplexed, and a performance which requires a certain degree of esthetic sensibility to be understood has, therefore, no chance with them for survival. Lewes writes with his usual levity and frankness; but, as always, there is profound truth in his joking: "We are rich and can patronize Art: what need, therefore, to feel it? . . . As for our own aesthetic taste—why—'*Tuppence more and up goes the donkey!*'—Ay, that is amusing: the donkey balanced on a human chin, and 'only tuppence!' "

The donkey in place of Art is Scribe in place of Racine, and Lewes makes his own preference very plain. He maintains that *Adrienne Lecouvreur* is vulgar and prosaic, a "melodramatic commonplace, admirably constructed." The conventional stage effects have no life, yet they are "placed with such tact that they amuse." Composed out of "the very frippery of the stage," the play lacks style, invention, wit, passion, and movement; and it is fundamentally inartistic: "If you really prefer that long exhibition of physical agony with which the poisoned Adrienne excites your applause, to the exhibition of mental agony in Phèdre, Camille, Hermione, or Roxane, say so; we have no objection; we merely tell you that it is the pathos of the Hospital, not the pathos of Art!" The part of Adrienne Lecouvreur, Lewes feels, is not worthy of Rachel's talents as an actress, and her real greatness emerges in her portrayal of the roles in the dramas of Racine. Her acting, no matter how perfect, does not compensate for the inherent weakness of Adrienne's character or for Scribe's inferiority as a dramatist.

What Lewes refers to as "the pathos of the Hospital" did not impress everyone so unfavorably. In the opinion of one critic, Rachel was at her best in the same scene that Lewes finds objectionable. The "highly-wrought dying scene, where she expires under the influence of a poison . . . is a fearfully satisfying exhibition of mental and corporeal pain." The "convulsive groan of physical agony" and the "stillness of death, representing a fine feeling for the imposing in attitude" are the high points of Rachel's performance; and the last scene "makes the fortune of the piece." [15] This opinion is the direct opposite of Lewes's, but it is in line with the standards of contemporary taste. A typical expression of Adrienne's sentiments in the "highly-wrought dying scene" demonstrates the truth of Lewes's assertion:

Ah! quelles souffrances! . . . Ce n'est plus ma tête, c'est ma poitrine, qui est brûlante . . . j'ai là comme un brasier . . . comme un feu dévorant qui me consume. . . . Mon Dieu! exaucez-moi! . . .laissez-moi vivre . . . quelques jours encore. . . . Je suis si jeune, et la vie s'ouvrait pour moi si belle![16]

(Ah, what suffering! . . . It is no longer my head, but it is my chest that is on fire . . . what I have here is like a hot coal . . . like a devouring fire that consumes me. . . . My God! Hear my prayer! . . . let me live . . . a few days more. . . . I am so young and life was beginning to be so beautiful to me!)

This indeed is "the pathos of the Hospital, not the pathos of Art," when compared with the speeches of Phèdre or Roxane. Yet the reviewer for the *Athenaeum*, John A. Heraud, finds that Adrienne Lecouvreur is Rachel's "most popular part in England" and that it contains "passages of elocution which have never been surpassed." The faults that Heraud finds with the performance are mostly with Rachel, not with the play itself.[17]

When Rachel returned to London in 1851 and acted in the same role, Lewes again expressed his disgust at its favorable reception, but tempered his scorn with a typical flash of levity: "After all, how few in a theatre appreciate Art! how few can discriminate between the bourgeois style of that épicier in art named Eugène Scribe . . . and that rare consummate artist Jean Racine! To them the pathos of the hospital . . . is more 'moving,' consequently more run after, than the pathos of Phèdre or Hermione; they like their wine brandied and their drama to match! Bordeaux? Pah! it gives a man the cholic—such thin wishy-washy stuff! Let me have wine with a 'body'—every glass a headache!" [18] His continued emphasis on the overwhelming superiority of Racine to Scribe, despite Scribe's immense popularity, is an illustration of Lewes's adherence to the highest standards of theatrical art. As a guardian of the public taste, he insisted that Scribe, "essentially a bourgeois," was "not for a moment to be classed beside the great writers," [19] and, as the subsequent history of Scribe's reputation demonstrates, he was right.

Lewes chides English audiences for their inability to appreciate Racine and ridicules their reasons for disliking him. "French Art is *so* French (as if *that* were wonderful!) and so unnatural (as if the aim of Art was to be natural!) and so cold (especially to us who do not feel the language!)." [20] But, though his poetry is "so French" and "frigid," Racine has tremendous dramatic power. In "mastery over passion," he ranks next to Shakespeare; and, in construction, he is "surpassingly fine." In *Andromaque*, Lewes writes that "the progress and movement of the story, the truth and fluctuations of passion, the culmination of interest and the wide-gathering sweep of the denouement, indicate the thought of a consummate artist." Racine's plays, Lewes concludes, are truly great, in spite of "a pauper unpoetical language, and the peculiar impress of the Court taste of Louis XIV," because they possess "that mastery over elemental passion, and that felicity of style which keep works eternally young, preserving their freshness through all the changes of centuries." [21]

This estimate of Racine differed widely from that of most of Lewes's contemporaries, most of whom thought that the French Classic drama represented an outworn tradition—if they thought about it at all. Critics often failed to comment on Racine when his plays were presented, or they praised him perfunctorily. One reviewer of Rachel's performances in 1853 remarks that the plays of Racine, "if they do nothing else, at any rate afford a fine scope for a tragic actress." [22] John Oxenford, in the London *Times*, reflects the same attitude when he writes that audiences do not go to the theater "to see this or that work, but . . . solely to see the portions which Rachel enlivens by her talent"; they "turn a listless ear" to the proceedings when she is not on stage.[23] The *Spectator* critic expresses the hope that English audiences will give the plays of Racine and Corneille a fair hearing, even though it has been the fashion to regard them as "mere negatives to Shakespeare." [24] These comments typify the attitude toward the French Classic drama of most of Lewes's contemporaries. As Lytton Strachey pointed out in 1908, the English conception of Racine had long been "as a stiff and pompous kind of dancing-master, utterly out of date and infinitely cold," whose style is "rhetorical, artificial, and monotonous."[25] Lewes's estimate of Racine, though very different from the conventional and accepted one, has been vindicated. Racine is now acknowledged, both in England and France, as unquestionably the greatest of the French tragedians.

Lewes's explanation of the reasons Racine's drama is not appreciated in England is consistent with the relativistic attitude he adopts in his criticism of fiction and poetry. Racine and others like him, such as Corneille and Alfieri, all wrote in the traditions of their age or their nation, and "are scouted because they are not Shakespearian." Schiller, Goethe, Sophocles, and Calderon, on the other hand, who did the same, are respected because they are Shakespearian. But the mere fact that a dramatist is not Shakespearian is no indication that he may not also be great.[26] In arriving at this conclusion Lewes was applying his theories about the flexibility of esthetic laws, which he had enunciated several years before in his observations on two German philosophers, G. W. F. Hegel and Augustus W. Schlegel. In the article on Hegel, written in 1842, he elaborated on his ideas about the changes of esthetic sensibility that take place from age to age, terming them "the temporalities in art."[27] The essay on Schlegel, published the following year, details his theories about the influence on criticism of the variations in the national origins of art.[28] Though the ideas in these essays are largely derivative, they form the basis of the relativistic philosophy that enabled Lewes to make critical judgments that are original and valid. He was able to see that popular opinion was wrong in refusing to acknowledge Racine's greatness because he was not an Englishman or because he was "frigid" or unnatural; for Racine was trying to abide by the rules of seventeenth-century French art, not to please a modern English audience. If the people in this audience cannot appreciate him, Lewes concludes, the cause is their ignorance—not Racine's deficiencies as a dramatist.

Lewes makes a valid point in applying his theories about the flexibility of esthetic standards to the judgments of professional critics. But he is not quite fair in berating theatergoers in the 1850's because they do not understand Racine. Even the highly selective group of spectators who attended the French plays at the St. James's Theatre could not be expected to appreciate fully the peculiarities and conventions of Racine's art. An understanding of these peculiarities and conventions requires considerable study by anyone who has been brought up in the tradition of Shakespeare, and most of these spectators were brought up in this tradition, as, indeed, most educated Englishmen and Americans were and still are. In addition, as Lewes also had pointed out in one of his early articles, there was a linguistic and cultural barrier.[29] The ability actually to "feel" spoken French—and such an ability is needed for a true appreciation of Racine—is rare in a person whose native language is English.

Perhaps Lewes was not altogether serious in expressing so forcibly his disapproval of popular critical standards, and it is also quite possible that he did not mean all the harsh things he said about the "public d'élite." But he may have felt that he could improve the quality of the drama in England by improving the taste of those upon whose favor the drama depended. He knew that, as long as people were satisfied with Scribe, Racine would have no chance of widespread acceptance. By calling attention to Racine's superiority, Lewes perhaps considered that he might contribute to a general appreciation of the real qualities of Racine's art and, in time, to a realization that the drama Racine stood for was better and more worth while than the genre of Scribe and his imitators.

Lewes's ideas about the French Romantic drama and its most famous exponent, Victor Hugo, constitute another interesting aspect of his criticism of modern tragedy. They were not so consistent as his ideas on Shakespeare and Racine and were influenced as much by contemporary opinion as they were by his own convictions. They changed substantially between 1840 and 1844 and, significantly enough, so did Hugo's reputation as a dramatist. *Hernani* and *Ruy Blas* had been received enthusiastically in France during the previous decade; but in 1843, Hugo's last play, *Les Burgraves,* was damned impartially in Paris by critics and spectators alike. Its failure marked the beginning of a reaction against the Romantic drama from which it never recovered.[30]

In one of his earliest major critical articles in the *Westminster Review,* Lewes defends both the Classic and Romantic schools. He attempts to justify the artificial rhetoric of Racine and the florid excesses of Hugo, whom he regards as the greatest of the

Romantic dramatists; and he maintains that the work of these two writers is representative of the finest productions of the French drama in two distinct spheres.[31] In this opinion Lewes was in direct opposition to most British critics, who, during the 1830's, had become more and more emphatic in their derogation of the French dramatists, especially of Hugo and the Romantics. Typical of the accepted view in England at this time is an indictment of Hugo in the *Quarterly Review* in which he is accused of thinking that "crime is grand" by exhibiting "in all their odious details, adultery, rape, incest, and murder." *Lucrèce Borgia, Marion de-Lorme* and *Marie Tudor* are reprobated for their grossness and improbability.[32] In an article in the *Edinburgh Review,* Hugo's novels are given a favorable criticism; but his dramas, particularly *Le Roi s'amuse* and *Lucrèce Borgia,* are deplored. Dealing as they do in a "mass of licentiousness, incest, and murder," they show that "the evil influences of his day" seem to be acquiring "a firmer hold" over Hugo's mind.[33] Even the liberal *Foreign Quarterly Review* describes the plays of the French Romantic writers as "dramas . . . than which nothing can be imagined more depraved in conception, or more objectionable in execution." [34]

In his opposition to these critical opinions Lewes went further than merely adopting a more tolerant attitude toward the French Romantic school. To illustrate Hugo's use of its principles, he analyzes *Marion deLorme,* which he considers one of Hugo's best works. Selecting this particular play for favorable criticism and defending its heroine's moral standards were radical violations of typical Victorian mores. Marion is a celebrated courtesan who, in the words of a contemporary, saves the man she loves *"by a sacrifice which we dare but hint at."* [35] Lewes is unperturbed; and, comparing her conduct with Isabel's in *Measure for Measure,* he finds that Marion is the more virtuous of the two. Shakespeare, with "marvellous judgment," has delineated Isabel as "a clap-trap heroine . . . a cold, selfish creature," because she acts as she does when her brother's life is at stake. But Marion, ruled by a noble passion, is not "so selfish as to stand upon her 'chastity' " when it is the price she must pay to save her lover.[36] These sentiments are again in marked contrast to those of Lewes's fellow critics, most of whom referred to Marion deLorme as a depraved and immoral woman, if they stooped to comment on her at all.

Though one historian of Hugo's reputation has called Lewes's

Westminster Review article "a milestone indicating the progress of French Romanticism in England,"[37] Lewes had completely changed his mind by 1844. Along with most of the critics on both sides of the channel, he saw the triumph of the Classic over the Romantic school in the failure of Hugo's *Les Burgraves* in 1843 and in the simultaneous success of Ponsard's *Lucrèce*. This development, Lewes wrote in 1844, heralded a return to "the healthy style of the French national drama." Audiences were attracted temporarily by Hugo's novelty, but Classical tragedies would always attract if they were well written because they are "truly national." In contrast to Racine, Hugo is a playwright, not a dramatist. Hugo's art is founded on falsehood, his characters and passions are unreal, his language is "by turns admirable and ludicrous," and his form is "anti-national."[38]

Lewes's comments in 1844 reflect what actually was happening to contemporary opinion in France. The damning of *Les Burgraves* ushered in a resurgence of respect for the Classical drama and was the beginning of the end for the French Romanticists. Hugo never again wrote for the theater, although some of his plays continued to be produced. Racine's tragedies resumed their place of supremacy on the French stage after the brief triumph of the Romantics had gradually faded. Lewes's observations about Hugo were in line with the opinions of most of his contemporaries in England as well as in France, although they directly contradict the views he expressed in his earlier defense of the Romantics. His turnabout in 1844 marks the beginning of his disenchantment with Hugo, and just why it occurred at this time is not difficult to understand. The *Westminster Review* article is in some ways based on immature judgments—after all, Lewes was only twenty-three when he wrote it; and, as his critical perceptions grew keener, his preference for the order and regularity that the Classical form implies becomes more evident. This preference, along with his increasing rationality and partiality for realism, is more than enough to account for his reaction against the exaggerations of the French Romantics.

Lewes did not change his mind again about Hugo and the Romantic drama. In 1845, when he wrote a review of *Virginie*, a five-act Classical tragedy by L. de Saint Ybars, he hailed its success as another indication of the "return to a healthy style—the national drama" in France, pointing to the "decay and downfall . . . of the noisy, tawdry, lifeless thing, called the Romantic School." He concedes that the Romantic dramatists have made some important discoveries: they have enlarged the sphere of the drama by destroying several outworn Classical conventionalities and by making people aware that tragedy is not confined to kings and queens, bringing forward "the eminently *human* nature of the drama." They also have improved certain notions of stagecraft and have taught dramatists "the value of situations." But, in spite of these contributions, in spite of "the grand discovery of the grotesque and deformed," Racine's fame "has remained unshaken, Racine's pathos still draws tears, Racine's mastery in art is still unrivalled." The Romanticists, Lewes concludes, "have had their day." [39]

Over the years Lewes remained consistent in this attitude. His chief objection to Hugo's plays was that they lacked verisimilitude; and, as we have seen, he attacked Hugo's fiction for the same reason. In 1852, in a criticism of *Ruy Blas*, he claims that Hugo, though he has talent, is neither a poet nor a dramatist because his pieces lack life and reality. *Ruy Blas* has the "unredeemable defect of seeming unreal from first to last." For this reason, Frédéric Lemaître, who played the principal role, was at a disadvantage. Lemaître's greatness, in Lewes's opinion, is in his "intense perception of the details which represent a real emotion"; but he is out of place as Ruy Blas because it is an "utterly unreal" part and "gives the actor no chance." [40] This view of Hugo's play and of his abilities as a dramatist was generally accepted in England during the 1850's; but by 1865, when Lewes wrote an adverse criticism of a new edition of Hugo's poems, his reputation had improved. Yet Lewes still felt constrained to write of Hugo that, "splendidly endowed" as he is, he has so few of "the cardinal qualities of Vision and Sincerity . . . that he excites little of the loving admiration which is so willingly given to poets who touch and teach." [41]

In general, though Lewes's opinions about Hugo may be open to doubt in some respects, very few of the later English critics, with the exception of Algernon Swinburne, have questioned either his condemnation of the French Romantic dramatists or his consistent admiration of Racine.[42] Although Hugo's plays are still performed in France, they are admired for their rhetoric, not for their qualities as drama. Racine's position in the French theater, on the other hand, corresponds very nearly to Shakespeare's in ours. Matthew Arnold, writing in 1879, terms Hugo "a great romance writer"; but he agrees essentially with Lewes on the subject of Hugo's defects as a tragic dramatist.[43] Two years later J. Brander Mathews called Hugo "a clever playwright, and artificer of dramas," but not a great dramatist.[44] In 1896 William Archer wrote that Lewes's estimate of Hugo and the French Romantic dramatists, whether right or wrong, certainly is "the modern judgment," and Archer's pronouncement has held up in view of Hugo's subsequent reputation.[45]

Lewes's comments on a tragedy by another French dramatist, Alexandre Dumas-*fils,* are less perceptive than his criticism of Hugo's plays; and they illustrate the influence of contemporary attitudes upon his judgment. *La Dame aux Camélias* was not a product of the French Romantic school, but Lewes objected to it anyway, not because of its dramatic deficiencies but because it outraged his Victorian sensibilities. There is no evidence that he had even seen the play when he wrote his criticism of it, yet he called it "an unhealthy idealisation of one of the worst evils of our social life" and deplored Dumas's skillful treatment of a subject "not only unfit to be brought before our sisters and our wives, but unfit to be brought before ourselves." [46] Practically everyone else in England seems to have agreed with him in this opinion. The Lord Chamberlain banned the play in 1853, with Lewes's wholehearted approval; and an English version, *Heartsease,* had to wait until 1880 before it was licensed to appear. *La Traviata,* the opera derived from it, was produced during the 1850's—but only after its setting had been radically altered to the period of Louis XIV.

Although a liberal in his politics, Lewes was essentially a Victorian in his views on morality. He was unable to tolerate the dramatic glorification of what he believed to be an utterly immoral human relationship. Considerations other than critical dulled the sharpness of Lewes's judgment of *La Dame aux Camélias,* and its subsequent consistent success has demonstrated how wrong Lewes and his fellow Londoners were about its value as an acting drama. But his biased comments on *La Dame aux Camélias* are not typical of Lewes's criticism of tragedy. For the most part, his attitudes were based upon esthetic values, not moral standards or popular conceptions of what was good or bad drama. He often disagreed with the opinions of his contemporaries; but many of his judgments have proved to be valid ones and have survived the test of time. He was almost alone in his rejection of Elizabethan techniques and conventions for use in the nineteenth-century theater. His deep respect for Racine and the French Classic drama, as well as his contempt for Scribe as a writer of tragedy, also were based on unconventional critical evaluations, although his estimate of Hugo, after his youthful attempt to defend him, was more acceptable. Lewes had particularly strong views on the French drama at this time because it exerted such a profound influence on the drama in England. His purpose was to make this influence salutary in line with his overriding objective: to improve the quality of serious drama on the British stage. Whatever the effects of his criticism may or may not have been, the writers of modern tragedy have stopped imitating the outworn conventions of the Elizabethans and have tried, as Lewes advised, to image forth "some reflex of the world that all men know, speaking their language, uttering their thoughts, espousing their idealisms." [47]

III *On Comedy*

In his criticism of comedy in the contemporary British theater, Lewes again had much to say about the French drama—in particular about the plays of Eugène Scribe. William Archer observes that it is "the strongest proof of Lewes's essential modernness that he foresaw from the first, and may be said instinctively to have headed, the reaction against Scribe." [48] This conclusion is based on Lewes's criticism of *Adrienne Lecouvreur,* in which, as we have seen, Lewes expressed his low opinion of Scribe as a tragic dramatist. But Archer does not take into account Lewes's comments on Scribe as a writer of comedy, for they indicate that Lewes recognized the significance of Scribe's contributions to the techniques of modern playwriting. Archer himself wrote in 1886 that "the whole theatrical history of the past fifty years would have been different" if Scribe had not lived.[49] Over thirty years before, Lewes had anticipated, at least in part, how important Scribe's influence was to be.

Emphatic as Lewes was in his opinion that Scribe was not to be compared with Racine, he never hesitated to acknowledge Scribe's capabilities as a playwright. In 1851 he called Scribe an "épicier in Art," but he qualified the term by admitting that he was "a wonderful épicier, no doubt, and one whose adroitness I am the last to despise." [50] Lewes's comments on Scribe's two comedies, *La Camaraderie* and *Une Chaîne,* are particularly interesting because they indicate that Lewes recognized the importance of Scribe's chief contribution to the drama: his mastery of the technique of constructing "la pièce bien faite"—the well made play—a technique that Lewes himself could have made good use of in the construction of some of his own plays, particularly *A Strange History* and *Chain of Events.*

The thesis of Lewes's criticism of *La Camaraderie* and *Une Chaîne* is that a good comedy must be well constructed. In *La Camaraderie* Scribe has "arranged all his lights so that the rays converge towards his central purpose"; taking his subject from "the breathing realities around us," he has "worked up a mere 'notion' into a work of 'art.'" *Une Chaîne* also is "a study of construction." Scribe has adopted one idea, the destruction of a young man's happiness by the liaison that has made him successful, and made a diverting play of it. Though neither comedy has much wit, both are entertaining and provide proof that "the dialogue may move amidst mere mediocrities, rising occasionally into humour, and the Comedy, nevertheless, be sparkling, animated, amusing." [51] Lewes acknowledged Scribe's talent for what it was, even though he saw clearly that much of Scribe's sentiment was specious and many of his devices were outworn and artificial. But Lewes did not allow his contempt for Scribe's abilities as a tragic dramatist to temper his admiration of him as a writer of "well-made" plays, and he saw that British playwrights would profit greatly by imitating him.

With the Congreve ideal still dominant, Lewes felt that the writers of comedy in England placed too much emphasis on stage "wit" and not enough on conversation and the portrayal of character. They wrote epigrams, not conversations; "any materials, however carelessly gathered, are thought good enough so that the 'jokes' be abundant." But they "disdain or overlook" certain necessary processes: "constructing a story as the development of some idea—grouping around that the characters which will most clearly set it forth—and subordinating the *writer* to the dramatist. . . ." The French writers, on the other hand, have concentrated on "the perfection of the construction and the representation of character rather than upon witty dialogue." For wit is "an exquisite superfluity . . . no more than the flying buttress to the building." If the dramatist takes his subject "out of Life," and his characters "from reality," and if he constructs his story "with the severity demanded by dramatic art," he can safely dispense with it.[52]

These are the fundamental tenets in Lewes's criticism of contemporary comedy in England. He felt that Scribe achieved his greatest success because he could depict lifelike characters and could write well-constructed plays. In these two aspects of dramatic art the British playwrights failed most completely. They did not relate their characters to reality, so that their plays had no bearing on the actualities of life; and they almost always made the mistake of introducing British stage "wit" for its own sake, without considering the requirements of the drama itself.

Lewes's attitude is also illustrated by his comments on two plays by Douglas Jerrold, *The Catspaw* and *Retired from Business*. Both were well received by their audiences and achieved a substantial success. They are also typical of the kind of comedy that was being written by the British dramatists whose technique Lewes disliked. Concerning *The Catspaw,* first performed in 1850, Lewes writes that the critic should "talk not of plot, situation, or construction; Jerrold has the marvelous power of dispensing with them. His wit is so exuberant and telling . . . that he abandons himself to it . . . careless of aught else." Comedies like this one are marred by "the slenderness of their tissue." They are "orgies of wit" but are "not works of art." Interest is aroused in the first two acts of *The Catspaw,* but it lags in the last three because there is "no action" and "no movement," although there is "perpetual activity." When the audience gets impatient, it is revived into merriment by "some irresistible joke," and so the play is carried off successfully.[53] But Lewes makes it clear that he thoroughly disapproves of Jerrold's method, even though the audience has been amused.

He is less equivocal in his criticism of *Retired from Business,* produced a year after *The Catspaw*. After expressing his admiration for Jerrold's talents, Lewes reproaches him with the admonition that *Retired from Business* "is not a comedy worthy of your powers." It has wit, satire, and feeling; but the plot is so poorly constructed that the play falls apart after the first act; and, though flashes of wit dazzle the audience and "laughter topples judgment," when laughter subsides, "judgment resumes its seat, and pronounces a stern verdict." [54] The defects were too glaring to be missed in Jerrold's comedies and in many others like them, and

Lewes was not alone in pointing out their structural inadequacies. Many critics agreed with him that the British dramatists had much to learn from the French, and that they should try to emulate the techniques of Scribe and his followers. Along with the rest of their species, Jerrold's plays have been forgotten; and it was the "pièce bien faite," not the series of all but unrelated witty remarks, that survived as the accepted form in the drama of the late nineteenth century. Popular as the Congreve model was in the 1850's, Lewes realized that it must inevitably be displaced by a more realistic style.

Another serious fault that Lewes found with the writers of comedy was that they paid no attention to the actualities of life and did not model their characters after real people. In his criticism of *All that Glitters is not Gold,* an adaptation from a French play, Lewes writes that the original comedy probably has "grace and verisimilitude" but that the English version lacks these qualities. The French "know what society is, and endeavor to depict it," while English dramatists are "ignorant of all the usages of society," apparently; and they depict "*not* what is daily enacted in our drawing-rooms and streets, but what the stage has traditionally handed down to us as the customs of certain classes. . . . They . . . rouge the cheek of truth—and that with no delicate hand—yet believe they have given it the ruddy glow of health." Lewes concludes that *All that Glitters is not Gold* is "immensely successful, if the purport of the drama be *not* to hold the mirror up to life . . . but rather to hold the mirror up to the stage. . . ."[55]

He finds that the same weakness characterizes the plays of most British dramatists. They take their characters and situations out of life as it is lived in the theater, not in everyday society. In *Love in a Maze,* a typically successful five-act comedy, the author, Dion Boucicault, borrows his characters, "like his dresses, from the theatrical repertory"; and he reproduces scenes and situations "that have become heirlooms." Every character and every incident "is unmistakably traceable to some other play or plays." Lewes goes into sufficient detail about the plot and characters to demonstrate that Boucicault has made good use of his materials, the "common property of the stage," but has added nothing to them. But then, Lewes asks, "Why add to what has already been found successful?" Perhaps "pedantic old *quidnuncs*" may believe that "the comic writer has a serious and laborious, no less than a noble task, that *observation* of life—the life which moves upon the world's stage—portraiture of character—invention and profound art—are all required to produce a comedy." But who regards the *quidnuncs*? And "what do we care about Life, when we have the Stage: what, after all, is the World compared with Inchbald's *British Theatre*?" [56]

Other reviewers of *Love in a Maze* did not agree with Lewes. The *Spectator* reviewer, for example, terms Boucicault a practical dramatist who has learned much from the "French School" and now has produced "an original weighty piece of great merit," which is reminiscent of the best specimens of the Parisian stage.[57] Heraud in the *Athenaeum* attributes the play's success to its "admirable structure" and its "moral vein and fine wit." [58] The *Play-Goer* critic, in a generally unfavorable review, finds that *Love in a Maze* is too long for its "meagre materials." [59] In none of these comments is there any mention of the principal deficiency Lewes sees in the play—the fact that it has no relationship with reality. Boucicault's failure to consider the actualities of life was not regarded as a very serious error; audiences and critics alike were indifferent to verisimilitude. Lewes was looking to the future when he declared that the comic writer's task was to observe "the life which moves upon the world's stage," for the requirements of realism had not yet begun to exert any appreciable influence in the theater. He was in advance of the taste of his time when he maintained that modern comedy must deal with the people and events of actual life, not with the familiar characters and threadbare stories that had been handed down as the heritage of the stage, just as he was in advance of his time when he declared, as we have seen, that the modern novel should deal with real people and events.

An inspection of almost any of the comedies that were being presented in the contemporary theater demonstrates that Lewes's opinions were well founded. The characters in them are stereotypes, the plots are artificial and far-fetched, and they are pervaded by the atmosphere of the Restoration comedy. Many of these plays were immensely successful when they were first produced, but none of them has survived either as drama for the stage or as literature for the study. Lewes anticipated the trend in dramatic writing that was to begin with the first important attempts at realistic comedy made by T. W. Robertson in the

1860's.[60] In Lewes's contention that situations and characters on the stage should have some bearing on the events of everyday life, he foresaw the problem comedies of Shaw and Ibsen, who were the most influential exponents of the Realistic style that has been so important in revitalizing the modern drama. The plays of Shaw and Ibsen and their followers are indeed a far cry from the stagy, artificial comedies that were popular a hundred years ago. Lewes was correct in his assertion that the drama would have to be regenerated if it were to continue to exist and that the sources of its regeneration must spring from life and reality—not from the outworn materials and usages of the theater.

IV *On Melodrama*

Lewes foresaw the decadence of melodrama at a time when it was still well thought of not only by the general public but also by the critics. Representative of his general opinion of it are his comments on Charles Kean's performance in Dion Boucicault's *The Corsican Brothers,* one of the most popular and successful examples of the genre. It opened at the Princess's Theatre in February, 1852; and Lewes's favorable reaction is a fine demonstration of his fair-mindedness, considering the fact that only three weeks before Kean had struck him off the free list, as we have noted above. But Lewes was impartial. Kean's acting in *The Corsican Brothers* proved that he is "unrivalled" in the field of gentlemanly melodrama, even though he is incapable of giving a really good performance in serious tragedy.[61] Despite Kean's animosity, Lewes never hesitated to praise him on this and other occasions whenever he acted in roles that suited his peculiar talents.

An interesting sidelight on Lewes's criticism of Kean's acting is the importance attached to it by Bernard Shaw, who wrote: "The one failure in Charles Kean's life that matters now is his failure to impress Lewes in anything higher than melodrama." [62] Shaw is probably right. One reason Lewes's opinion counts for so much is that the other critics who saw Kean act were almost unanimous in their praise of his work in melodrama, but they neglected to add —as Lewes did—that he was not so great an actor in serious tragedy. The fact that Lewes held to his standards and insisted on describing Kean's limitations, as well as his talents, demonstrates Lewes's integrity as a critic and enhances the reliability of his judgments.

In his criticism of the play itself, Lewes finds that *The Corsican Brothers* is "the most daring, ingenious, and exciting melodrama I remember to have seen." But the conclusion, a bloody duel "represented with minute ferocity of detail," is "gratuitously shocking"; and Lewes discerns a generic weakness in the intensity of the horror of this scene. It is the fatality of melodrama "to know no limit. The tendency of the senses is *downwards*. To gratify them stimulants must be added and added, chili upon cayenne, butchery upon murder. . . . And herein lies the secret weakness and inevitable failure of Melodrame . . . in the fact that Melodrame appeals to the lowest faculties, the avenues to which are very limited, consequently the influence is soon exhausted; whereas Drama appeals to the highest faculties, and *their* avenues are infinite." [63]

Lewes recognizes the same symptoms of decadence in art and the public taste in his criticism of *Sextus V*, another melodrama of the same type as *The Corsican Brothers*. He sees in the success of *Sextus V*

> an omen of inevitable decay: decay not only of Art, which is one of the sacred influences; but decay even of the vulgar artifice that takes its place. Whoever knows anything of the human organization knows that the more you excite the public by *sensuous* stimulants the more you destroy the palate and pervert its taste. The four hours of tumult and surprise on Monday night will render more tumult and surprise necessary for the next piece; and so on till the whole stock is exhausted. . . . By substituting the material for the moral such is always the result.[64]

The facts of subsequent theatrical history bear out Lewes's prophecy that melodrama would not survive as a respected form of art. As he foresaw, the appeal of melodrama, as he and his contemporaries knew it, gradually limited itself to lower and lower tastes because of the extravagancies and exaggerations inherent in the species itself. Its ultimate evolution into burlesque was unavoidable.

Other critics often recognized the same deficiencies in melodrama that Lewes did, but few of them acknowledged the implications of its popularity or attempted to deal with questions of taste or art. The *Literary Gazette* reviewer, for example, calls *The Corsican Brothers* "probably . . . the greatest 'hit' of the season" and concludes that its success "was immense and deserved," even though the duel scene called forth "several expressions of disapprobation." [65] The critics were not so enthusiastic in their praise of *Sextus V*. Heraud, in the *Athenaeum,* writes that the general impression he received of it was one of "extreme tediousness," despite the elaborate scenery and fine acting, and the *Play-Goer* reviewer calls it "a thoroughly impossible and extravagant melodrama." [66] In general, the criticisms of these plays and others like them are typified by long, detailed résumés of the plots and by glowing accounts of the scenic effects; but they rarely contain observations on anything more important than these immediate impressions. Lewes's contemporaries were interested primarily in recording the events that occurred on the stage before their eyes; they did not concern themselves, as Lewes did, with the significance or the effects of melodrama as a decadent influence in the theater.

Lewes also deals with what he terms the "Material" or "Fast" School of art in his criticism of melodrama. He designates "situation," "stage effect," and "incident" as the watchwords of this school. At the expense of these elements, poetry, psychology, and truth to life are mercilessly sacrificed. Lewes does not object to the technical aspects of the "Material School" but to the degeneration of dramatic art which its conditions demand. He feels that situation, stage effect, and incident are good in themselves; for many years he has been "preaching the absolute *necessity* of such things in dramas intended for representation." But, when he subjects the "Fast School" to "a little philosophical analysis," he finds that it places undue emphasis upon these purely mechanical considerations. A "situation" should not be inserted into a drama merely because it may be interesting as such, for it is "only the embodiment of an idea." It is interesting "not for its *own* sake, but for the sake of what it expresses." The function of a "stage effect" is as "the culmination and material presentation of some passion or some thought," but it is not important in and of itself.[67]

Lewes uses a striking analogy to illustrate his idea of the proper relationship between the drama and the means whereby dramatic effects are conveyed. When an artist paints a picture, he must choose a single moment, "one phasis of the action," to represent his story; his selection, consequently, "must be that moment which best gathers into one the whole thread of the action." This comprises "the difficulty of conception." The painter's next step is his design, "the distribution of the figures with reference to their significance in expressing the whole." Like the dramatist, he must produce his results by means of situation, incident, and stage effects—the "Representative Conditions" of his art. Likewise, the dramatist must remember that the drama, "as an Art, is the material representation of an ideal conception. It places before our eyes the progress and culmination of some passion, the story of some ideal life. But, inasmuch as it must represent and not imitate —inasmuch as it must affect us in the space of a few hours with the emotions of many nights or years, it is thereby limited to what I may call Representative Conditions." [68]

Lewes concludes that the dramatist and the artist have, in a sense, the same materials to work with and the same difficulties to overcome. They must select the right moments to depict their "ideal conceptions," and they must use the "Representative Conditions" of their respective mediums in such a way as to set off these conceptions in the most effective manner. To pretend to despise these conditions, Lewes maintains, is to show ignorance; but to "pretend . . . to elevate them into the first rank is to suppose that paintings depend on colours, not upon the artistic *employment* of colours." The "Fast School" commits the error of presuming that dramas depend on situation and stage effects alone, not upon the judicious use of these materials in representing an "ideal conception" of something above and apart from them.[69]

These are the principles underlying Lewes's criticism of the "Fast School" of the drama. He applies them in his conclusions concerning *Sextus V:* "For four mortal hours the strangest adventures, perils, escapes, captures, reëscapes, and recaptures are crowded pellmell together. The clash of swords, the click of muskets, the tumult of mobs, the pealing of organs, the chanting of nuns . . .—all the ancient repertory of Mrs. Radcliffe, Dumas and the melodramatists. . . ." As far as "effects" go, the most ravenous appetite is satisfied. "But, what then?" Lewes asks. "What are these effects? Colours scattered on a palette!" The piece itself "did not interest me in the slightest degree. The horrors had no awe, the perils no danger, the sorrows no tears, the despair no pang: the bodily presentment of all these things wanted an 'o'er-informing spirit.'" [70] There were the materials of drama in limitless profusion, but no drama: brilliant colors, but no picture.

Lewes calls attention to the same deficiencies in his criticisms of other plays of the same type as *Sextus V*. *The Templar*, he writes, is effective because of its movement, situations, and spectacle—"properties" usually sneered at by poets, but "necessary as the vehicle even for the finest poetry." But its "poverty of thought, imagery, psychological revelations, and the superficiality of its passions" make it "dramatically *insignificant*." It conveys no real impression, but is forgotten when the curtain falls.[71]

His fellow critics were hardly more enthusiastic about *The Templar* than Lewes was, but they again failed to comment on the reasons for its weakness. The reaction of the *Spectator* reviewer is typical; he terms *The Templar* "a clever melodrama of an elevated kind" and blames the audience if it is disappointed in its expectations, "for now-a-days a good melodrama is, after all, not to be despised." Oxenford's remarks in the *Times* are along the same line; the play is a "first-rate melodrama," which is "better than an abortion of a higher genus"—a somewhat equivocal compliment.[72] Both critics are generous in their praise of the scenery and acting, but neither is concerned with what Lewes considers the characteristic defect of the piece: the sacrifice of artistic merit at the expense of spectacle and sensation.

Lewes makes an interesting comparison in his review of *The Templar* between Shakespeare's tragedies and the "Fast School." *Hamlet, Macbeth,* and *Othello,* like *The Templar,* are all "melodramatic" in theatrical structure. Shakespeare too depends heavily upon plot, sensation, and movement. His tragedies, then, are melodramas, but with the addition of "noble poetry, the masterly exhibition of character, thought, beauty, grace and fancy"—in short, the things that make the difference between real and specious dramatic art.[73] Shakespeare employs the "Representative Conditions" of the drama in their proper function, as a means to convey dramatic effects, but these effects are not ends in themselves, as they are in the work of the "Fast" writers. In a later criticism of *Hamlet,* Lewes points out that it contains "the elements for several Fast dramas," but it is at the same time "the most thoughtful and philosophical of poems." [74] The essential difference between Shakespeare and the "Material School" is that Shakespeare, possessing all the abilities of the melodramatists, was also a great poet. The writers of "Fast" drama, with the same materials at their disposal that Shakespeare had, are not poets; and their plays, despite their constructive ingenuity and exciting situations, are failures because they lack the indispensable ingredients of poetry and human interest.

Related to Lewes's ideas concerning the "Fast School" are his observations about the harmful effects of the policies employed by some London theater managers, who insisted on subordinating the finer elements of the drama to scenery and stage effects. Typical of Lewes's views on what he considered a misplaced emphasis on showmanship at the expense of esthetics is his criticism of Kean's production of *Sardanapalus,* with which he was so disgusted that he refrained from commenting on it until a week after he had seen it. But, even after simmering down, he found two "fatal objections" to the performance that he could not forgive: first, that "the sum total of all this splendour, all this archaeology, all this 'business,' is overpowering dullness; and, second that in a drama the accessories are but accessories, subordinate and not to be brought into the first rank. In proportion as the drama claims a hearing in right of its poetical conception and execution . . . as it appeals to the higher faculties, not to the lower appetites . . . the accessories become unimportant, and their prominence becomes impertinent." [75] Here Lewes expresses his strong objection to the tendency among theater managers to cater to the lower "appetites" in order to score a popular success, despite the effects of their policy upon the drama itself.

Contemporary critics, who found no such faults with *Sardanapalus,* apparently were as captivated as the audiences by the elaborate splendor of the production. The *Spectator* and *Athenaeum* reviews, which are typical, consist chiefly of panegyrics on the stage effects. The *Spectator* critic calls the play a magnificent spectacle, and particularly admires the "Assyrian antiquities," including the Hall of Nimrod, "with its strangely costumed guests and its big Assyrian man-lions." Heraud in the *Athenaeum* regrets that Byron's poem has been abridged, but he praises the performance as "an unrivalled whole—such as never previously in modern times at least was seen on any stage, native or foreign." [76]

Lewes compares Kean's acting in *Sardanapalus* with Macready's, which he had seen some twenty years before; and he finds that Macready's vastly superior acting talents made his performance far more memorable. Basing his judgment on the dramatic aspects of the presentation, not on its qualities as an exhibition, Lewes finds that Kean's interpretation of the role completely disregards Byron's original conception of it. The drama and poetry of the original are sacrificed to sensation and spectacle, and, although "Charles Kean is so bad an actor, and his troupe is so incompetent" that this policy is "undeniable from *his* point of view," yet it is based on completely false esthetic standards. But, Lewes asks in his despairing conclusion—laced as usual with a little levity—"how about the public? Why not give up the drama altogether, and make the Princess's Theatre a Gallery of Illustration?" [77]

Although the equivalent of the "Fast School," with all its implications, has survived until the present—and has in fact achieved a healthy maturity not only on the stage but also in the movies and television—the distinction between it and higher forms of drama has become relatively clear. One of Lewes's major quarrels with the contemporary theater stemmed from the fact that this distinction did not exist and that, as a consequence, authors and managers "hampered Amusement with the necessary conditions of Art" or degraded Art "by making it secondary to Amusement." [78] Melodrama, in Lewes's opinion, comes under the head of "Amusement," even though it is sometimes classed with a more reputable type of drama; but it will continue to satisfy the public—"good, stolid, stupid public"—as long as it remains so undiscriminating. In lugubrious resignation, Lewes writes at the conclusion of his spirited criticism of *Sextus V:* "Enough, enough! I croak in vain. What is logic against a full house? I write my protest and pass on." [79]

V *On Shakespeare*

Lewes's ideas about Shakespeare's plays also were most unusual. At a time when most critics felt that Shakespeare was a poet who had more or less accidentally adopted the drama as his medium of expression, Lewes claimed that he was a dramatist who wrote his plays in poetic form because it was considered the accepted mode of dramatic presentation in the Elizabethan theater where he intended for them to be produced. In the early decades of the century the Romantic critics were in almost unanimous agreement with Charles Lamb's dictum that Shakespeare's plays are "less calculated for performance on a stage than those of almost any other dramatist whatever." [80] Coleridge wrote that "chance and the necessity of his genius combined to lead Shakespeare to the drama," not the desire to write plays for the stage.[81] In Goethe's opinion Shakespeare's fame and excellence "belong to the history of poetry," and the reader gains "so much the purer pleasure" from the plays if he never sees them acted.[82] Most Shakespearians in England, as well as in Germany, were in substantial agreement with these conceptions in 1849 when Lewes, rejecting them completely, declared: "It is a curious illustration of the absence of fixed principles that two such critics as Goethe and Charles Lamb (not to mention others), should have gravely maintained that Shakespeare's very excellence as a dramatic Poet prevented the success of his works, on the stage," and that his "excellencies" were so great that "they *failed* to produce the very effects for which they were employed!" [83]

Lewes's consistent viewpoint was that Shakespeare should be regarded primarily as a dramatist and secondarily as a poet and that any critical appreciation of his work should depend on his achievements as a writer for the theater. In adopting this attitude Lewes was in direct opposition to most contemporary criticism, but he was anticipating the modern concept of Shakespeare—that he was a dramatist whose chief concern was to write and produce plays that would be successful in the Elizabethan theater. But Lewes was not one-sided in his criticism; he appreciated Shakespeare's genius as a poet, while insisting on taking into account his genius as a dramatist as well. His plays were masterpieces because he could combine beautiful poetry with "the most effective modes of stage representation." In criticizing the plays, Lewes concluded that they should be considered both as poetry and drama because Shakespeare wrote them for the theater and that, consequently, any valid criticism must place proper emphasis on the art of the theater as an important aspect of his technique.[84]

Most critics of Lewes's generation, as well as his predecessors, did not share his attitude. As Lewes pointed out, those who did regard Shakespeare as a dramatist tested him, "absurdly enough . . . according to the classic rules, the rules of French tragedy, and, finally, to those of German philosophy," but not according to those of the theater. Johnson, Pope, and Voltaire in the eighteenth century, and the Schlegels in the nineteenth, even though they may have considered Shakespeare's dramatic abilities, consistently judged his plays by standards that were not applicable to them. On the other hand, the English Romantic critics, led by Coleridge, Lamb, and Hazlitt, concentrated on his poetry and neglected his genius as a dramatist; they even considered it an honor to Shakespeare to call him "essentially untheatrical," and they maintained that "the plays which he above all things meant for representation . . . are really ill adapted to representation!" [85]

This view Lewes regarded as an "extraordinary fallacy" because Shakespeare's plays are far more effective as drama for the stage than as reading for the study. Though theatrical presentation has some disadvantages, so that our impressions of the plays sometimes are degraded when we see them acted, these impressions are also intensified. There is no comparison between the vividness of a play that is performed and a poem that is read. For example, the characters of Shylock and Othello, as Charles Kean played them—in spite of Kean's shortcomings as an actor—"produced an infinitely grander effect than could have been reached by any closet reading." [86] In a review of *Shakespeare*, by G. G. Gervinus, Lewes remarks on the German critic's perspicacity in noting that *A Midsummer Night's Dream*, though the "most difficult" of all the plays, is better and more easily understood when it is acted than when it is read. This view opposes that of the revered Hazlitt, who felt that stage representation converts a delightful fiction into a "dull pantomime," in which the "airy shape" of poetry becomes an "unmanageable reality." The reality is at fault, not the play, Lewes points out. Hazlitt is right when he complains about the lack of proper actors in Shakespearian companies—though "fairies are not incredible," fairies six feet high are. But in the Elizabethan theater they were not six feet high, but "deft and tiny children," writes Lewes; and it was in this theater that *A Midsummer Night's Dream* originally was intended for performance. Inept presentations, not the play itself, make the acting versions unpalatable to contemporary audiences.[87]

Lewes summarizes his opinions about critics who think that Shakespeare's plays should be read rather than acted by declaring that, even if the plays "*on* the stage are not immensely amusing" to these men, "what then? . . . Shakespeare is in our blood. . . ." [88] *Hamlet, Othello, Macbeth,* and even *King Lear* still "charm the uncultivated crowd in suburban theaters"; and

"*That* is a sufficient answer to all who may be disposed to doubt his theatrical excellence, in consequence of their seeing in him beauties beyond and above the reach of a mere playwright." [89] But Lewes still appreciated the "beauties" of Shakespeare's poetry even though he insisted that the plays were plays first and poems second, and he went so far as to dispute Samuel Johnson's time-honored pronouncement that "Addison speaks the language of poets, Shakespeare of men." In Lewes's view, it is Shakespeare, not Addison, who speaks the language of poets, because it is superior as poetry to Addison's. The vividness of Shakespeare's representations of nature is a result of his knowledge of humanity, his "intensity of poetic power, and the brightness of the medium through which it passes"—his poetic style. "Had Shakespeare spoken the language of men, as distinguished from that of poets," declares Lewes, "he would never have delighted thousands upon thousands of all ranks and characters"; and his plays would not have remained popular for more than two centuries.[90]

Shakespeare's extraordinary ability to delineate character is an aspect of his art that both Lewes and the Romantic critics agreed on, but Lewes felt that this ability was not alone an indication of Shakespeare's poetic powers, as they did, but of his dramatic powers as well. By his "slight touches," he reveals the "preceding conditions of the mind and affections" of his characters. Their "involuntary demonstrations of qualities studiously guarded from the public gaze" interpret their interests and prejudices; and "gusts of passion sighing into tender recollections and then roused again to fury disclose the innermost secrets of their hearts." [91] But—and on this point Lewes deviates from Coleridge and his followers—Shakespeare used his remarkable character studies as integral elements in the dramas and did not intend that they should be regarded as anything else. The greatness of his art, Lewes asserts, "is not shown in the mere portrayal of mental states, but in the *adaptation* of these mental states to the purposes of the drama." Where the poet delineates the peculiar and individual qualities of a character, the dramatist must make these qualities "*dramatic agents*" in the development of his story. In the portrayal of Othello, for example, Lewes points out that Shakespeare does not analyze the character in extensive detail; he displays just those facets most necessary to an understanding of the play. The audience learns enough about Othello to obtain a proper appreciation of his function, no more. If Shakespeare had introduced additional traits of character, which, "though consistent in themselves, yet had no bearing on the general picture," he would have ruined the dramatic interest.[92]

In contrast to Lewes, Coleridge attributed little importance to what Lewes called the "acting qualities" of Shakespeare's plays. When Coleridge summarizes their distinguishing features, he comments on their adherence to the laws of nature and their high moral tone; but he does not mention their effectiveness in the theater. He even implies that they are defective in dramatic structure, by suggesting that "everything will remain" in the plays if certain omissions are made. For example, he feels that it would be no loss to *King Lear* or to *The Merchant of Venice* if the opening scenes are left out because these scenes contribute nothing to Lear's and Shylock's characterization.[93] But Coleridge's recommendations would convert these plays into two series of disconnected character sketches with no regard for the requirements of dramatic representation. Lewes was acutely aware of these requirements when he declared that Shakespeare purposely included in the plays enough about his characters to arouse interest in them and no more, so that the audience can understand their motives as "dramatic agents" in the development of the action. Although important for their own sakes, Shakespeare's characters must always be considered parts of the drama, not self-sufficient, mutually independent creations operating in an esthetic vacuum. The characters are, of course, indispensable; but the drama itself is just as indispensable.

It is worth noting that Lewes's opinions about the dramatic function of Shakespeare's characters are held by such recent critics as A. C. Bradley and E. E. Stoll. Bradley agrees with Lewes that it is a mistake to say that Shakespeare's interest lay in "*mere* character," for "he was dramatic to the tips of his fingers," and rarely, if ever, did he concentrate on characterization apart from action.[94] E. E. Stoll's observation that a play by Shakespeare is not "a cluster of studies embedded in a story" but "an individual, unbroken whole" accords with Lewes's idea that the characters function as "dramatic agents" in the development of a unified plot.[95] Stoll also repeats in substance what Lewes said about the emphasis Shakespeare places on the relationship between plot and characterization and about the dramatic effect of this relationship upon the audience. Stoll asserts that "Shakespeare is careful not so much for the single character, as for the drama; indeed, he observes not so much the probabilities of the action, or the psychology of the character, as the psychology of the audience for whom both character and action are framed." [96] Some seventy-five years previously, Lewes had made the same point, in perhaps more specific terms: "What did Shakespeare think of, when he sat down to write a play? You will answer, if you answer honestly,—'To fill the Globe theatre!' " And Shakespeare succeeded in filling it because he wrote to amuse his audiences, not to teach or uplift them. He realized that people "do not go to the theatre to learn Moorish customs or to analyze character, but to see a drama." [97]

The versification of Shakespeare's plays was another source of disagreement between Lewes and most of his predecessors and contemporaries. Again, his opinions were based on dramatic rather than purely poetic considerations. He maintained that Shakespeare's dramatic verse was irregular and inconsistent metrically because it was meant to be spoken, not read, and that Shakespeare did not correct the deficiencies and redundancies because he never prepared his plays for publication. These irregularities may be "intolerable in the reading," but they are perfectly acceptable, and may even gain "welcome variety" in recitation.[98] Lewes felt that the eighteenth-century critics simply forgot that the plays were meant to be acted on the stage when they judged that any verses containing lines with more than ten syllables were faulty simply because they did not read metrically. The nineteenth-century critics, on the other hand, thinking that everything that Shakespeare did must be perfect, assumed that his metrical irregularities were the result of his "exquisite art," and that they actually were not irregularities. To Lewes, Leigh Hunt's statement that Shakespeare "has almost sanctified a *ten syllable regularity of structure scarcely ever varied by a syllable*" is a "strange assertion." [99] Both schools of critical thought were in error, according to Lewes. Shakespeare's verses are "both correct and incorrect: fit for the stage, unfit for the closet." They contain numerous metrical irregularities, some intentional, others merely careless. If Shakespeare had published his plays, Lewes concludes, he would have corrected these careless errors; but on the stage he knew that they would not be noticed.[100]

This view of Shakespeare's general attitude about the publication of his plays is still held by most modern scholars. Lewes knew that Shakespeare revised his poems and sonnets carefully before allowing them to be printed and circulated because he felt that his literary reputation would depend on them. But he never prepared the plays for publication; they were meant to be acted in the theater, and his chief concern was "for the stage, and for the stage only." [101] These sentiments are substantially repeated by Hardin Craig in his recent edition of the plays, when he writes that Shakespeare did not prepare his manuscripts "with any expectation of their appearing in printed form" but that he wrote "with one idea in mind—that of producing plays that would act well on the stage." The poems, on the other hand, were "no doubt more highly regarded by Shakespeare himself and his contemporaries than were the plays, since plays were thought of as ephemeral if not mercenary." [102]

Shakespeare's carelessness in versification was not the only thing Lewes was heretical about: he felt that Shakespeare's humor was often outmoded and in bad taste. Since much that was amusing in Shakespeare's day is not so now, it is a mistake to "consecrate as beauties" the "defects which a wiser homage would have admitted to be blemishes." [103] The puns, quibbles, conceits, and other comic devices that made the plays so popular with the Elizabethans should not, therefore, be considered virtues to be emulated but weaknesses to be avoided. Recognizing the greatness and universality of Shakespeare's genius, Lewes still did not hesitate to acknowledge that the plays are not suitable in some respects for presentation on the modern stage—an opinion that few if any of his contemporaries dared to express, but one that ties in with his feelings about the other Elizabethan dramatists, as we already have seen. He felt that the characteristics of their plays that are "temporal and peculiar" to the Elizabethan age, far from being assets, were disadvantages to Shakespeare, whose works have survived as living drama not because of these characteristics but in spite of them.[104]

In this opinion he also anticipated the ideas of many modern critics. H. Granville-Barker, for example, writes in the introduction to his *Prefaces to Shakespeare* that, despite the danger of tampering with the text of the plays, some changes might improve their dramatic effectiveness. He suggests the omission of some of Shakespeare's obscene jokes and topical passages because they now are in bad taste and meaningless.[105] These are the sort of "defects" Lewes refers to, which "a wiser homage" admits to be "blemishes." And in his emphatic disparagement of the Elizabethan drama as an art form Lewes anticipated such later critics as Bernard Shaw and G. L. Strachey. In 1895 Shaw went even further than Lewes did, writing along much the same lines: "What Shakespeare got from his 'school' was the insane and hideous rhetoric which is all that he has in common with Jonson, Webster, and the whole crew of insufferable bunglers and dullards whose work stands out as vile even at the beginning of the seventeenth century." [106] Some twenty years later G. L. Strachey almost repeats Lewes, when Strachey writes that Shakespeare's plays have survived not because he adhered to the Elizabethan tradition but because he was not "subdued" by it.[107]

Another unusual quality that distinguishes Lewes's criticism is that he was willing, when he felt like it, to comment adversely on the plays themselves. With the cult of Shakespeare idolatry still at its height, he was extremely brash in daring to express sentiments not unequivocally praising anything and everything that Shakespeare ever wrote. But, while Lewes was drama critic for the *Leader,* he always tried to judge the plays from the point of view of their suitability for the contemporary theater, without considering their reputation as great literature. By his own admission, he sometimes found it difficult not to allow his critical perceptions to be dimmed by his profound respect for Shakespeare's genius; but on several occasions he was outspoken in his criticism of what he thought were palpable faults.

For example, he declared that *The Merry Wives of Windsor,* despite its merits, is one of Shakespeare's worst plays, "for the wit for the most part is dreary or foolish, the tone is coarse and farcical, and the characters want the fine distinctive touches he so well knew how to give." [108] In another criticism, Lewes referred to *The Merry Wives* as "this dirty, disagreeable play"; and he bluntly defended his use of the words "dirty" and "disagreeable" with the remark that "if your reverence for the Swan makes you think otherwise, mine does not." [109] This view is in marked contrast to the more typical one of a contemporary who wrote that *The Merry Wives* is "perhaps the most acceptable" of all Shakespeare's comedies, because the audience invariably is "pleased with the amusing nature of its incidents" and appreciates "the pictures of jovial English life which it represents." [110]

Lewes also made some uncomplimentary remarks about two other plays, *Much Ado About Nothing* and *The Merchant of Venice.* He felt that *Much Ado* is so weak as a comedy that it can be successfully staged only when it is performed by actors of the highest excellence. The story "hovers so constantly on the unpleasant . . . the wit is often so forced and (burn me, idolators!) feeble, that unless the insolence of youth and beauty, and the confidence and animal spirits be represented as such . . . the play becomes mere impertinence and is unpleasant." [111] *The Merchant of Venice* Lewes considered a great and powerful play, but not perfect. Its chief defect lies in the conception of Jessica, which Lewes termed "a serious blunder in art." He felt that Shakespeare would have done far better if he had shown "how the overmastering passion of *love* conquered all the obstacles" confronting Jessica and had made her "sacrifice everything" to it, instead of portraying her as "a heartless and frivolous girl" who has respect for neither her father nor her heritage. If she had been motivated by love, she would not be the altogether "odious" character that she is. "Were a modern poet so to outrage nature and art," Lewes concludes, "no mercy would be shown him." [112]

In his judgments of the three plays, there is no question but that Lewes was influenced as much by his desire to explode the myth of Shakespeare's infallibility as he was by his own honest opinions. Though many subsequent critics have expressed reservations about them, and modern scholars have found that *The Merry Wives* is indeed a "dirty" play—and Lewes certainly could not have known how very dirty—the fact remains that they are still favorites in the Shakespeare repertory. Lewes perhaps did not mean all the harsh things he said about them; he was reacting against the unrestrained "Shakespearolatry" that was then in fashion. In any event, he fully realized how radically he deviated from popular opinion, as the "burn me, idolators!" in the *Much Ado* criticism indicates. He also added to his reproaches against Jessica, cited above, that "I have little doubt that many readers are indignant at my temerity in accusing Shakespeare of such gross errors!" And, when he wrote about the unsuitability of Shakespeare and the Elizabethans as models for modern dramatists, he prefaced his remarks with the exhortation to "Light the fagots! clear your throats for execration! ransack your memory for epithets like stones to cast at our heretical heads! we are about to utter heresy of so black a dye that it will take the breath from some of you!" [113]

But his heresy was not of "so black a dye" as he thought, at least in the light of what many later critics of Shakespeare have written. As we have seen, both Bernard Shaw and G. L. Strachey were in complete agreement with him in rejecting the dramatic art of the Elizabethans. Among others, both A. C. Bradley and Walter Raleigh have endeavored to disseminate a more reasonable view of Shakespeare's genius than that of the nineteenth-century Romantics, and they also have evaluated the plays as drama for the stage rather than as poetry or philosophy for the study.[114] We can conclude, therefore, that Lewes was one of the most perceptive of the nineteenth-century Shakespearian critics, and one of the least prejudiced. He had such a sincere admiration for Shakespeare's genius and such a profound understanding of it that he was fully conscious of what he was doing when he found faults in the plays. When praise was due, he could heap it with the most effusive of the idolators; but he refused to assume that Shakespeare was always perfect simply because he was Shakespeare. Lewes regarded him as a dramatist who wrote his plays for the stage and for the stage only, and he tried to judge them by standards that were applicable to them as acting drama, not as beautiful poetry. In adopting this point of view, Lewes was perhaps the only critic of his time who looked upon Shakespeare not as a poet or philosopher who accidentally took to writing plays, but as a genius whose major strength and capabilities were directed toward the creation of great drama for the theater.

CHAPTER 6

Man of Diverse Interests

LEWES'S dramatic and literary criticism is his most significant contribution to the literature of his time, although he made his mark in other fields of intellectual endeavor as well. He was also a philosopher, a scientist, a biographer, a psychologist, and an editor, and in all these capacities he achieved considerable distinction at one time or another during his relatively short but very active career.

I *Philosophy, History, Science*

Lewes's philosophical writings are chiefly derivative and explanatory. His most impressive work is the *Biographical History of Philosophy*, an evaluation of philosophical thought by means of individual accounts of the lives and ideas of the great philosophers, from Thales and the other ancient Greeks to Auguste Comte. First published in four parts in 1845–46 in a two-volume edition, the *Biographical History* was in Charles Knight's popular series of shilling "Weekly Volumes" of widely circulated, cheap editions of worthwhile works. It gained considerable fame for Lewes among amateurs who were interested in learning the elementary principles of philosophy. One contemporary, G. J. Holyoke, recollects in a memoir that at first it "fascinated all students who were beginning to turn their attention to philosophy," but that the later editions, which included erudite and sometimes irrelevant notes and references, were valued by scholars but not by the "far larger class" that Lewes had formerly "interested, instructed, and inspired."

Holyoke adds an intriguing note when he mentions that the *Biographical History* actually was more popular in the United States than in England and that "American backwoodsmen" read it by the light of their campfires far into the night—a revealing insight, if true,[1] into the intellectual propensities of the American pioneer spirit. George Saintsbury's final verdict still stands as the most realistic: the *Biographical History* is "occasionally superficial" and is written with "an excellent though sometimes a rather treacherous clearness, and a unity of vision which is perhaps more valuable for fairly intelligent readers than desultory profundity." But it "can hardly take rank as a book of philosophical scholarship, though it is almost a brilliant specimen of popular philosophical literature." [2]

Holyoke was right in pointing out that the extensive notes Lewes added to the later versions of the *Biographical History* do not add anything by way of clarification to the original. They actually detract from the general effectiveness of the book by lending an impression of ponderous and rather forbidding scholarship. Five more editions were published in England during the half century after it first appeared, and it remained standard reading for beginning students throughout most of the period.[3] In 1875 a plush "Library Edition"—some seven hundred pages—was published in the United States, "Much Enlarged and Thoroughly Revised"; because of its size and weight, it was probably not the one that our intrepid backwoodsmen presumably perused as they brooded over their campfires.

Lewes's chief original contribution to philosophical thought was his exposition and dissemination of Auguste Comte's ideas on Positivism. They exerted a profound influence on philosophy both in England and America. Deeply committed to Positivism himself in several of its aspects, Lewes wrote many articles about it during the 1840's in addition to the long discussion of it in the *Biographical History*. His most sustained effort to explicate it is the series he wrote for the *Leader* between April and August, 1852, which he enlarged on and published the following year, as a volume in "Bohn's Scientific Libraries." Its most available reprint is the edition of 1883, with the imposing title, *Comte's Philosophy of the Sciences: Being an Exposition of the Principles of the Cours De Philosophie Positive of Auguste Comte*. This book would be the logical place to start with the ascertainment of the nature and implications of Comte's theories; but for our purposes it is enough to know that Positivism is a system of philosophy that attempts to account for all phenomena on the basis of scientific fact.

As Lewes explained in his review of the first volume of Comte's *Système de Politique Positive*, the "Positive" method of government leads to a science of society by studying morals and politics "in the same scientific spirit as astronomy or biology."[4] There also were "Positive" systems that applied to religion, sociology, family life, economics, and language—in short, to the whole spectrum of philosophical thought that maintains a close connection with scientific phenomena. According to Lewes's interpretation, throughout the Positivist view one "peculiar" consideration is constant: the "theory of social order is rigorously deduced from, and limited by, the theory of individual organism," leading to the conclusion that Comte "makes Biology the basis of Sociology" and science the basis of all his philosophy.[5] In general, Lewes followed Comte's ideas closely in his own thinking, although he eventually disagreed with his rather radical conclusions about religion.

The tendency to embrace fact and to reject philosophic intuition—which Lewes regarded as out and out "Metaphysics"—had the effect of increasing Lewes's interest in pure science, to which he devoted more and more of his time and energies in the late 1850's and early 1860's. His experiments in biology led to the publication of "Seaside Studies," a series of articles that ran in *Blackwood's Magazine* in 1856–57 and appeared in book form in 1858. They consist mainly of accounts of his discoveries in marine biology and physiology made among the flora and fauna in the waters off Tenby and the Scilly Isles, where he visited periodically with George Eliot. His researches also resulted in articles on allied subjects, such as sea anemones, early forms of animal life, animal heat, blood circulation, and respiration, many of which were included in his *Physiology of Common Life*, published in 1859, reprinted and translated into German in 1860, and reissued in 1876. Yet another series in *Cornhill Magazine* developed into *Studies in Animal Life*, which appeared in 1862. Another manifestation of his chief preoccupation was his "History of Science," launched in the early 1860's; but the only apparent result of this research was his *Aristotle: A Chapter from the History of Science*, published in 1864 as part of an obviously larger project that Lewes never completed.

As the decade wore on, his interests turned more and more toward the connections between the sciences and philosophy, rather than toward pure science; he also involved himself in experiments in which he attempted to relate physiology and biology to the then young science of psychology. He took up such matters as the differences between "Spiritualism" and "Materialism"—a burning question to the Victorians; the relationship between objective and subjective reality; and the correspondence between ideas and facts. In general, Lewes was reaching toward the formation of a theoretical ground on which to bring abstract philosophy into a coherent relationship with biological science. He started assembling his findings during the 1860's into what he hoped would be his most important book, *Problems of Life and Mind,* on which he was still at work when he died in 1878.

The first major division of this monumental undertaking, *The Foundations of a Creed,* came out in two volumes in 1874–75. The American philosopher and psychologist, William James, reviewed it favorably in the *Atlantic Monthly,* though he reserved his right to disagree with some of Lewes's Positivist ideas. James prophesied that Lewes's work would be "a most important ferment in the philosophic thought of the immediate future," despite its "diffuseness and repetition."[6] The third volume, *The Physical Basis of Mind,* appeared in 1877. Frederick Harrison—a lawyer, writer, ardent Positivist, and intimate friend of Lewes—attributed to it major significance as a masterpiece in the synthesis of the two sciences of psychology and biology.[7] The final two volumes, *The Study of Psychology,* came out posthumously in 1879, under the editorial guidance of George Eliot.

Although *Problems of Life and Mind* remains as a sort of philosophic and scientific curiosity because Lewes's findings have long since been outmoded, his work in elucidating the philosophy of Auguste Comte retains its vitality as a contribution to the understanding of Positivism in the English-speaking world.[8] Lewes's development of a scientific approach to certain aspects of physiology and psychology also was of considerable importance to nineteenth-century thinking about the relationship between man's mental processes and the physical properties of his brain and nervous system. Lewes occupies the place of a pioneer in these fields, but the influence of his ideas has diminished in the light of the strides forward that science and psychology have taken in the twentieth century. His output of viable scientific and philosophic writings is remarkable in itself, and is a tribute to his versatility as well as to his industry.

II *Biography*

This output is all the more remarkable when we remember that he also was a biographer, an editor, and a man of letters during much of the time that he occupied himself with the problems of philosophy, science, and psychology. His best known work in biography is *The Life of Goethe.* It first came out in 1855, went into several editions in both English and German during Lewes's lifetime, and is still in print. One contemporary commented that it received "the highest tributes of respect which can be paid to a book of the kind: in Germany it has been translated and admired, and in France it has been plagiarized." [9] It was considered the most reputable biography of Goethe until well into the twentieth century, although judged by modern standards it is in many respects ponderous and wordy, with much superfluous detail and sometimes too exhaustive criticisms of the works. But students of Goethe still refer to it, and it remains one of the most important biographies ever written of him. As a sort of picturesque appendage, Lewes wrote in 1867 a series of sprightly explanatory notes for an elaborate folio volume of engravings by the German artist, William Kaulbach, called *Female Characters of Goethe.* For modern readers it is considerably more lively and vivid than some parts of the *Life.*

Lewes's other major biography is his *Life of Maximilien Robespierre,* written in 1848—a most propitious year in European history for such a subject. In his "Dedicatory Preface" Lewes maintains that his aim is to marshal together all the facts of Robespierre's career, but not to pass judgment on him. On the whole, the book is objective and capably conceived, though there is too much in it about Rousseau's "Social Contract," along with extensive elaborations on liberal ideas on society that were congenial both to Lewes and Robespierre. Heavily dependent on outside sources, the biography makes no original contribution to an understanding of the French revolutionary's life or times; and it is—as Lewes himself admits in the Preface—a chronicle of previously known facts, not a work of art or history.

III *The Editor*

Turning to his activities as an editor, we find that Lewes also was an active supporter of liberal causes in this capacity, particularly during the years from 1850 to 1854 when he was on the staff of the *Leader*. Besides writing his literary and drama reviews, he contributed numerous articles on scientific and philosophic subjects, as we have seen, and was influential in matters of general editorial policy. With Thornton Hunt, the co-editor, he wrote a good deal along such ultra-liberal lines as universal sufferage, academic freedom, the obligation of journalists to speak honestly even when their opinions are not "respectable" according to Mrs. Grundy, and the desirability of a more Socialist bias in the thinking of British politicians. Thomas Carlyle observed in 1850, when the paper was just starting publication, that Lewes and Hunt "are thinking of the *Socialist* line," although he doubts if anything will come of the venture since Hunt doesn't know what he is talking about when he advocates revolution by the lower classes to alleviate social injustice—an attitude that presumably was shared by Hunt's partner in editorial "crime." [10]

In addition to the expression of his liberal social views in the *Leader*, Lewes wrote many light, incidental pieces that he probably regarded as space fillers. They deal with such matters as love, marriage, and beautiful women; are written in a charming, easy style; and usually are signed "Vivian," who is repeatedly designated as a carefree bachelor—perhaps wishful thinking on Lewes's part, in view of what was happening to his domestic situation during these years. For example, in "A Gentle Hint to Writing-Women," Vivian asks his colleagues in the weaker sex to stop writing so many books and do the things women are supposed to do—such as cooking, sewing, and taking care of their husbands.[11] And in "A Flight of Authoresses" he again complains that women not only are monopolizing the writing market but are also eating his dinners and occupying his seats at the opera; they would be much better off, and so would he, Vivian concludes, if they would stay in the country.[12] But he still sympathizes with them in "Two Old Owls," a little "Apologue" about a husband who is tempted to desert his faithful wife—and is advised not to, by Vivian himself.[13]

Lewes's later work as an editor was more staid than his activities on the *Leader*. Well established in the late 1850's and 1860's as a versatile and productive literary man, he was asked at various times to take charge of editorial policies for three new periodicals that eventually took their places among the most reputable in

England, the *Cornhill Magazine,* the *Pall Mall Gazette* and the *Fortnightly Review.* During the 1860's he functioned in editorial capacities on all three, starting in 1862 with *Cornhill,* shifting to the *Fortnightly* at the urgent request of Anthony Trollope early in 1865, and becoming an adviser on the *Pall Mall Gazette* from 1865 to 1868. Because of the strain on his health and the extra time these activities took, he gave up his position with the *Fortnightly* late in 1866. His editorial work during the 1860's was distinguished throughout by his usual industry and thoroughness. He wrote numerous pieces himself, obtained articles from some of the best writers of the day, and contributed materially to the future reputations of all three of the periodicals he was connected with.

IV *The Significant Contribution*

Though Lewes's work in several fields was in many ways significant—as philosopher, scientist, psychologist, biographer, historian, and editor—it was as a man of letters that he achieved his greatest distinction, specifically as a critic of literature and the drama. The scientific bent of his mind, together with his Positivist beliefs in the supreme efficacy of factual, systematic thinking, combined to produce an eminently rational criticism that was in marked contrast to the Romantic effusions of most of his predecessors and to the expressions of indefinite and sometimes biased opinions of most of his contemporaries.

As we have seen, his literary criticism was in general well conceived, fair, and perceptive; and the great majority of his literary judgments have been vindicated by the test of time. As the first English exponent of Realism and as the first among his contemporaries to give meaning to the term, he was instrumental in encouraging other critics and authors to move in the direction of truth and reality as criteria of excellence in prose writing. Particularly in his judgments of nineteenth-century fiction he was able to set a standard of quality that has lasted for over a century, and his evaluations of such figures as Jane Austen, the Brontës, Thackeray, and Dickens have proven to be largely valid in the light of current opinions about them. He always subjected the works he scrutinized to the light of truth; and he tried to judge them on the basis of definite esthetic criteria, equipped as he was with firmly based ideas on what was good and bad.

But his method of criticism was better suited to the novel than to poetry because of its factual bases, and his judgments of poetry sometimes were not so perceptive as those of fiction. Yet his appraisals of the work of such poets as Wordsworth, Shelley, and Arnold have held up remarkably well. He was also among the first of the English critics to recognize that an indigenously American literature was being born on the other side of the Atlantic. His unbiased views on literature of all types and origins can be accounted for largely on the basis of the fact that he seldom deviated from a consistent esthetic in arriving at his judgments; and, in the possession of such an esthetic, valid and reliable as it was, he was almost unique among the critics of his time.

His criticism of the drama has a similar basis. In general, because he was better prepared for it, it was more consistent in quality than his criticism of other literary forms; and it entitles Lewes to a permanent place among the great figures in the field. Unlike most of his fellow critics, he was intimately acquainted with the practical aspects of the theater through his experiences as an actor and playwright, as we have seen. But again the really significant difference between Lewes's judgments and those of most other critics of his time—and ours, for that matter—is that they were firmly based on a well-integrated body of philosophic theory that provided him with an esthetic that enabled him to evaluate works of art on the basis of consistent standards.

Lewes's view of the strengths of Racine and Shakespeare was as keen and steady as his perceptions of the weaknesses of Eugène Scribe and the "Fast School," although he was able to recognize the good as well as the bad aspects of various kinds of drama. His relativistic convictions about the "temporalities in art" and the differences in the national origins of art enabled him to arrive at a series of valid, unbiased judgments of the drama created in other eras and cultures. Because of his practical experience in the theater, he could differentiate between what in the drama of both the past and the present was good and appropriate for modern presentation and what was outworn and antiquated; and he did not hesitate to point out both the unsuitability of the Elizabethans and the incompetence of his contemporaries as creators of a viable drama for presentation in the contemporary theater.

Lewes also brought to his criticism the benefits of an eminently readable literary style, which enabled him to write down his observations with brilliance, verve, and humor. In his hands, the functions of the drama critic and the book reviewer included edification and entertainment for his readers, not merely information; and he set a standard of excellence in critical writing that has been equalled by few of his successors. Though there were some weaknesses in his critical conceptions, they usually were the results of his environment. His Victorian standards of morality prevented him from seeing the merits of certain works in which these standards were completely violated—as in a play such as *La Dame aux Camélias* or a novel like *Tom Jones*. But moral standards did not interfere very often with his criticism, and his rare errors in judgment usually occurred because of his temporary neglect of his own rigid critical requirements.

We can conclude that, as a critic, Lewes was one of the foremost figures of the nineteenth century. In his criticism of literature, and in particular fiction, he foresaw the trend toward Realism and psychological insight that has distinguished the great novelists of the late nineteenth and twentieth centuries. In his criticism of the theatrical aspects of the drama, he foresaw the most important trends in dramatic art that were to take place in the same period: the ascendency of the well-made play as a model for English writers, the advent of Realism in style and content as the criterion of excellence in modern tragedy and comedy, and the decline of melodrama as a reputable form of serious entertainment.

Most of Lewes's contemporaries who turned their attention to criticism were not equipped with comparable intellectual abilities, as my references to typical examples of their work have shown. Among his immediate predecessors, Hazlitt and Coleridge probably are his only peers, as is Arnold among his contemporaries. Lewes stood almost alone in the nineteenth century in his treatment of Shakespeare as a dramatist rather than exclusively as a poet, as we have seen. His status as a drama critic is equal—if not superior—to that of such later English critics as William Archer, Henry Arthur Jones, and Bernard Shaw—who went out of his way to acknowledge Lewes's importance. That he stood head and shoulders above most of the critical writers of his time has, I believe, been demonstrated; and his place in the literary and cultural history of the nineteenth century is secure. No doubt the light of his fame will remain, to a considerable extent, the reflection of George Eliot's glory. But some light surely belongs to him in his own right as a man of letters. His ideas, his writings, and the impact of his thoughts and personality were highly significant—if not spectacular—influences in making the Victorian period what it was and in shaping the age that was to come.

Notes and References

Chapter One

1. John Forster, *Life and Times of Oliver Goldsmith* (London, 1877), II, 334ff.

2. See John Lewes' comment in his Advertisement to the *Memoirs.* He claims that the Biographical Sketch which prefaces the *Comic Sketches* is a product of the unknown author's "superior inventive powers."

3. *On Actors and the Art of Acting* (New York, 1878), p. 15.

4. *Life of Goethe,* 2nd ed. (London, 1864), p. 26, note.

5. *Leader,* IV (June 18, 1853), p. 597. *Sardanapalus* was performed on April 10, 1834.

6. Cf. Anna T. Kitchel, *George Lewes and George Eliot* (New York, 1933); Frederick Locker-Lampson, *My Confidences* (London, 1896); and Francis Espinasse, *Literary Recollections and Sketches* (London, 1893).

7. See Leslie Stephan's biography of Lewes in the *Dictionary of National Biography* and Lewes' "Journal X" in the Beinecke Library, Yale University.

8. See "Spinoza," *Fortnightly Review,* IV (April, 1866), 385–406, for a full account of this episode.

9. *Ibid.*

10. See W. B. Scott, *Autobiographical Notes* (London, 1892), I, 129ff.

11. *Ibid.,* p. 133.

12. Accounts of these incidents are in the *Leader,* Nov. 2, 1850, p. 763, and in the *Pall Mall Gazette,* I (July 5, 1865), 1427.

13. *Ranthorpe* (London, 1847), p. 86.

14. Mrs. Lynn Linton, *My Literary Life* (London, 1899), pp. 18ff.

15. Francis Espinasse, *Literary Recollections* (New York, 1893), pp. 281–82.

16. Margaret Fuller Ossoli, *Memoirs* (London, 1852), II, 185–86.

17. *Leader,* Feb. 14, 1852, pp. 158–59.

18. Clement Shorter, *The Brontës—Life and Letters* (London, 1908), II, 143.

19. See Lewes's biography in the *New Quarterly Magazine,* II (July and Oct., 1879), pp. 356ff. All subsequent references to this incident derive from this source, but I have found no trace of a performance of *The Guardian* in 1841 in any of the contemporary theatrical records, and in fact no trace of a Whitehall Theatre.

20. *Times,* May 16, 1848, p. 8.

21. For further details on Barry Sullivan's rather acrid reactions to Lewes, see W. J. Lawrence, *Barry Sullivan: A Biographical Sketch* (London, 1893), p. 34, and R. M. Sillard, *Barry Sullivan and His Contemporaries* (London, 1901), I, pp. 137ff.

22. *Selections from the Letters of Geraldine Endsor Jewsbury to Jane Welsh Carlyle,* ed. Mrs. Alexander Ireland (London, 1892), in a letter dated March 5, 1849.

23. For further details on the *Leader,* see W. J. Linton, *Threescore and Ten Years 1820 to 1890 Recollections* (New York, 1894), and G. J. Holyoke, *Sixty Years of an Agitator's Life* (London, 1893), *passim.*

24. *The George Eliot Letters,* ed. Gordon S. Haight (New Haven, 1954), II, 166. (Hereinafter referred to as *Letters.*)

25. Lewes's Journal X in the Beinecke Library.

26. George Eliot's first use of the name was as the signature on a letter to William Blackwood, dated Feb. 4, 1857. See the *Letters,* II, 292.

27. *Letters,* III, 40. The manuscript of *Adam Bede* now is in the British Museum.

28. Lewes's Journal X.

29. *Letters,* VI, 109. The letter is dated Jan. 3, 1875.

30. *Ibid.,* pp. 246–47, in a letter dated May 6, 1876.

Chapter Two

1. In the Beinecke Library at Yale University in MS. On the front cover is written, presumably in Lewes's hand, "Extracts made by G. H. Lewes (Interesting)."

2. *Leader,* Dec. 18, 1852, p. 1211.

3. *Ranthorpe* (London, 1847), p. ii.

4. *Ibid.,* p. 350.

5. *Principles of Success in Literature* (London, 1898), p. 146. Hereinafter referred to as *S.i.L.*

6. "Balzac and George Sand," *Foreign Quarterly Review,* XXXIII (July, 1844), 145–62.

7. *Rose, Blanche and Violet* (London, 1848), II, 205–6.

8. See "Recent Novels: French and English," *Fraser's Magazine*, XXXVI (Dec. 1847), 686–95.

9. Clement Shorter, *The Brontës—Life and Letters* (London, 1908), I, 367.

10. *Ibid.*, pp. 409–10, in a letter to W. S. Williams, dated April 26, 1848.

11. *Ibid.*, pp. 411–12.

12. *Ibid.*, pp. 412–13.

13. *Ibid.*, p. 413.

14. *Letters of Charles Dickens*, ed. Walter Dexter (Bloomsbury, 1938), II, 90. The letter was dated May 20, 1848, and signed "Yours heartily."

15. *Letters and Memoirs of Jane Welsh Carlyle*, ed. James A. Froude (New York, 1883), I, 245–46. The letter was dated April 13, 1848.

16. *British Quarterly Review*, VII (May 1848), 332–46.

17. *Fraser's Magazine*, XXX (Oct., 1844), 394–412. The second episode appeared in the November issue, pp. 563–71.

18. *Douglas Jerrold's Shilling Magazine*, V (1847), 161–71.

19. *Ibid.*, VI (1847), 517–34.

20. *Blackwood's Magazine*, LXXIX (1856), May, pp. 562–78; June, pp. 676–91; LXXX (1856), July, pp. 61–76.

21. Quoted from an ALS in the National Library of Scotland, written to John Blackwood. It is undated, but probably was written early in May, 1856, and was sent by the same post as the last instalment of "Metamorphoses."

22. In Part I, *Blackwood's*, LXXIX (May, 1856), 564.

23. Quoted from the ALS referred to in Note 22. The subsequent letter is another ALS in the National Library of Scotland. Probable date is May 19, 1856.

24. *Alexandre chez Apelles* was first performed at the Théâtre du Vaudeville on Dec. 27, 1852. The authors were MM. Bayard and Dupin.

25. *Blackwood's*, LXXXIX (May, 1861), 537–54.

26. *Alexandre chez Appeles*, sc. viii, p. 20, in Vol. 68 of "Bibliothèque Dramatique," a collection of published French plays bound in series in the Yale Library.

27. The scene is on pp. 35ff. of the MS of "The Fox Who Got the Grapes" in the Beinecke Library. Pencilled across the cover, presumably in Lewes' hand, is the notation, "Turned into 'Mrs. B's Vengeance' in Blackwood."

28. *Leader*, Nov. 19, 1853, 1125. The remarks are included in

Lewes's criticism of a one-act comedy, *A Nice Farm*, by Tom Taylor.

29. *S.i.L.*, p. 17.

Chapter Three

1. "Percy Bysshe Shelley," *Westminster Review*, XXXV (April, 1841), 313.
2. *Ibid.*, p. 307.
3. *Principles of Success in Literature*, p. 101.
4. "Victor Hugo's Last Romance," *Blackwood's*, XCII (Aug., 1862), 172–73.
5. "Percy Bysshe Shelley," pp. 315–20.
6. "Balzac and George Sand," *Foreign Quarterly Review*, XXXIII (July, 1844), 159.
7. "Recent Novels: French and English," *Fraser's*, XXXVI (Dec., 1847), 691–92.
8. *Ibid.*, p. 693.
9. *Ibid.*
10. *Ibid.*, p. 687.
11. "*Shirley:* a Tale, By Currer Bell, Author of *Jane Eyre*," *Edinburgh Review*, XCI (Jan., 1850), 159.
12. *Ibid.*
13. *Ibid.*, p. 160.
14. "A Word about *Tom Jones*," *Blackwood's*, LXXXVII (March, 1860), 331–41.
15. "Recent Novels: French and English," p. 687.
16. "A Word about *Tom Jones*," pp. 334ff.
17. *Ibid.*, p. 338.
18. *Ibid.*, p. 339.
19. *Ibid.*, p. 341.
20. "The Lady Novelists," *Westminster Review*, LVIII (July, 1852), 71.
21. "Realism in Art: Recent German Fiction," *Westminster Review*, N. S., XIV (Oct., 1858), 493–99.
22. *Ibid.*, pp. 498–99.
23. *S.i.L.*, p. 27.
24. "Victor Hugo's Last Romance," pp. 176–77.
25. *Ibid.*, p. 179.
26. *Ibid.*, pp. 180–82.
27. "The Lady Novelists," p. 73.
28. "The Novels of Jane Austen," *Blackwood's*, LXXXVI (July, 1859), 102–4.
29. *Ibid.*, pp. 105ff.
30. René Wellek, *A History of Modern Criticism: 1750–1950* (New Haven, 1965), IV, 150.

31. See George H. Ford, *Dickens and His Readers* (Princeton, 1955), p. 131, and Franklin Gary, "Charlotte Brontë and GHL," *Publications of the Modern Language Association,* LI (1936), 525ff.
32. *Essays of George Eliot,* ed. Thomas Pinney (New York, 1963), p. 271. The quotation is from "The Natural History of German Life," *Westminster Review,* LXVI (July, 1856), 51–79.
33. "Girardin's Lectures on the Drama," *Foreign Quarterly Review,* XXXIII (Apr., 1844), 33.
34. *S.i.L.,* p. 136.
35. Wellek, *op. cit.,* IV, 150.
36. These remarks are in Lewes's own hand in one of his Autographed Notebooks in the Beinecke Library. The Notebook is undated, but almost certainly was written during the 1840's.
37. From an A.L.S. in the Speck Collection at Yale.
38. The title of the article is "The Life and Works of Goethe," *British and Foreign Review,* XIV (1843), 78–135.
39. See Anna Kitchel, *George Lewes and George Eliot,* pp. 26ff. Miss Kitchel indicates November, 1842, as the date of Mill's letter to Lewes praising the article, showing that Mill must have read it in manuscript.
40. "T. B. Macaulay—History of England," *British Quarterly Review,* IX (Feb., 1849), 1–41. Lewes's remarks on style appear on pp. 12ff.
41. *Ibid.,* pp. 7–8.
42. *Leader,* June 11, 1853, p. 571.
43. "A Pleasant French Book," *Blackwood's,* LXXXIV (Dec., 1858), 675–76.
44. "Realism in Art: Recent German Fiction," *Westminster Review,* N.S., XIV (Oct., 1858), 490.
45. *Leader,* Jan. 3, 1852, p. 17.
46. "Criticism in Relation to Novels," *Fortnightly Review,* III (1865), 354–55.
47. *Ibid.,* p. 355.
48. *Ibid.,* p. 361.
49. *Fraser's Magazine,* XXXVI (1847), 688–90.
50. The review of *Shirley* was in *Edinburgh Review,* XCI (Jan., 1850), 153–73.
51. See, for example, Earl A. Knies, "Art, Death, and the Composition of *Shirley,*" *Victorian Newsletter,* No. 28 (Fall, 1965), 22–24.
52. *Leader,* Feb. 2, 1853, p. 163.
53. "Ruth and Villette," *Westminster Review,* LIX (Apr., 1853), 245–54.
54. *Ibid.,* pp. 246ff.
55. *Ibid.,* pp. 251ff.

56. *Ibid.*, p. 254.
57. "The Lady Novelists," *Westminster Review*, LVIII (July, 1852), 70–72.
58. *Ibid.*, pp. 70–71.
59. *Ibid.*, pp. 71–72.
60. *Ibid.*, p. 72.
61. *Ibid.*, p. 73.
62. *Ibid.*
63. *Ibid.*, p. 74.
64. "Balzac and George Sand," *Foreign Quarterly Review*, XXXIII (July, 1844), 162.
65. *Ibid.*, p. 151.
66. "The Lady Novelists," p. 76.
67. *Ibid.*, pp. 75ff.
68. See Mrs. Linton's *My Literary Life* (London, 1899), pp. 18ff.
69. "The Lady Novelists," p. 77.
70. *Morning Chronicle*, Mar. 6, 1848, p. 3.
71. *Letters and Private Papers of William Makepeace Thackeray*, ed. Gordon Ray (Cambridge, 1946), II, 353–54. The letter is dated March 6, 1848.
72. *Ibid.*, p. 354.
73. *Leader*, Dec. 21, 1850, p. 929.
74. *Leader*, Nov. 6, 1852, pp. 1071–72.
75. "Benjamin D'Israeli," *British Quarterly Review*, X (Aug., 1849), 120ff.
76. *Leader*, Nov. 27, 1852, pp. 1141–42.
77. "Dickens in Relation to Criticism," *Fortnightly Review*, XVII (Feb., 1872), 152.
78. For details, see G. S. Haight, "Dickens and Lewes on Spontaneous Combustion," *Nineteenth Century Fiction*, X (June, 1955), 53–63.
79. For details on this and other aspects of their long friendship, see G. S. Haight, "Dickens and Lewes," *Publications of the Modern Language Association*, LXXI (Mar., 1956), 166–79.
80. "Dickens in Relation to Criticism," p. 142.
81. *Ibid.*, p. 143.
82. *Ibid.*, pp. 144–45.
83. *Ibid.*, p. 146.
84. *Ibid.*, p. 147.
85. *Ibid.*, p. 150.
86. *Ibid.*, pp. 150–51.
87. *Ibid.*, p. 151.
88. John Forster, *Life of Charles Dickens* (London, 1899), II, 337–338.

89. *The Complete Works of Swinburne,* Bonchurch Edition (1925–1927), XVIII, 477.

90. George H. Ford, *Dickens and His Readers* (Princeton, 1955), p. 154.

91. *Ibid.,* p. 151.

92. *Ibid.,* p. 229.

93. *Ibid.,* p. 256.

94. See G. S. Haight, "Dickens and Lewes," p. 178, and Anthony Trollope, "George Henry Lewes," *Fortnightly Review,* XXXI (Jan., 1879), 23.

95. "Dickens in Relation to Criticism," pp. 152–54.

96. Ford, *op. cit.,* p. 229.

97. *Ibid.,* p. 149.

98. *Leader,* June 14, 1851, p. 560.

99. *Leader,* Dec. 14, 1850, p. 905.

100. *Leader,* Nov. 30, 1850, pp. 856–57.

101. "Shelley and the Letters of Poets," *Westminster Review,* LVII (Apr., 1852), 272.

102. *Ibid.*

103. *Leader,* May 14, 1853, p. 473.

104. *Principles of Success in Literature,* p. 186.

105. *Ibid.*

106. *Ibid.,* p. 199.

107. "Percy Bysshe Shelley," *Westminster Review,* XXXV (Apr., 1841), 321.

108. *S.i.L.,* pp. 205ff.

109. *Leader,* Nov. 26, 1853, pp. 1146–47.

110. *Leader,* Dec. 3, 1853, pp. 1170–71.

111. "The Study of Poetry" originally appeared as the General Introduction to *The English Poets,* ed. T. H. Ward (London, 1880).

112. See S. M. B. Coulling, "Matthew Arnold's 1853 Preface: Its Origin and Aftermath," *Victorian Studies,* VII (March, 1964), 233–63, for a detailed analysis of the critical ideas Arnold expressed in the Preface and the reaction to it of other contemporary critics besides Lewes. This summarizing quotation is on p. 263.

113. *Leader,* Dec. 3, 1853, pp. 1170–71.

114. In "The Antigone and Its Critics," *Foreign Quarterly Review,* XXV (Apr., 1845), 56–73.

115. *Leader,* Dec. 3, 1853, p. 1171.

116. See "The Function of Criticism at the Present Time," in Arnold's *Selected Essays* ed. Noel Annan (London, 1964), *passim.*

117. "Robert Browning and the Poetry of the Age," *British Quarterly Review,* VI (Nov., 1847), 491.

118. "The Function of Criticism . . . ," Arnold's *Selected Essays*, pp. 14–15.

119. "The Roman Empire and Its Poets," *Westminster Review*, XXXVIII (July, 1842), 33.

120. *Ibid.*, p. 53, note.

121. "Leigh Hunt on the Italian Poets," *Foreign Quarterly Review*, XXXVI (Jan., 1846), 181–82.

122. *Leader*, Oct. 1, 1853, pp. 953–54. These remarks are in a review of Robert Carruthers' new edition of Pope's *Poetical Works*.

123. The most substantial of Lewes's poetic effusions I have come across is "The Remorse of Pontius Pilate," in the *Leader*, Dec. 7, 1850, p. 860, but dated 1843 at the end of the poem. It is written in rhymed four-line stanzas and tells the story of Pontius' despair, wandering, madness, and death after the Crucifixion. A headnote explains that the poet means to give it the coloring that an ancient Christian might have given it, not the feeling of a Roman governor. The poem is distinguished neither for its qualities as verse nor for its intellectual or spiritual profundity. As far as I have been able to determine, Lewes wrote no other poetry except for a few short verses, apparently composed on the spur of the moment for occasional use in his *Leader* columns and not worthy of comment here.

124. "Robert Browning and the Poetry of the Age," *British Quarterly Review*, VI (Nov., 1847), 495–97.

125. *Ibid.*, pp. 507ff.

126. *Leader*, Apr. 27, 1850, p. 111.

127. "Shelley and the Letters of Poets," *Westminster Review* LVII (Apr., 1852), 268–72.

128. *Ibid.*, p. 272.

129. *Leader*, June 22, 1850, pp. 303–4.

130. *Leader*, Nov. 20, 1852, p. 1116.

131. *Leader*, July 5, 1851, p. 635.

132. The excerpt from Smith's poem and Lewes' defense of it are in the *Leader*, Jan. 3, 1852, p. 15. The poem was an untitled Sonnet, the first line of which reads "Last night my cheek was wetted with warm tears . . ." See Smith's *Poems* (Boston, 1853), p. 185.

133. "Poems of Alexander Smith," *Westminster Review*, LIX (Apr., 1853), 270–71.

134. *Ibid.*, pp. 272ff.

135. For a detailed account of the "Spasmodic" poets, see Hugh Walker, *The Age of Tennyson* (London, 1928), pp. 246–52.

136. "Life of Keats," *British Quarterly Review*, VIII (Nov., 1848), 329–30, 328–43.

137. *Ibid.*, pp. 330–31.

138. *Ibid.*, p. 331.

139. Albert C. Baugh, ed., *A Literary History of England* (New York, 1948), p. 1251.
140. "Life of Keats," pp. 335–36.
141. *Ibid.*, p. 343.
142. In Hunt's *Imagination and Fancy* (New York, 1845), p. 230.
143. "Shelley and the Letters of Poets," p. 271.
144. *Leader*, Aug. 17, 1850, pp. 496–97.
145. *Ibid.*
146. *Ibid.*
147. Clarence Gohdes, *American Literature in Nineteenth Century England* (Carbondale, Ill., 1944), p. 132.
148. The review is in the *Leader*, Nov. 8, 1851, p. 1067.
149. *Leader*, July 3, 1852, pp. 636–37.
150. *Leader*, June 21, 1851, pp. 587–88.
151. See Stanley Williams, "Nathaniel Hawthorne," in *Literary History of the United States* (New York, 1955), p. 432.
152. *Leader*, July 10, 1852, pp. 663–64.
153. Williams, *op. cit.*, p. 435.
154. *Leader*, Oct. 16, 1852, p. 996. Lewes was not exaggerating. *Uncle Tom's Cabin* sold over 300,000 copies during 1852.
155. *Leader*, Sept. 25, 1852, p. 931.
156. *Leader*, Feb. 14, 1852, pp. 158–59.
157. *Leader*, Mar. 30, 1850, p. 16.

Chapter Four

1. See *The Noble Heart* (London, 1850), pp. iii–iv. The offending lines are in Act. II, sc. 1, p. 23.
2. *Examiner*, Feb. 23, 1850, p. 117.
3. *Times*, Feb. 19, 1850, p. 6.
4. *Spectator*, XXIII (Feb. 23, 1850), 180.
5. *Literary Gazette*, Feb. 23, 1850, p. 149.
6. *The Noble Heart*, p. iv.
7. See George C. D. Odell, *Annals of the New York Stage* (New York, 1931), VII, 181. The Boston Museum playbill is in the Harvard Theater Collection.
8. See "Recent Tragedies," *Westminster Review*, XXXVII (1842), 334–35.
9. In *The Life of Charles Mathews*, ed., Charles Dickens (London, 1879), II, 263. Lewes's remarks are in the article in *Pall Mall Gazette*, II (Oct. 11, 1865), 683.
10. See John Hollingshead, *My Lifetime* (London, 1895), I, 65–66, for a vivid—and variant—version of the conditions under which Lewes wrote his translation of *The Game of Speculation*.
11. *Leader*, Oct. 4, 1851, p. 949.

12. *Leader,* Dec. 27, 1851, pp. 1238–39, in a letter from Paris signed "Le Chat Huant," Pigott's usual pseudonym.

13. See Hollingshead, *My Lifetime,* I, 66, and *Dramatic Essays,* ed. William Archer (London, 1896), Introduction, p. xxxiv.

14. In *The Game of Speculation* (London, n.d.), Vol. V of "Lacy's Acting Edition of Plays, Dramas, Extravaganzas, Farces, Etc . . . ," Act I, Sc. 1, p. 4. Hereinafter referred to as "Lacy's."

15. *Mercadet,* Act I, Sc. 1, in Balzac's Théâtre Complet (Paris, 1874), II, 156.

16. *The Life of Charles Mathews,* II, 267.

17. Originally a drama in seven acts by Auguste Anicet–Bourgeois and Michel Masson, *La Dame de La Halle* is in Vol. LIII of "Bibliothèque Dramatique," a collection of published French plays bound in series in the Yale University Library.

18. In the *Spectator,* XXV (Apr. 17, 1852), 366, and the *Examiner,* same date, p. 247.

19. The text of *A Chain of Events* is in Vol. XXI of "Lacy's." Beverley became scenic director for the Covent Garden operas in 1853, and painted immensely popular scenes in various London theaters over a thirty-year period. Mathews' record is in the *Life,* II, App. B. pp. 320ff.

20. Sc. 1, p. 3, in the reprint of *Tambour Battant* in Vol. 49 of "Bibliothèque Dramatique," and Sc. 1, p. 2 of *Taking by Storm!* in Vol. 6 of "Lacy's."

21. GHL's criticism is in the *Leader,* June 5, 1852, p. 547, that in the *Spectator* on the same date, p. 535.

22. See Odell, *Annals of the New York Stage,* VI, 235, for the play's history in New York, where it ran at the National Theater for three nights, opening May 16, 1853. The authors of *Marianne* were the same as those who wrote *La Dame de la Halle.*

23. *Leader,* Apr. 2, 1853, pp. 333–34.

24. *A Strange History* is in Vol. X of "Lacy's," subtitled "A Dramatic Tale in Eight Chapters."

25. Written by P. F. P. Dumanoir and L. F. Nicolai, it opened in Paris at the Théâtre Gymnase on Aug. 9, 1852.

26. *Times,* May 20, 1853, p. 5. Lewes quotes this account in the *Leader,* May 21, p. 501, instead of reviewing the play himself.

27. *Spectator* XXVI (May 21, 1853), 494–95.

28. Act I. Sc. 5, p. 12 of *Les Avocats,* in Vol. LXI of "Bibliothèque Dramatique" and Act I, Sc. 1, p. 9 of *The Lawyers,* in Vol. 2 of "Lacy's."

29. For a more serious discussion of spontaneous combustion see the *Leader,* Feb. 5, 1853, pp. 137–38 and Feb. 12, pp. 161–63.

30. For Lewes' review, see the *Leader,* Mar. 25, 1854, p. 284. My only evidence that he wrote the farce is that Slingsby Lawrence is mentioned as the author of it on the title pages of the published editions of *A Cozy Couple* and *Give a Dog a Bad Name,* in Vol. 24 of "Lacy's."

31. Written by Théodor Barrière and Jules Lorin, the play was first performed at the Théâtre du Vaudeville on Apr. 30, 1853, and is in Vol. 82 of "Bibliothèque Dramatique."

32. *Times,* Apr. 19, 1854, p. 12, and the *Leader,* Apr. 22, p. 380.

33. Madame Girardin's version had opened at the Théâtre Français on Feb. 25, 1854. Lewes's review was in the *Leader,* May 27, 1854, p. 499.

34. *Times,* June 17, 1854, p. 9, and *Spectator,* XXVII, same date, p. 639.

35. In *La Joie Fait Peur,* Sc. 8, *Oevres Complètes de Madame Émile de Girardin* (Paris, 1860), VI, 390, and in *Sunshine Through the Clouds,* French's Acting Ed. (London, 1854), p. 11.

36. *Spectator,* XXVII (June 17, 1854), 639.

37. *Athenaeum,* Mar. 24, 1855, p. 354, and *Spectator,* XXVIII, same date, p. 311.

38. In *Le Village,* Sc. 8, in Octave Feuillet, *Théâtre Complet* (Paris, 1892), I, 281–82, and in *A Cozy Couple,* in Vol. 24 of "Lacy's," pp. 27–28.

39. *Times,* June 30, 1855, p. 12.

40. *Buckstone's Adventures with a Polish Princess,* in Vol. 22 of "Lacy's," p. 10. The siege of Sebastopol in the Crimea was going on during the summer of 1855.

41. Lewes' review of *Ranelagh* is in the *Leader,* Feb. 18, 1854, p. 164. The description of the changes in *Stay at Home* is in the *Leader,* Feb. 16, 1856, p. 164, in a review that was almost certainly not written by Lewes. My further impressions of the play all are based on contemporary reviews, because I have been unable to find a copy, and I am quite certain that it has never been published.

42. *Spectator,* XXIX (Feb. 16, 1856), 187, and *Times,* Feb. 12, 1856, p. 10.

43. See Lewes's Journal No. XI (1859–66) in the Beinecke Library. Details on those negotiations appear in the entry for Nov. 30, 1860. Receipt of the £100 is recorded in Lewes' Literary Receipt Book.

44. *New York Times,* May 30, 1864, pp. 6 and 7, and subsequent issues.

45. *Ibid.,* June 6, 1864, p. 5.

46. *Frank Leslie's Illustrated Newspaper,* XVIII (June 18, 1864), 195.

47. *Albion*, XLII (June 4, 1864), 271.
48. The prompter's copy of *Captain Bland* is in the New York Public Library.
49. *Captain Bland*, Prompter's Copy (New York, 1864), Act III, p. 19.
50. *Ibid.*, Act I, p. 21.
51. "The Prize Comedy and the Prize Committee," *Westminster Review*, XLII (1844), 112.
52. The MS of *Pretension*, written entirely in Lewes's hand, is in the Beinecke Library. He wrote "*Copied* Nov., 1843" on the last page, probably indicating that he completed the fair copy for submission to a theater on that date, though he may have finished writing the play previously.
53. In *Ranthorpe*, p. 134, completed at about the same time that he wrote *Pretension*, Lewes describes an aspiring playwright's attempt to sell a tragedy, not knowing that three hundred plays "are every season sent in to each patent theatre—about three or four plays are produced!" Another indication that he knew about the troubles of playwrights first-hand is in "The Drama: Authors and Managers," *Westminster Review*, XXXVII (1842), 72, where he writes that he has himself "suffered many of the grievances" of which the "unacted" dramatists complain.
54. *Pretension*, Act I, pp. 4 and 5, and Act III, pp. 43ff.
55. *Ibid.*, Act I, p. 8.
56. *Leader*, Mar. 15, 1851, p. 254.
57. *Pretension*, Act V, pp. 77ff.
58. *Ibid.*, Act I, p. 8.
59. *Ibid.*, Act III, Sc. 1, p. 39.
60. *Leader*, Jan. 18, 1851, p. 67.
61. *Drat that Dick!*, p. 1.
62. *Ibid.*, pp. 26–27.
63. *Ibid.*, p. 36.

Chapter Five

1. Bernard Shaw, *Our Theatres in the Nineties* (London, 1931), III, 163.
2. *Ibid.*, II, 169–70. The review appeared originally in the *Saturday Review* on June 20, 1896.
3. *Leader*, Aug. 2, 1851, p. 735.
4. *Leader*, Feb. 7, 1852, p. 137.
5. *Ibid.*
6. *On Actors and the Art of Acting* (New York, 1878), p. 63.
7. "Recent Tragedies," *Westminster Review*, XXXVII (1842), 334–35.

8. *Leader,* Aug. 3, 1850, p. 451, in an article called "The Old and Modern Dramatists," occasioned by a performance of Marston's *Malcontent* at the Olympic Theatre on July 29. Italics are Lewes's.

9. *Leader,* Nov. 30, 1850, p. 859, in a review of a performance of *The Duchess of Malfi* at Sadler's Wells Theatre on Nov. 20.

10. *Play-Goer,* Jan. 25, 1851, p. 2.

11. Macready staged some of Byron's tragedies with reasonable success in the 1830's, but his acting was more attractive to the audiences than Byron's abilities as a dramatist.

12. *Leader,* Aug. 3, 1850, p. 451.

13. Allardyce Nicoll, *British Drama* (New York, 1933), p. 322.

14. Elisa Rachel Felix (1820–1858) was one of the most successful and influential actresses on the French stage. *Adrienne Lecouvreur* was written expressly as a vehicle for her. The performance Lewes reviewed was at the St. James's Theatre on July 8, 1850, presented by a group of French actors. The review appears in the *Leader,* July 13, 1850, p. 379.

15. *Spectator,* XXIII (July 13, 1850), 659.

16. Scribe and Legouvé, *Adrienne Lecouvreur* (New York, 1917), Act. V, Sc. 5, pp. 178–79.

17. *Athenaeum,* July 13, 1850, p. 747.

18. *Leader,* June 14, 1851, p. 565.

19. *Leader,* July 20, 1850, p. 403.

20. *Leader,* July 6, 1850, p. 355.

21. *Leader,* July 20, 1850, p. 403.

22. *Spectator,* XXVI (June 25, 1853), 606.

23. *Times,* July 2, 1850, p. 8.

24. *Spectator,* XXVI (July 2, 1853), 631.

25. Lytton Strachey, *Books and Characters, French and English* (London, 1922), p. 18.

26. *Leader,* July 20, 1850, p. 403.

27. "Hegel's Aesthetics," *British and Foreign Review,* XIII (1842), 48.

28. "Augustus Wilhelm Schlegel," *Foreign Quarterly Review,* XXXII (1843), 175ff.

29. "The French Drama: Racine and Victor Hugo," *Westminster Review,* XXIV (1840), 290ff.

30. *Les Burgraves* was presented at the Comédie Français on March 7, 1843, and was withdrawn after a few performances.

31. "The French Drama: Racine and Victor Hugo," pp. 287–324.

32. "State of the French Drama," *Quarterly Review,* LI (1834), 184ff.

33. "French Literature—Recent Novelists," *Edinburgh Review,* LVII (1833), 345.

34. *Foreign Quarterly Review,* XV (1835), 272–73.

35. "State of the French Drama," p. 186. *Marion deLorme* opened in Paris at the Porte St. Martin Theatre on Aug. 11, 1831, and was not a popular success.

36. "The French Drama: Racine and Victor Hugo," pp. 316–22.

37. K. W. Hooker, *The Fortunes of Victor Hugo in England* (New York, 1938), p. 84.

38. "Criticism in France," *British and Foreign Review,* XVI (1844), 360–61.

39. "The New Classic Drama in France," *Foreign Quarterly Review,* XXXVI (1845–46), 32–37. *Virginie* was first produced at the Théâtre Français on Apr. 5, 1845.

40. *Leader,* Mar. 27, 1852, p. 306. *Ruy Blas* appeared at the St. James's Theatre on Mar. 19.

41. "Victor Hugo's Latest Poems," *Fortnightly Review,* III (1865–66), 190.

42. See A. C. Swinburne, "The Works of Victor Hugo," *Nineteenth Century,* XVIII (1885), 14–29 and 294–311, one of his characteristically eulogistic and biased accounts of Hugo.

43. Matthew Arnold, "The French Play in London," *Nineteenth Century,* VI (1879), 228–43.

44. J. B. Mathews, *French Dramatists of the 19th Century* (New York, 1881), p. 41.

45. William Archer, "George Henry Lewes and the Stage," *Fortnightly Review,* LXV (1896), 226.

46. *Leader,* Apr. 2, 1853, p. 333. *La Dame aux Camélias* was based on a novel by Dumas of the same name and had an immediate and lasting success after its opening in Paris at the Théâtre du Vaudeville on Feb. 2, 1852.

47. *Leader,* Aug. 3, 1850, p. 451.

48. *Dramatic Essays,* Introduction, p. xliii.

49. William Archer, *About the Theatre* (London, 1886), p. 297.

50. *Leader,* June 14, 1851, p. 565.

51. *Leader,* May 17, 1851, pp. 469–70. *La Camaraderie* was performed at the St. James's on May 9, *Une Chaîne* on the 12th.

52. *Ibid.,* p. 470.

53. *Leader,* May 11, 1850, p. 162, in a review of a performance of *The Catspaw* at the Haymarket Theatre on May 9.

54. *Leader,* May 10, 1851, pp. 446–47. *Retired from Business* opened at the Haymarket on May 3.

55. *Leader,* Jan. 18, 1851, p. 67.

56. *Leader,* Mar. 15, 1851, pp. 253–54. *Love in a Maze* opened at the Princess's on Mar. 6.

57. *Spectator,* XXIV (Mar. 8, 1851), 226–27.
58. *Athenaeum,* Mar. 8, 1851, p. 275.
59. *Play-Goer,* Mar. 15, 1851, p. 62.
60. Robertson's first successful play, *Society,* opened in London at the Prince of Wales's Theatre on Nov. 11, 1865.
61. *Leader,* Feb. 28, 1852, p. 209. *The Corsican Brothers* opened at the Princess's on Feb. 24, 1852, and was an immediate and lasting success. Boucicault adapted it from *Les Frères Corses,* also a popular success in France. The original version was a novel by Alexandre Dumas.
62. *Our Theatres in the Nineties,* II, 168.
63. *Leader,* Feb. 28, 1852, p. 209.
64. *Leader,* Feb. 22, 1851, p. 182. Boucicault adapted *Sextus V* from a French melodrama called *L'Abbaye di Castro.* It first appeared in London at the Olympic Theater on Feb. 17.
65. *Literary Gazette,* Feb. 28, 1852, p. 212.
66. See the *Athenaeum,* Feb. 22, 1851, p. 226, and the *Play-Goer,* same date, p. 38.
67. *Leader,* Feb. 22, 1851, pp. 181–82.
68. *Ibid.*
69. *Ibid.*
70. *Ibid.*
71. *Leader,* Nov. 16, 1850, p. 812, in a review of *The Templar,* first produced at the Princess's on Nov. 9.
72. See the *Spectator,* XXIII (Nov. 16, 1850), 1089, and the *Times,* Nov. 11, p. 5.
73. *Leader,* Nov. 16, 1850, p. 812.
74. *Leader,* June 19, 1852, p. 594.
75. *Leader,* June 25, 1853, pp. 620–21. The revival of *Sardanapalus* opened at the Princess's on June 13.
76. See the *Spectator,* XXVI (June 18, 1853), 584, and the *Athenaeum,* same date, p. 745.
77. *Leader,* June 25, 1853, p. 620.
78. *Leader,* June 28, 1851, p. 614.
79. *Leader,* Feb. 22, 1851, p. 182.
80. Charles Lamb, "On the Tragedies of Shakespeare, considered with reference to their fitness for stage representation," in *Correspondence and Works* (London, 1870), III, 88. The eassy first appeared in Leigh Hunt's *Reflector* in 1811.
81. S. T. Coleridge, "Shakespeare a Poet Generally," in *Complete Works,* ed. W. G. T. Shedd (New York, 1884), IV, 50. The essay was first published in 1818, in *Essays and Lectures.*
82. Translated from Goethe's "Shakespeare als Theaterdichter," a

section of his essay called "Shakespeare und Kein Ende!" in *Werke* (Weimar, 1902), XLI, Vol. 1, pp. 64ff. The essay first appeared in 1816.

83. "Shakespeare's Critics: English and Foreign," *Edinburgh Review*, XC (1849), 62.

84. *Ibid.*, pp. 76ff.

85. *Ibid.*, p. 68.

86. *Ibid.*, pp. 62–63. Lewes does not specify here whether he is referring to Charles Kean rather than his father Edmund, but it is almost certain that he was, since Edmund left the stage in 1832.

87. *Leader*, Mar. 30, 1850, p. 15. Gervinus' *Shakespeare* later came out in an English translation by F. E. Bunnètt as *Shakespeare Commentaries.* The observations about *A Midsummer Night's Dream* are in the 1875 edition of the *Commentaries*, pp. 201ff. Hazlitt's review originally appeared in the *Examiner*, July 21, 1816.

88. *Leader*, Sep. 18, 1852, p. 907.

89. "Shakespeare's Critics: English and Foreign," p. 64.

90. *Ibid.*, p. 55. Lewes quotes from Johnson's "Preface to Shakespeare," in the *Works* (Troy, N. Y., 1903), XII, 17.

91. "Spanish Drama: Lope de Vega and Calderon," *Foreign Quarterly Review*, XXXI (1843), 506.

92. "Shakespeare's Critics: English and Foreign," pp. 42–44.

93. "Recapitulation and Summary of the Characteristics of Shakespeare's Dramas," in Coleridege's *Complete Works*, IV, pp. 61ff.

94. A. C. Bradley, *Shakespearean Tragedy*, 2nd ed. (London, 1916), p. 12.

95. E. E. Stoll, *Art and Artifice in Shakespeare* (Cambridge, England, 1938), p. 49.

96. *Ibid.*, p. 168.

97. "Shakespeare's Critics: English and Foreign," pp. 42–45.

98. "Shakespeare and His Editors," *Westminster Review*, XLIII (1845), 60.

99. Quoted from Leigh Hunt's Preface to the *Legend of Florence*, 2nd ed. (London, 1840), p. xi. Italics are Lewes's.

100. "Shakespeare and His Editors," pp. 69–71.

101. *Ibid.*, p. 60.

102. *The Complete Works of Shakespeare*, ed. Hardin Craig (Chicago, 1951), pp. 50 and 425.

103. "Shakespeare's Critics: English and Foreign," p. 45.

104. *Leader*, Aug. 3, 1850, p. 451.

105. Introduction, *Prefaces to Shakespeare*, 1st series (London, 1927), *passim.*

106. Shaw, *Our Theatres in the Nineties*, I, 137.

107. Strachey, *Landmarks in French Literature* (New York, 1912), pp. 91ff.
108. *Leader,* Nov. 29, 1851, p. 142, in a review of a performance of *The Merry Wives* at the Princess's Theatre on Nov. 22.
109. *Leader,* May 21, 1853, p. 502.
110. *Literary Gazette,* Nov. 29, 1851, p. 829.
111. *Leader,* Dec. 3, 1853, p. 1173.
112. *Leader,* Nov. 9, 1850, p. 787.
113. *Leader,* Aug. 3, 1850, p. 451.
114. Cf. A. C. Bradley, *Shakespearean Tragedy,* and Walter Raleigh, *Shakespeare* (New York, 1907), *passim.*

Chapter Six

1. George J. Holyoke, *Sixty Years of an Agitator's Life* (London, 1893), I, 244.
2. George Saintsbury, *A History of 19th Century Literature* (New York, 1931), p. 355.
3. Dates of the subsequent English editions were 1857, 1867, 1871, 1880, and 1891.
4. "Contemporary Literature of France," *Westminster Review,* N.S., I (Jan., 1852), 346.
5. "Contemporary Literature of France," *Westminster Review,* N.S., II (Oct., 1852), 615ff.
6. William James, "Lewes' Problems of Life and Mind," review in *Atlantic Monthly,* XXXVI (1875), 361–63, reprinted in James's *Collected Essays and Reviews* (New York, 1920), pp. 4–11.
7. See Harrison's obituary account of Lewes in *The Academy,* Dec. 7, 1878, pp. 543–44.
8. See R. L. Hawkins, *Positivism in the United States, 1853–1861* (Cambridge, Mass., 1938), for details on Lewes's part in popularizing Comte in this country.
9. *The Times,* Dec. 3, 1878, p. 7.
10. *New Letters of Thomas Carlyle,* ed. Alexander Carlyle (London, 1904), II, 90–91.
11. *Leader,* May 18, 1850, p. 189.
12. *Ibid.,* June 15, 1850, p. 284.
13. *Ibid.,* Nov. 19, 1853, p. 1123.

Selected Bibliography

PRIMARY SOURCES

1. *Books by George Henry Lewes*

A Biographical History of Philosophy. 2 vols. London: Charles Knight & Co., 1845–46. Later eds., 1857, 1867, 1871, 1880, 1891. American ed., New York: D. Appleton & Co., 1875.

The Spanish Drama. Lope de Vega and Calderon. London: C. Knight & Co., 1846.

Ranthorpe. London: Chapman & Hall, 1847.

Rose, Blanche and Violet. 3 vols. London: Chapman & Hall, 1848.

The Life of Maximilien Robespierre; with Extracts from his Unpublished Correspondence. London: Chapman & Hall, 1848.

Comte's Philosophy of the Sciences: Being an Exposition of the Principles of the Cours De Philosophie Positive of Auguste Comte. London: H. G. Bohn, 1853. Later ed., 1883.

The Life of Goethe. London: D. Nutt, 1855. Later eds., 1864, 1875, 1882, 1890, 1906, 1908, etc. First American ed., Boston: Ticknor & Fields, 1856.

Seaside Studies at Ilfracombe, Tenby, the Scilly Isles and Jersey. London: William Blackwood & Sons, 1858. Later ed., 1860.

The Physiology of Common Life. 2 vols. London: William Blackwood & Sons, 1859.

Studies in Animal Life. London: Smith, Elder & Co., 1862.

Aristotle: A Chapter from the History of Science. London: Smith, Elder & Co., 1864.

Selections from the Modern British Dramatists. Introduction and Biographical Notes. 2 vols. in one. Leipzig: F. A. Brockhaus, 1867.

Female Characters of Goethe. From the Original Drawings of William Kaulbach. With Introduction and Explanatory Notes by George Henry Lewes. New York: T. Stroefer [1868]. Introduction dated 1867. Later ed., 1874.

On Actors and the Art of Acting. London: Smith, Elder & Co., 1875. American ed., New York: Henry Holt, 1878.

Problems of Life and Mind:
The Foundations of a Creed. 2 vols. London: Trübner & Co., 1874–1875.
The Physical Basis of Mind. London: Trübner & Co., 1877.
The Study of Psychology. 2 vols. London: Trübner & Co., 1879.

The Principles of Success in Literature. San Francisco: Albert S. Cook, 1885. Later eds., London: Walter Scott, Ltd., [1898]; New York: Allyn & Bacon, 1917.

Dramatic Essays, [by] John Forster [and] George Henry Lewes. Ed. William Archer and Robert W. Lowe. London: Walter Scott, Ltd., 1896.

Literary Criticism of George Henry Lewes. Ed. Alice R. Kaminsky. Lincoln, Nebraska: University of Nebraska Press, 1964.

2. *Literary and Dramatic Criticism in Periodicals*

N.B.: Unsigned articles have been identified usually by reference to Lewes's Literary Receipt Book that is in manuscript in the Berg Collection of the New York Public Library and was published for the first time in *The George Eliot Letters,* cited below.

Blackwood's Magazine
"A Pleasant French Book," LXXXIV (1858), 675–87.
"The Novels of Jane Austen," LXXXVI (1859), 99–113.
"A Word About *Tom Jones,*" LXXXVII (1860), 331–41.
"Victor Hugo's Last Romance," XCII (1862), 172–82.

British and Foreign Review
"Hegel's Aesthetics," XIII (1842), 1–49.
"The Life and Works of Goethe," XIV (1843), 78–135.
"State of Criticism in France," XVI (1844), 327–62.
"Alfieri and the Italian Drama," XVII (1844), 357–90.
"The Three Fausts," XVIII (1844), 51–92.

British Quarterly Review
"Robert Browning and the Poetry of the Age," VI (1847), 490–509.
"Forster's Life of Goldsmith," VII (1848), 1–25.
"Historical Romance—Alexandre Dumas," VII (1848), 181–204.
"Charles Lamb—His Genius and Writings," VII (1849), 292–311.
"Life of Keats," VIII (1848), 328–43.
"T. B. Macaulay—History of England," IX (1848), 1–41.
"Benjamin D'Israeli," X (1849), 118–38.
"Spanish Literature," XI (1850), 200–29.

Cornhill Magazine
"The Miseries of a Dramatic Author," VIII (1863), 498–512.
"Shakespeare in France," XI (1865), 33–51.

Edinburgh Review
"Dramatic Reform—Classification of Theatres," LXXVIII (1843), 382–401.
"Lessing," LXXXII (1845), 451–70.
"Shakespeare's Critics: English and Foreign," XC (1849), 39–77.
"Shirley: A Tale, by Currer Bell, Author of *Jane Eyre*," XCI (1850), 153–73.

Foreign Quarterly Review
"Spanish Drama: Lope de Vega and Calderon," XXXI (July, 1843), 502–39.
"Augustus Wilhelm Schlegel," XXXII (Oct., 1843), 160–81.
"Girardin's Lectures on the Drama," XXXIII (Apr., 1844), 33–43.
"Balzac and George Sand," XXXIII (July, 1844), 145–62.
"The Antigone and Its Critics," XXXV (Apr., 1845), 56–73.
"The Rise and Fall of European Drama," XXXV (July, 1845), 290–334.
"The New Classic Drama in France," XXXVI (1845–46), 32–39.
"Leigh Hunt on the Italian Poets," XXXVI (1845–46), 179–90.
"Abelard and Heloise," XXXVI (1845–46), 139–57.
"George Sand's Recent Novels," XXXVII (1846), 12–20.

Fortnightly Review
"Victor Hugo's Latest Poems," III (1865), 181–90.
"Criticism in Relation to Novels," III (1865), 352–61.
"Dickens in Relation to Criticism," XVII (1872), 141–54.

Fraser's Magazine
"On the History of Pantomimes," XXXIII (1846), 43–45.
"The Condition of Authors in England, Germany and France," XXXV (1847), 285–95.
"Recent Novels: French and English," XXXVI (1847), 686–95.
"The Life and Works of Leopardi," XXXVIII (1848), 659–69.

Leader, I–VIII (1850–57). Miscellaneous articles and reviews, as indicated in footnotes. These are identified in Lewes's personal file of *Leader* articles in the Beinecke Library, or are signed "Vivian," except those written between 1854 and 1857, which I have otherwise identified.

Paul Mall Gazette, I–IV (1865–66), Miscellaneous articles and reviews, as indicated in footnotes, signed "L."

Westminster Review
"The French Drama: Racine and Victor Hugo," XXXIV (1840), 287–324.
"Percy Bysshe Shelley," XXXV (1841), 303–44.
"The Drama: Authors and Managers," XXXVII (1842), 71–97.

"Recent Tragedies," XXXVII (1842), 321–47.
"The Roman Empire and Its Poets," XXXVIII (1842), 33–58.
"The Errors and Abuses of English Criticism," XXXVIII (1842), 466–86.
"Strafford and the Historical Drama," XLI (1844), 119–28.
"The Prize Comedy and the Prize Committee," XLII (1844), 105–116.
"Shakespeare and His Editors," XLIII (1845), 40–77.
"Historical Romance," XLV (1846), 34–55.
"Shelley and the Letters of Poets," LVII (1852), 268–72.
"The Lady Novelists," LVIII (1852), 70–77.
"Ruth and Vilette," LIX (1853), 245–54.
"Poems of Alexander Smith," LIX (1853), 270–76.
"Realism in Art: Recent German Fiction," N.S., XIV (1858), 488–518.

3. *Other Significant Periodical Articles*

On Comte's *Systeme de Politique Positive:*
"Contemporary Literature in France," *Westminster Review*, N.S., I (Jan., 1852), 346–56; and *Westminster Review,* N.S., II (Oct., 1852), 614–30.

On History as a Social Science:
"Modern French Historians," *Westminster Review,* XXXVI (Oct., 1841), 273–308.
"Bushey and Dannon on the Science of History," *Foreign Quarterly Review,* XXXII (Jan., 1844), 176–88.

On Philosophy and Science:
"Spinoza," *Fortnightly Review,* IV (1866), 385–406.
"On the Dread and Dislike of Science," *Fortnightly Review,* XXXIX (1878), 808–15.

On Physiology and Psychology:
"Voluntary and Involuntary Actions," *Blackwood's,* LXXXVI (1859), 295–306.
"Great Wits, Mad Wits?" *Blackwood's,* LXXXVIII (1860), 302–11.

4. *Printed Plays*

Buckstone's Adventures with a Polish Princess. By "Slingsby Lawrence." London: T. H. Lacy, 1855(?). In Vol. XXII of "Lacy's Acting Edition of Plays, Dramas, Extravaganzas, Farces, etc., etc., as Performed at the Various Theatres."
A Chain of Events. By "Slingsby Lawrence." London: T. H. Lacy, 1852(?). In Lacy, XXI.

A Cozy Couple. By "Slingsby Lawrence and Charles Mathews." London: T. H. Lacy, 1854(?). In Lacy, XXIV.
The Game of Speculation. By "Slingsby Lawrence." London: T. H. Lacy, n.d. In Lacy, V.
Give a Dog a Bad Name. By "Slingsby Lawrence." London: T. H. Lacy, 1854(?). In Lacy, XXIV.
The Lawyers. By "Slingsby Lawrence." London: T. H. Lacy, n.d. In Lacy, II.
The Noble Heart. London: Chapman & Hall, 1850.
A Strange History. By "Slingsby Lawrence and Charles Mathews." London: T. H. Lacy, n.d. In Lacy, X.
Sunshine Through the Clouds. By "Slingsby Lawrence." London: T. H. Lacy, 1854(?). In Lacy, XV.
Taking by Storm! By "Frank Churchill." London: T. H. Lacy, 1852(?). In Lacy, VI.

5. *Manuscript and "Lost" Plays*

N.B.: An Asterisk indicates that the play was acted. A double asterisk denotes that the whereabouts of the text of the play is unknown —if it is even in existence.

* *Captain Bland,* Prompter's Copy. 1864. New York Public Library. (Written in 1855–56.)
Drat that Dick!. By "Slingsby Lawrence." 1852(?). Beinecke Library at Yale University.
The Fox Who Got the Grapes. 1854. Beinecke Library. Converted into a short story, "Mrs. Beauchamp's Vengeance," and published in *Blackwood's Magazine,* LXXXIX (1861), 537–54.
Marguerite, n.d. Beinecke Library.
The Miser's Niece. n.d. Beinecke Library.
Pretension, or The School for Parvenus. 1843. Beinecke Library.
** *Stay at Home.* 1853(?). (Acted in 1856).
** *Wanted a She-Wolf.* 1854(?).

N.B.: In addition to the plays, there is considerable unpublished material in MS by and about Lewes in the Beinecke Library, including his Journals, many letters, and several miscellaneous notebooks. Some are published in *The George Eliot Letters.*

1. *Books*

N.B.: No full-length biography of Lewes has as yet appeared. Of the many books that contain extensive references to him, most of which are referred to in my footnotes, this list includes only those that are of particular interest or significance as supplementary materials.

EVERETT, EDWARD. *The Party of Humanity: The Fortnightly Review and Its Contributors, 1865–74*. Chapel Hill, N.C.: University of North Carolina Press, 1939. Extensive account of the first decade of the *Fortnightly*'s existence, with considerable comment on Lewes's work.

The George Eliot Letters. Ed. Gordon S. Haight. 6 vols. New Haven: Yale University Press, 1954–55. Best, most comprehensive source of information about Lewes and George Eliot, a *sine qua non* for all scholars. Contains many letters to and from Lewes, his Literary Receipt Book, excerpts from his Journals, and a wealth of information about his activities, publications, and accomplishments.

George Eliot's Life, as Related in her Letters and Journals. Ed. J. W. Cross. 3 vols. London: William Blackwood & Sons, 1885. For many years the only published version of these materials. One of the chief elements of interest in the selection is the frequency of the omissions of references to G. H. Lewes.

HAIGHT, GORDON S. *George Eliot and John Chapman*. New Haven: Yale University Press, 1940. Includes one of the first full and frank accounts of the relationship between Lewes and George Eliot, and its important consequences.

———. *George Eliot, A Biography*. New York: Oxford University Press, 1968. The definitive account of George Eliot's life, based on *The George Eliot Letters,* referred to above, and much additional hitherto unpublished material. Contains a thorough, sensitive analysis of the full implications of the George Eliot–G. H. Lewes relationship.

KITCHEL, ANNA T. *George Lewes and George Eliot*. New York: The John Day Co., 1933. The only attempt at a biography of Lewes. Much interesting information about his early life. Concentrates on his relationship with George Eliot in the account of his later years. A comprehensive and well-written work.

LINTON, MRS. LYNN. *My Literary Life*. London: Hodder & Stoughton, 1899. Extensive and rather biased account of Lewes's married life with Agnes, and George Eliot's role in the early 1850's, with an attempt to vindicate Thornton Hunt.

Autobiographical Notes of the Life of William Bell Scott. Ed. W. Minto. 2 vols. London: Osgood, McIlvaine & Co., 1892. Informative and entertaining on Lewes's early life in London, with an interesting description of a later encounter.

2. *Periodicals*

ARCHER, WILLIAM. "George Henry Lewes and the Stage," *Fortnightly Review,* N.S. LIX (1896), 216–30. Reprinted in substance in Lewes's and Forster's *Dramatic Essays,* this is a relatively brief but inclusive account of Lewes's activities as a critic, with some references to his acting.

BRETT, R. L. "George Henry Lewes, Dramatist, Novelist and Critic," *Essays and Studies,* XI (1958), 101–20. On the basis of Lewes's intellectual breadth and philosophical acumen, concludes that his claim to rank as "the most important critic between Coleridge and Arnold is a considerable one." (p. 120).

GARY, FRANKLIN. "Charlotte Brontë and George Henry Lewes," *Publications of the Modern Language Association,* LI (1936), 518–542. A readable and complete account of the relationship between Charlotte Brontë and Lewes, with some interesting conclusions about his influence on her and on the course of nineteenth century fiction.

GREENHUT, MORRIS. "George Henry Lewes as a Critic of the Novel," *Studies in Philology,* XLV (1948), 491–511. Able summary of some of Lewes's views on the novel, culled from a selection of his best articles and reviews. Concludes that Lewes had "a coherent aesthetic of the novel as a literary form." (p. 491).

———. "G. H. Lewes' Criticism of the Drama," *Publications of the Modern Language Association,* LXIV (1949), 350–68. Competent analysis of some of Lewes's most important contributions to dramatic criticism.

HAIGHT, GORDON S. "Dickens and Lewes on Spontaneous Combustion," *Nineteenth Century Fiction,* X (1955), 53–63. An amusing account of the dispute between the two friends on the scientific possibilities of spontaneous combustion as Dickens wrote about it in *Bleak House.*

———. "Dickens and Lewes," *Publications of the Modern Language Association,* LXXI (1956), 166–79. Traces the evolution of their friendship from the early days to Lewes's controversial article about Dickens in the *Fortnightly.*

HIRSHBERG, EDGAR W. "*Captain Bland* on the New York Stage," *Bulletin of the New York Public Library,* LXII (Aug., 1953), 382–88. Full account of the performances of Lewes's wandering melodrama in New York and reactions to it.

KAMINSKY, ALICE R. "George Eliot, George Henry Lewes, and the Novel," *Publications of the Modern Language Association,* LXX (1955), 997–1013. Interesting and convincing presentation of the case for Lewes as a salutory influence on George Eliot.

KAMINSKY, JACK. "The Empirical Metaphysics of George Henry Lewes," *Journal of the History of Ideas,* XIII (1952), 314–32. Explication of the naturalistic aspects of Lewes's philosophy.

SULLY, JAMES. "George Henry Lewes," *New Quarterly Magazine,* II

(1879), 356–76. Unsigned. The best and most reliable of the many obituary accounts of Lewes's life, together with Trollope's, cited below.

TROLLOPE, ANTHONY. "George Henry Lewes," *Fortnightly Review*, N.S. XXV (1879), 15–24. Adulatory, with some revealing insights on Lewes's personality.

Index